THE NATIONAL
GEOGRAPHIC TRAVELER
ROME

THE NATIONAL GEOGRAPHIC TRAVELER
ROME

Sari Gilbert and Michael Brouse

Contents

How to use this guide 6–7 About the authors 8
Areas of Rome 35–222 Excursions 223–234 Travelwise 235–64
Index 265–69 Credits 270–71

**Page 1: Fountain of the
Four Rivers, Piazza Navona
Pages 2–3: The Colosseum
Left: Picturesque
courtyard on one of the
city's quieter backstreets**

How to use this guide

See back flap for keys of text and map symbols

The *National Geographic Traveler* brings you the best of Rome in text, pictures, and maps. Divided into three main sections, the guide begins with an overview of history and culture. Following are 11 area chapters with sites selected by the authors for their particular interest and treated in depth. Each chapter opens with its own contents list for easy reference. A final chapter suggests excursions from Rome.

A map introduces each area of the city, highlighting the featured sites and locating other places of interest. Walks, all plotted on their own maps, suggest routes for dis-

covering the most about an area. Features and sidebars offer detail on history, culture, or contemporary life. A More Places to Visit page generally rounds off the chapters.

The final section, Travelwise, lists essential information for the traveler—pre-trip planning, getting around, communications, money matters, and emergencies—plus a selection of hotels and restaurants arranged by chapter area, shops, and entertainment possibilities.

To the best of our knowledge, site information is accurate as of the press date. However, it's always advisable to call ahead.

Color coding

Each area of the city is color coded for easy reference. Find the area you want on the map on the front flap, and look for the color flash at the top of the pages of the relevant chapter. Hotel and restaurant listings in **Travelwise** are also color coded to each area.

Colosseo

- Map p. 57
- Piazza del Colosseo
- 06 700 5469
- $$
- Bus 75, 81, 85, 87, 117
- Metro: Linea B (Colosseo). Tram: 30B from Circus Maximus or San Lorenzo

Visitor information

Practical information is given in the side column next to each major site (see key to symbols on back flap). The map reference gives the page number where the site is shown on a map. Further details include the site's address, telephone number, days closed, entrance charge in a range from $ (under $4) to $$$$$ (over $25), and nearest public transportation stop. Visitor information for smaller sites is in italics and parentheses in the text.

TRAVELWISE

PIAZZA DI SPAGNA TO VILLA BORGHESE — Color-coded area name

HOTEL — Category name

HASSLER VILLA MEDICI
$$$$$ ★★★★★ — Hotel name, price ranges & star rating

PIAZZA TRINITÀ DEI MONTI 6, 00187
TEL 06 699 340
FAX 06 678 9991 — Address, telephone & fax numbers

Its enviable position at the top of the Spanish Steps is matched by elaborate interior design and bustlingly attentive service. — Brief description of hotel

🛏 100 plus suites 🅿
🚇 Spagna 🔄 🆂 🚫 All major cards — Hotel facilities & credit card details

RESTAURANTS

CAFFE DELLE ARTI
$$$ — Restaurant name & price range

VIA A. GRAMSCI 73, 00197
TEL 06 3265 1236 — Address & telephone number

Set in the glorious surroundings of the Gallery of Modern Art in Villa Borghese. Fine food, especially fish dishes. — Brief description of restaurant

🪑 130 seats 🅿 🚇 116
🔒 Closed D Mon. — Restaurant facilities & credit card details

Hotel and restaurant prices

An explanation of the price bands used in entries is given in the Hotels and restaurants section (see pp. 243–55).

AREA MAPS

- A locator map accompanies each area map and shows the location of that area in the city

WALKING TOURS

- An information box gives the starting and ending points, time and length of walk, and places not to be missed along the route.

AREA/EXCURSION MAPS

- Towns and sites described in the Fuori le Mura (Outside the Walls) and Excursions chapters are highlighted in yellow on the map. Other suggested places to visit are also highlighted and shown with a red diamond symbol.

THE NATIONAL GEOGRAPHIC TRAVELER

ROME

About the authors

Sari Gilbert was born and bred in New York City and became interested in things Mediterranean while still attending Hunter High School there. She spent part of her junior year in Italy, at Syracuse University's semester abroad program in Florence. After receiving her B.A. in political science from Syracuse, Sari returned to Italy to attend the Johns Hopkins Bologna Center, and subsequently received an M.A. and a Ph.D. in international relations from the School of Advanced International Studies in Washington, D.C. Her doctoral dissertation was on Italian foreign policy. In 1972 Sari returned again to Rome, where she lives in the heart of the ancient Trastevere district and, for almost 20 years, has worked as a correspondent for important U. S. newspapers and magazines. She speaks Italian and French and is currently a roving correspondent for a major Italian daily.

Michael Brouse is a native San Franciscan who spent much of his childhood in Hawaii. After graduating from high school in Marin County, Michael attended the Santa Clara University where he received a B.A. in history, but only after spending his junior year abroad, in Rome. Like Sari, Michael returned to Rome in 1972 where, after a stint of teaching English, he worked for many years in men's fashion. His ongoing passion for history and art history found an outlet in popular walking tours he conducts for visitors to the city. Michael is fluent in Italian, French, and German and is an accomplished translator. Three years ago he returned to teaching, and is now a history instructor at an international high school. Most mornings on his way to work he walks through the Roman Forum.

Travelwise author Jane Shaw is a writer, editor, and translator based in Rome. She has contributed to a wide range of guidebooks on Rome and the rest of Italy.

History & culture

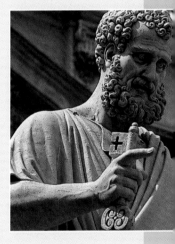

St. Peter with the keys to the Kingdom of Heaven

Rome today

LUCIAN, THE SECOND-CENTURY GREEK RHETORICIAN, DESCRIBED IT AS "a bit of Paradise"; the 15th-century Tuscan scholar, Gian Francesco Poggio Bracciolini, writing centuries later, described the city of Rome as "the most beautiful and magnificent of all those that either have been or shall be"; and in the early 19th century, the English poet, Percy Bysshe Shelley, said the impression of "that majestic city… exceeds anything I have ever experienced in my travels." These are opinions that have survived through time, and today manage to survive even the difficulties of life in modern-day Rome. Labor strikes, pollution, urban disarray, and heavy-handed bureaucracy cannot obscure the beauty and fascination of what is truly the Eternal City.

You can visit this city countless times, or live here for years, and its magnificent light, its colors (soft reds, ochers, and oranges mixed with the off-white and gray of marble and travertine), its harmonies of marble bridges across a curving river, its tree-shaded Renaissance villas and parks, its skyline of domes and *campanili*, will still take your breath away. The Pantheon, the Colosseum, the Campidoglio at sunset, the Roman Forum in the flattening afternoon light—these are timeless wonders that over past centuries (and future ones) make this city a destination for anyone who loves history and admires the artistic capacities of man. While the rampant building speculation that took place after the war has turned the city's outskirts into prosaic cement canyons, the area within the still resistant Aurelian walls and particularly the *centro storico* (historic center) has—despite uncivilly parked cars, buzzing *motorini*, and ubiquitous dog poop—lost little of its magic.

Rome, of course, has always had its critics. Scan the centuries for the reports of more or less known travelers (or talk to some of today's inhabitants) and words such as decay, dirt, noise, and traffic will literally jump off the pages. Even Poggio Bracciolini, writing in the early 1400s, was moved to dismay, speaking of a city "stripped of beauty, lying prostrate like a giant corpse, decayed and everywhere eaten away." At that time the popes had recently returned from self-imposed exile in Avignon (France), to find a city that plague and factional strife had reduced to severe urban dirtiness and disarray. Other low points were the three-day invasion in 410 by the barbarian Visigoths; the aftermath of the bloody (4,000

dead) Sack of Rome in 1527 by the French and German troops of the Holy Roman Emperor, Charles V; and the brutal German occupation which ended only in 1945 with the Allied liberation.

Italy's capital since 1870, Rome gradually recovered after World War II, thanks largely to the Marshall Plan and to the Italians' natural resilience. The new, democratic party system that was grafted onto the roots of pre-Fascist liberalism, grew quickly, if chaotically. And despite all the problems that have ensued— corruption, government instability, strikes, and terrorism—Rome is now the flourishing capital of a major, and wealthy, European power. Largely a service and administrative center (as well as a tourist destination), its stores and boutiques are elegant (and often expensive). Its restaurants are full. Its parks are lovely and provide bikers, strollers, and mothers and small children with some 21,000 acres (8,400 ha) of green. Its middle-class families are well enough off to give their teenagers motorbikes that go for $2,000 a throw. Conspicuous consumption is thriving and it's hard to find a Roman who doesn't have— and constantly use—a *telefonino* or *cellulare* (cell phone).

A CITY IN TRANSITION
Rome today is a city of almost three million people, most of whom have come from the

Louis XV of France helped pay for this 18th-century monumental staircase, which ironically has always been called the Spanish Steps. A central feature of the city, it is used for fashion and flower pageants.

surrounding Lazio region or from the Italian south. Drawn to the capital by the possibility of work and the political contacts that, in this Mediterranean country, can be oh-so-useful to business, they have helped the city to expand far beyond its original perimeters. Never an industrial capital, for decades Rome's 20-odd government ministries were swollen repositories of political patronage. The head-quarters of most of the country's major banks are located here as are the airlines, the unions,

and of course the unbelievable, and still expanding, plethora of Italian political parties. Many young Italians have poured into Rome to attend its three open-admission public uni-versities and some newer private ones. And, of course, Rome is the capital of the Alta Moda (High Fashion or couture) industry as well as the home of the Vatican and of the pope. It thus attracts hundreds of thousands of tourists and pilgrims and, according to statistics supplied by the City Hall, the num-

Ancient art and artifacts, authentic or not, are part of Italian culture and are everywhere in this city. At the Sunday flea market at Porta Portese, buyers look for images of the past.

ber of visitors per year is now approaching six million, two-thirds of whom are foreigners, with the three biggest groups being Americans, Japanese, and Germans. The Roman Catholic Jubilee of the year 2000 is expected to attract 30 million visitors.

Despite this influx from without, for decades Rome was strongly resistant to most foreign influences. Until recently, the capital (like most of Italy) boasted a society that was almost stiflingly homogeneous: Almost everyone was white and Catholic (at least nominally). As recently as the mid-1970s, the number of foreign restaurants could be counted on two hands. Now all this has changed and Rome appears to be on the brink

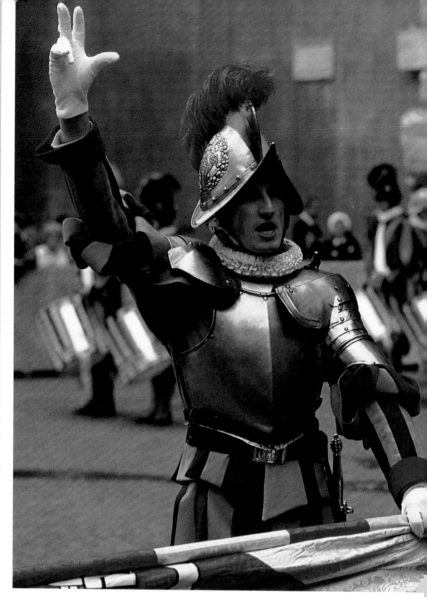

of recapturing the multiracial and polyglot atmosphere it surely had during the imperial period, when people from all corners of the empire came here, albeit—in the case of slaves—not always voluntarily.

In less than a decade, the arrival of tens of thousands of immigrants from Africa, Asia, and the Middle East, have set in motion an ethnic revolution that in the long run is bound to have profound social and cultural implications, not least because the Italian birthrate is currently the lowest in the world. Many are illegal, many others have succeeded, thanks to Italy's frequent amnesties, in getting work papers. At present, the biggest foreign group is from the Philippines. They are followed, in order, by Americans, citizens of the former Yugoslavia, Poles, Spaniards, Brits, Indians, Somalis, and Brazilians. Immigrants from developing countries work as domestic help, construction workers, housepainters, or home aides for the elderly. Many Senegalese

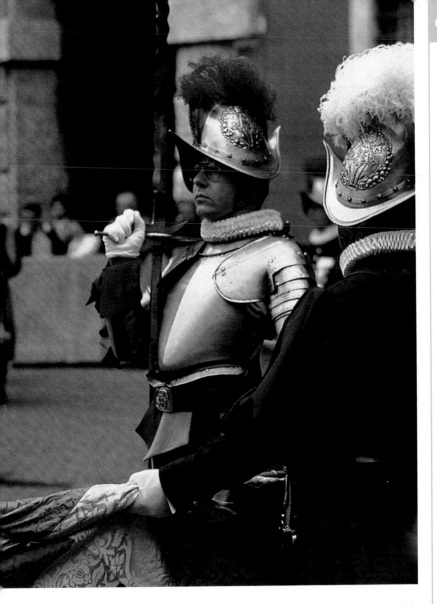

are street peddlers. Chinese run the city's dozens of Chinese restaurants and carry-outs. Egyptians work in restaurant kitchens and may have cooked that luscious *all'amatriciana* that you are eating.

LA DOLCE VITA, ROMAN STYLE

Most of the new arrivals from developing countries have come to Rome for very clear, work-related reasons. They are part of a huge south–north, east–west migration toward

The Swiss Guard was instituted in the 16th century to protect the pope. The uniform has been unchanged since then.

Europe that reflects the sharp differences in living standards that afflict our world. In contrast, foreigners who have come to Rome from developed countries such as the U.S. and the U.K. are generally motivated by totally different considerations. First, they know that this city is an open-air museum where the ruins and records of the near and more distant past can be found at almost every turn in the road.

Furthermore, Rome would also appear to have an inside track on sensuality, relaxation, and overall hedonism. And how could it be otherwise in a society that puts beauty and pleasure first and foremost? Although they frequently lose their tempers in traffic, Romans have turned being laid-back into an art form. Two thousand years of history, with all its vagaries, appear to have left the average Roman with one major conviction: Nothing is more important than the here and now, and the best way to enjoy it.

How do you know when it's spring in Rome? Because at the first warming of the sun's rays, everyone is outdoors, chatting on street corners, filling sidewalk cafés, or taking prolonged and possibly undeserved coffee breaks. How do you know when it's summer? Because everyone has left the city for the near-

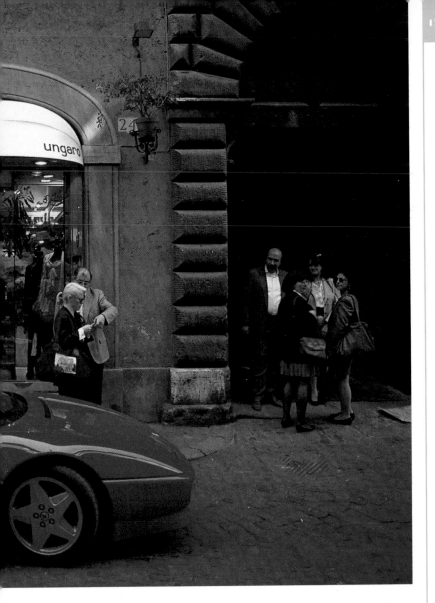

by beaches to soak up the sun, hopefully becoming even more beautiful in the process. During other seasons, they opt for the *gita in campagna*, a country jaunt, or a short trip to some nearby lovely village, especially if there's a good restaurant in the area. In the evenings, except when it's raining or when a soccer match is being telecast, Romans pour into the streets, particularly in neighborhoods such as Trastevere, Testaccio, and the area around the Pantheon. Many head for the local trattorias,

Conspicuous consumption and a passion for luxury products have always been key elements in the dolce vita.

since eating is definitely the number one Roman sport. An after-dinner *caffè* or *gelato*, a bit of people-watching, and some gossip are other favorite pastimes of the average Roman, especially since his *telefonino* allows him to keep in touch with his friends and, if necessary, head for a different destination. ∎

History of Rome

ROME IS ONE OF THE FEW CITIES IN THE WORLD TO HAVE BEEN CONTINU-
ously inhabited for the last 2,700 years, which is why so few traces of early settlement have
been found. Centuries have passed but the influence of its ancient heritage remains para-
mount and holds the key to understanding its later development.

THE FOUNDING OF ROME

From a literary point of view it sounds great:
Aeneas flees Troy by boat, carrying his aged
father Anchises on his back and leading his
small son Ascanius by the hand. He lands in
Italy and founds the city of Lavinium on the
coast. When Ascanius grows up, he founds
Alba Longa in the Alban Hills but because of
family squabbles over the throne in the suc-
ceeding generation, Romulus and Remus are
thrown into the Tiber River and wash up on
the slopes of the Palatine Hill where they are,
in short order, suckled by a she-wolf and res-
cued by a shepherd. The boys grow up, and set
about founding their own city. In the process
they quarrel: Remus is killed and Romulus
becomes the first king of Rome.

Unfortunately, very little of this may be
true. The Romans, in fact, were just one of the
many various peoples to inhabit the central
portion of the peninsula in the late Iron Age,
and which included the Etruscans, the Latins,
and the Samnites. The original population of
the area occupied by the future city of Rome
was therefore probably composed of an aggre-
gation of local tribes. In this context, the legend of the Sabine women makes sense. The
women were probably kidnapped by
Romulus's men because of a real shortage
of females.

What is surely true, according to the
traces that have been found of Rome's early
Iron Age dwellings on the Palatine Hill, is
that whoever settled this area probably had
an instinct for survival and then some.
The Palatine was, after all, the most strategic
location for a primitive settlement: A hill
that was easy to defend, but at the same
time was close to a major river with natural
port facilities. Even more to the point the
hill was not too distant from the most
fordable spot on the river, where the
existence of Tiber Island made crossing
considerably easier.

ROYAL & REPUBLICAN ROME

Romulus, then (or someone like him), was
Rome's first king, and legend tells us that he
was the first of seven, the others being Numa
Pompilius, Tullus Hostilius, Ancus Marcius,
Tarquinius Priscus, Servius Tullius, and
Tarquinius Superbus ("the proud"). The
existence of the first rulers cannot be proved.
But all indications are that the last three,
all with Etruscan names, did exist, and their
Etruscan origin testifies to the likelihood of
some degree of tribal intermingling. Another
clue is that the Etruscans had highly developed
engineering skills and it was precisely then, in
the sixth century B.C., that the marshy area
between the Palatine and Capitoline Hills, the
future Roman Forum, was drained.

Tarquinius Superbus is believed to have
been deposed in 509 B.C. and the monarchy
was then replaced by a republic with two consuls elected annually by the men of the city.
The consuls appointed the members of an
advisory council which eventually became
known as the Senate. Formally at least, this
political system was to last until the advent of
imperial rule under Octavius, or, as he preferred to be called after 27 B.C., Augustus. But
over the centuries it evolved and changed. At
first, the government was dominated by a
patrician elite whose influence derived largely
from the wealth that allowed them to lead the
republic's armies and, later, when qualifica-
tions including wealth and land owning were
set, to dominate the Senate. The result was
years of conflict with the unlanded and the
unwealthy plebeians. During the fourth
century B.C., after skillful manipulation of
public opinion in the Forum's open-air assem-
blies, the dispossessed finally won the right to
equal representation. In fact, say historians,

**The pontiff performs ceremonial rites at
his altar under Bernini's bronze canopy in
St. Peter's Basilica.**

Rome's first expansionist forays into surrounding areas may have been designed to acquire territory needed to distribute among the newly enfranchised.

THE ROMAN EMPIRE, ITS RISE & ITS DECLINE

Rome had an empire long before it had an emperor. In fact, despite the on-going conflict between plebeians and patricians (or perhaps because of it!), the Roman Republic gradually gained control of the city's hinterland. The twin deities, Castor and Pollux, are said to have lent a hand during the Battle of Lake Regillus in 496 B.C., where the Romans defeated the Latin League. Be that as it may, this proved to be the start of an almost unbroken series of military successes, ending with the conquest of all the other peoples of Latium (the area surrounding Rome), be they Latins, Etruscans, Volsci, or Aequi to name but a few. And if the invasion of central Italy by the Gauls in 390 B.C. looked like it was about to become a major setback, it didn't: The young republic was saved when the Veneti attacked the Gauls on their northern flank, forcing them to head back home.

By the middle of the third century B.C., Rome's armies had conquered most of southern Italy. It was in this period that the major consular roads, beginning with the Via Appia to the south and the Via Aurelia and Via Flaminia to the north, were built to facilitate both troop movements and trade. Expansion almost to the shores of Sicily, until then considered to be a part of Carthage's sphere of influence, brought Rome into open conflict with that North African stronghold. The three Punic wars, lasting on and off for 118 years (264 B.C. to 146 B.C.), ended with the destruction of what was then Rome's only major rival for power in the western Mediterranean, and, at the same time, witnessed the first Roman expansion outside the confines of the Italian peninsula: Sardinia, Corsica, and Illyria (today's Dalmation coast) fell under Roman sway, soon followed by Macedonia, Greece, and parts of Asia Minor.

When Julius Caesar appeared on the scene in the first century B.C., Rome's attention had for almost a century been focused on political and social problems at home rather than on

further expansion, although during his reign Caesar did manage to defeat and annex Gaul. The social unrest of the era, however, allowed Caesar increasingly to concentrate power in his hands, a trend that was to continue and be further reinforced by Augustus. Under Augustus, who defeated Mark Antony and Cleopatra, Egypt became a Roman province, Spain was completely subjugated, and the empire's borders were extended as far as the Rhine and the Danube. The next hundred years saw more of the same. Britain was conquered, Palestine was annexed, and under Trajan (A.D. 98–117) the empire reached its maximum limits of expansion, stretching from the British Isles to Asia Minor.

By the second half of the second century A.D., however, barbarian tribes had begun to pose a real threat. Hadrian's decision to build his famous defensive wall in England, completed in A.D. 136, was significant. As Roman competence on the battlefield declined (the empire's overextension was one reason for this), barbarian encroachments increased. In A.D. 325, Constantine founded Constantinople, which soon became the administrative capital of the empire. Not many years after Constantine's death in A.D. 337, the empire was divided in half. The Eastern Empire, governed from Constantinople, was strong enough to survive for another thousand years. Disaster loomed in the west, however, where repeated barbarian invasions took place. In 410, the Visigoths, led by Alaric, descended on Rome, pillaging for three days and putting an end to the city's

Statues from the garden at Villa Borghese are stored in a shed to protect them from vandalism and theft.

reputation of invincibility. In 476, the Germanic warrior, Odovacar, deposed the last emperor, Romulus Augustulus, but a teenager. Despite its unhappy end, the achievements of the Roman Empire cannot be minimized. Military prowess, combined with an ability to incorporate conquered peoples into its social and political system brought unparalleled success. The proof? Five Latin-based Romance languages (Italian, French, Spanish, Portuguese, and Romanian), the 26-letter western alphabet, the continued use of Roman numerals, and a calendar of 12 months and 365 days.

CHRISTIANITY & THE PAPACY

It was under Roman rule that Jesus was crucified. It was in Rome that both Peter and Paul
suffered martyrdom and where the shrines so
dear to future pilgrims were built over their
graves. Rome is the center of Catholicism
because the popes, in a direct line of Apostolic
succession, are considered heirs of St. Peter.
The history of Christianity is thus inextricably
intertwined with that of the Roman Empire.
Indeed, in the Middle Ages many believed that
the Roman Empire had been part of a divine
plan to provide a stable geographical area and
a fertile terrain for the spread of Christianity.
Having achieved its purpose, the pagan
Roman Empire could decline and disappear,
to be replaced by the new universal, but
Christian, empire. Unfortunately, things were
not quite so cut and dried.

Peter and Paul both died in Rome, probably during the early Neronian persecutions
between A.D. 64 and 67. For centuries, however, Christianity remained only one of many
cults exported to Rome from the East. And
even after it had become the favored sect of
the imperial family under Constantine, there
were problems. Much of the Roman elite
remained fiercely pagan. Indeed, it was only in
the fifth century that Christianity became
strong enough to step, definitively, out of the
closet. It was in this period, in fact, that the
first grandiose churches, such as Santa Sabina
(see pp. 208–209), were built.

As the papacy began to reign supreme in
spiritual matters, it also gradually assumed
responsibility for the temporal welfare of
Rome's population, filling in increasingly for
the absentee rulers in Constantinople. In the
aftermath of the disastrous sixth-century
Gothic wars, Pope St. Gregory the Great
(590–604) was forced to provide food and
shelter for a population swollen with impover-
ished refugees. Diaconates were created for the
distribution of food, and in the ninth century
defensive structures were built around the
Vatican by Leo IV to protect it from the
marauding Saracens. Greater power meant a
larger bureaucratic apparatus and, particularly
after the reign (1073–1085) of Gregory VII, an
increased determination to remain independent of any temporal authority, be it king or
emperor. This led to the famous conflict over
who had the authority to appoint (or invest)
bishops, the so-called Investiture Controversy,
between the Holy Roman Emperor Henry IV
and Pope Gregory VII, which continued to
rankle even after the compromise solution of
the Concordat of Worms (1122).

If the 12th and 13th centuries witnessed
the papacy's transformation into a first-rate
European political power, a gradual decline in
status and effective political clout was
inevitable. By the beginning of the 1300s,
other European nations, as well as the increasingly prosperous Italian city-states, were
emerging as independent power brokers. In
Rome, rampant factionalism and bitter
rivalries among the city's noble families led
the popes to move the Holy See to Avignon in
France (the so-called Babylonian Captivity),
where they were to remain for much of the
14th century. During this period a vast
reorganization of Church agencies and administration was begun, as were reform measures
for the clergy. The close connection to the
French court, and the consequent tensions
with England and Germany, ended by damag-
ing the papacy's prestige.

RENAISSANCE

Historians have been discussing the true
significance of the Renaissance (literally
"rebirth") almost since its inception. What is
not questioned, however, is its outcome (the
birth of modern Europe) and its place of origin (Italy). The upsurge of renewed interest in
the learning and values of classicism was
probably inevitable in Italy with its abundance
of classical ruins. The result was humanism, a
philosophy propounded by secular men of letters as well as Church scholars whose primary
emphasis was on the intellectual and artistic
capacities of man. This period of heightened
artistic expression was to really take off when
the prosperous and ambitious princes of the
burgeoning Italian city-states, such as the
Medici in Florence, summoned to their courts
some of the era's most prestigious painters,
sculptors, architects, and draftsmen.

The papacy, always resilient, was to reach
new heights in the rarefied atmosphere of the
Renaissance (and again in the 1500s) in
response to the birth of Protestantism, becoming an incomparable patron of the arts. By the

Andrea del Pozzo, a 17th-century Jesuit, painted "The Entry of St. Ignatius into Paradise" on the ceiling of St. Ignatius Church.

middle of the 15th century, the pontiffs had reasserted their authority over the Eternal City and, applying their vast resources to the city's embellishment, had shifted the center of the Renaissance from Florence to Rome. Starting about 1450, a series of ambitious, wily, and even (occasionally) erudite popes, dedicated much of their attention to beautifying their city. Tuscan and Umbrian artists such as Fra Angelico, Pinturicchio, and Michelangelo were brought to Rome to decorate Vatican interiors such as Nicholas V's chapel, the Borgia apartments, and, of course, the Sistine Chapel, which for close to 60 years kept many famous artists occupied. In architecture, too, the Renaissance was to leave its mark on Rome and here, as well, the Church was to prove a major patron. An eloquent example was Donato Bramante, considered the creator of High Renaissance architecture, who designed the classically inspired Tempietto at San Pietro in Montorio (see p. 189) and then, appointed

Papal Architect by Julius II (1503–13), produced the first designs for the new, gigantic St. Peter's.

COUNTER-REFORMATION & THE BAROQUE

The religious movement identified as the Counter-Reformation was to have a profound effect on its capital, Rome, as well as on the psychology of its governing elite. At its inception, it was a reaction to the Protestant Reformation begun by Martin Luther in the early part of the 16th century. The reforms set off by the challenge of that breakaway movement were to stimulate an era of intense religious fervor, bringing to the fore zealot saints such as St. Philip Neri, St. Theresa of Avila, and, of course, St. Ignatius of Loyola. The latter's soldier mentality (he was once quoted as declaring that he had "never left the army") left its mark on the quasi-military structure of his newly created order, the Society of Jesus (the Jesuits), who were often referred to as the "pope's legions."

The Counter-Reformation also represented a period of serious self-analysis on the part of the Roman Catholic Church. If the three-part Council of Trent (1545–1563) was to establish the doctrinal foundations and the institutional structures that would help the Church

Streets, piazzas, monuments, and high schools throughout Italy are named after Giuseppe Garibaldi.

to survive the Protestant challenge, it also outlined the basic tenets that would govern the life of ordinary Catholics until the Second Vatican Council (1962–65). Primarily conservative in nature, the Trent Council confirmed that the Church alone could interpret Scripture, reformed monastic and religious orders, created a new catechism, and adopted the Tridentine Latin Mass. The renewed vigor brought to the papacy by the Counter-Reformation and the Council of Trent was to give it a new lease on political life and two more centuries as a truly important player on the European stage. The emergence of a new world of young nation-states changed things, however, gradually pushing the Holy See to the political sidelines.

IL RISORGIMENTO & NATIONAL UNIFICATION

Il Risorgimento (from the Italian verb, *risorgere*, to rise again) was the prime force in 19th-century Italy. The ideological and bureaucratic groundwork laid by the French Revolution and the Napoleonic Wars had set in motion a desire for national unification. Three great men were on hand to make it happen: Giuseppe Mazzini, a democratic nationalist; Giuseppe Garibaldi, a firebrand general whose father was a fisherman; and Count Camillo Cavour, a Piedmontese aristocrat and skilled politician-diplomat. Their combined efforts resulted in the proclamation of the Kingdom of Italy in March 1861. Only two pieces were missing: Venice (to be conquered from Austria in 1866) and Rome, which, thanks to French acquiescence, was to be taken from the pope by Italian armies on September 20, 1870.

Papal rule and the overweening influence of the fractious Roman nobility had not done much for the city. At the end of the 18th century, Rome, with a population of under 200,000, was still a backwater provincial capital, but intellectual currents were running swift. A 15-year period of occupation by Napoleon's armies had infected many Romans with the virus of liberalism and republicanism, and in 1848 Pope Pius IX granted a constitution. This didn't satisfy Mazzini and his supporters who in 1849 proclaimed the short-lived Roman Republic. Despite a valiant defense by the "Garibaldini" and others, the French, acting for the pope, retook the city. But time was running out for the papacy.

Before 1859, as Austria's Metternich had put it, Italy was only "a geographical expression." Divided into eight separate states, it was subject to the domination of foreign powers, mainly France, Spain, and Austria, while the popes still controlled a broad swathe of central Italy. The desire for unification was to snowball, however, particularly after Cavour became prime minister of Piedmont in 1852. Allied with the French, in 1859 the Piedmontese took Lombardy from the Austrians and the next year annexed Umbria and the Marches. In the south, Garibaldi and his Thousand defeated the Bourbon armies, conquering Sicily and then Naples. The remaining Italian states chose union with Piedmont. Rome remained in papal hands, but not for long, although attempts by Garibaldi to capture the city in 1862 and 1867 were unsuccessful. In 1870, with France weakened by its war with Prussia, Italy had its chance. On September 20, Italian troops opened a breach in the city walls (at Porta Pia) and entered Rome. After a plebiscite, Rome became Italy's capital.

FASCISM, WAR, & DEMOCRACY

Rome's population grew rapidly after 1870. By the onset of World War I it had hit 500,000 and by 1930 there were over one million inhabitants. The city had now also expanded well beyond the old Roman walls built by Aurelian. Given the imperial ambitions of the Fascist dictator, Benito Mussolini, it is not sur- prising that the Fascist regime undertook important archaeological excavations that brought to light or restored many of the mon- uments of ancient Rome. It was at that time, too, that a major impetus was given to the transformation of the city into a modern capi- tal: The then avant-garde EUR section (for a projected 1942 international fair) was built, as were the new, grandiose avenues such as Fori Imperiali and Conciliazione, although the lat- ter two cost the city the loss of two important medieval neighborhoods.

As the capital of Italy, the 20th century saw an enhancement of the administrative charac- ter that the city had already acquired under its popes. But the social stresses and strains of building a nation (and of "making Italians" as the 19th-century statesman, Metternich, had put it) were to have disastrous consequences. Neutral when the Great War began, Italy joined up in hopes of territorial gains, but the war was unpopular and the loss of 600,000 men made it particularly hard to swallow the Triple Entente's refusal to give Italy Dalmatia and Fiume, now part of Croatia, leading nationalists to bemoan a "mutilated victory." Serious postwar economic problems—includ- ing galloping inflation and soaring unemploy- ment—increased the social unrest that led both to the growing popularity of the Left and to the rise of the Right. Mussolini's October 1922 march on Rome won him the govern- ment, but within two years he had already eliminated democracy, disbanding most of

Italy's constitutional system, banning free speech and association, bridling the press, and, in the late 1930s, introducing anti-Semitic laws. Nevertheless, many aspects of the regime were genuinely popular.

Following Italy's censure by the League of Nations (for invading Ethiopia), Mussolini moved closer to Hitler. The military alliance

This was a favorite pose of Benito Mussolini, the fascist dictator. His urban renovations destroyed medieval areas.

with Germany was to have disastrous economic and military consequences. In July 1943, following the Allied invasion of Sicily, Mussolini was dismissed and arrested and an armistice signed. The Germans immediately occupied Rome and the Italian army disintegrated. Despite the valiant efforts of the Resistance, more active farther north, it was only in June 1944 that the city was liberated by the Allies. After World War II, which had left the country devastated and Rome demoral- ized, the foundations were laid for a democra- tic system. In 1946 Italians voted to end the monarchy and found a republic. The new 1948 constitution established a multiparty, parlia- mentary system which, although chaotic and confusing, has allowed Italy to regain a place of respect within the family of nations. ∎

The arts

THE BEAUTY OF THE ETERNAL CITY IS NOT OF THE CONTEMPORARY KIND.
The two major influences on Rome's artistic heritage were, without a doubt, the Roman
Empire and the papacy and these have left their indelible mark on the city.

ARCHITECTURE & ART

The Emperor Augustus reportedly claimed
that he had found a city made of brick and left
one made of marble. In a sense this is true.
Like his adoptive father, Julius Caesar,
Augustus learned early on that public works
constituted an effective way, not just to
embellish an imperial city and heighten its
prestige, but to gain the good will, or at least
the tolerance, of public opinion. Architectural
extravaganzas were not undertaken simply
because there was an empty space to fill. From
the Colosseum to the Arch of Titus, from the
refurbished Temple of Vesta to the Baths of

Caracalla, the political significance was funda-
mental. The concept that art "is the handmaiden of politics" has been around for a long
time. Perhaps no other country, and its capital,
has so benefited from the ambitions and, yes,
megalomania of its rulers, be they emperors,
popes, or princes. The final result is layer upon
layer of artistic and architectural glory. Look
around you at the ruins of so many past
regimes. The stratification is such that if you
observe carefully, you can usually identify the
successive layers of Rome's past majesty, often
in the very same structure.

Architecture had its first real boom with

the advent of the Imperial Roman era. Some emperors built for their own enjoyment alone: Nero and his Golden House come to mind. But in most instances, their major building projects were destined for public use. And the largely unknown architects of ancient Rome did wonders: Some of their constructions—the Pantheon, the Colosseum, Trajan's Markets, the Arches of Titus, Septimius Severus, and Constantine—still stand today, mute witnesses of past glories, silent embellishments even today of man's all too brief existence.

Just how different from the emperors of Rome were the popes of the Eternal City? Was not the construction of Santa Sabina in the early fifth century in the midst of an elegant,

The restoration of the Sistine Chapel was completed in 1989. Here, a craftsman works on Michelangelo's "Last Judgment."

and until then largely pagan, aristocratic quarter, a political affirmation of Christianity's march toward primacy? In fact, Catholicism's decision to convert many ancient Roman structures into churches (thereby ensuring their survival), was hardly made on practical grounds alone: The symbolic and psychological content of certain gestures, for example moving the doors of Julius Caesar's Senate to the Basilica of San Giovanni in Laterano, appears obvious. But once again, we are the beneficiaries. Whether we are Catholic, Protestant, Jew, Muslim, or Buddhist, our lives have been enriched by the political decisions of Rome's past secular and religious rulers.

Naturally, some of Christianity's constructions were largely idealistic in inspiration. In some of the early churches, built near or over the shrines of early martyrs, or like Santa Maria in Cosmedin, on the site of an early diaconate, you can almost physically sense the aura of Christian faith. Later on, vigorous building campaigns by the papacy, especially in the 9th and 13th centuries, served a dual purpose: New structures were needed to welcome the faithful, but glorification of the mother institution was also part of the process. The building of St. Peter's in the 16th and 17th centuries may have been the most blatant example of architectural self-glorification. The papacy also used interior decoration to effectively reaffirm its precepts; the examples of decorative work with an explicit political undertone are numerous. One of the most eloquent examples from the Middle Ages is the series of 13th-century frescoes in the St. Sylvester chapel in the church of the Quattro Coronati near the Colosseum. The decision to depict events in the life of the Emperor Constantine in such a way as to make him appear subservient to Pope Sylvester is propaganda at its best. How else to explain the final scene in which Constantine, on foot, humbly holds the reins of the pope's donkey!

From the Renaissance on, mosaic work— for centuries the most widely used decorative medium in the classical world—was replaced by sculpture and painting, perfect tools for the expression of political concepts and conceits. For centuries, statuary as a medium had been reserved for the representation of gods and secular rulers. One thinks, for example, of the equestrian statue of Marcus Aurelius (long believed to be Constantine) or the statue of Augustus from Livia's villa at Prima Porta. In the 13th century, the popes, too, began to commission statues of themselves—as rulers rather than religious leaders—to be displayed in public. So only a few feet away from Arnolfo di Cambio's statue of Charles of Anjou (dressed as a Roman senator) in the Capitoline Museum are Bernini's statue of Pope Urban VIII, a Barberini, and Algardi's statue of Innocent X, a Pamphili. And you can't miss the political overtones of Raphael's paintings in the so-called Rooms of Raphael in the Vatican Museums. The "Expulsion of Heliodorus from the Temple," for example, was a clear allusion to Pope Julius II's military campaign to expel usurpers from Church lands.

Gian Lorenzo Bernini, "sovereign of the arts, to whom popes, princes and peoples reverently bowed" (see the plaque on his house on Via della Mercede, near the corner with Propaganda Fide), was undoubtedly a genius. The baroque style, of which he is indisputably one of the major creative protagonists, is perhaps the maximum example of art used to convey concepts—primarily faith in the Church and in its doctrines—that transcend the purely ornamental. Designed to combat the rapidly spreading Protestant Reformation and, at the same time, to emphasize the importance of the Catholic religion, the baroque was blatantly propagandistic: All the plastic arts (architecture, painting, sculpture) were used to make an appeal to the faithful that was both sensory and emotional. The magnificence of Rome's baroque churches such as Il Gesù (the mother Jesuit church) or Santa Maria della Vittoria was successfully intended to underscore the magnificence and importance of the papacy, to impress the viewer, and convince him that the Roman Catholic Church was the oldest, the best, and the only institution qualified to decipher Divine Will (and scripture) for the faithful. A sharp contrast with the sense of Martin Luther's reforms which stressed the necessity for individual interpretation of scripture.

It was also a lucky break for the Vatican (and for Rome) that three of the great baroque

The gloriously decorated **Sala Regia** was the room in the **Apostolic Palace** where rulers came to pay homage to the pope.

geniuses (Bernini, Francesco Borromini, and Pietro da Cortona) were contemporaries and spent most of their creative lives in the Eternal City. The extravagant characteristics of their styles (rich colors, gold decoration, unlimited movement, endless depth, diagonal lines, whether concave or convex, dramatic lighting, and theatricality) were utilized in complex compositions to overwhelm the senses, to impress, to underline the importance of the clergy and the Church as an institution, and, through an appeal to the senses, to stimulate piety and devotion. The overall effect—dynamism and movement in sharp contrast to the stability and unambiguous definition of Renaissance painting and sculpture—is often overwhelming.

The Church also encouraged and utilized musicians. Palestrina, from the nearby town of the same name, a major innovator of contrapuntal composition, composed at least 105 Masses while in Rome, many of which he dedicated to Pope Julius III, for a while his patron.

Subsequently, in the 17th century, the Italian baroque was exported abroad and was adopted by secular rulers elsewhere—Versailles in France and the Tsars' Winter Palace in St. Petersburg are good examples—for their own purposes. The situation was different, the message was the same: I am powerful, I am to be admired, feared, and—above all—respected.

In the 20th century, the Fascist government continued (albeit less successfully) with the traditional use of art and architecture by autocratic governments as a means of reinforcing power and prestige. In the 1920s and '30s, Mussolini's regime fostered a style which, although presented in a modern guise, adopted many ancient Roman motifs. The idea was to reinforce its legitimacy as the true heir to the ancient grandeur of Rome. The present-day Via dei Fori Imperiali was, at its inauguration, called the Via dell'Impero. Some might have thought the reference was to the empire that the Italians were then seeking to create through the annexation of territory in North Africa, but just as likely was the desire to be seen as successors to the "Impero" that, with far greater success, had existed two thousand years before.

The sprawling Foro Italico sports complex was begun by Mussolini's fascist regime. In 1960 it was the site of the Olympic Games.

LITERATURE

In the early days of ancient Rome, educated people used Greek for learning and for literary expression. By the first century B.C., Latin had asserted itself as an artistic medium. Plautus, a comic poet, used colloquial Latin for his plays as did Ennius with his epics and tragedies. By the second half of the first century B.C., there were many writers of distinction, including Julius Caesar. But Cicero—philospher, orator, and poet—stands out for his use of Latin in the expression of complex, abstract thought. Virgil was not a Roman, but in the capital he became part of an elite circle of poets close to the Emperor Augustus, and his works—

particularly the *Aeneid*—became an inspiration. The poet Horace was lauded for the perfection of form of his *Odes* and *Epistles*. Ovid wrote witty and elegiac poetry. Poems were recited in literary circles and in public, and great importance was given to structure and euphony. Whereas Livy and Tacitus excelled in history, Seneca chose tragedy, and Juvenal, satire. The post-Augustan period, while more subject to political suppression, still produced writers as skillful as Petronius, Statius, Martial, and Suetonius. Later, Romans began to write in Greek again, in fact, the greatest work by a Roman in the first centuries A.D., Marcus Aurelius's *Meditations*, was written in Greek.

In the intervening centuries, most writing in Latin was done by prelates or people trained in church schools. The 13th century, however, brought the first examples of literature in the vernacular and the emergence of major Italian writers such as Dante, Petrarch, and Boccaccio, none of whom were Roman, although Petrarch, was crowned with laurel at the Campidoglio in 1341. Torquato Tasso, who was born in Sorrento and lived in Urbino, Venice, Padua, Ferrara, and Paris, was also supposed to be made Poet Laureate of Rome, but died shortly after arriving (1595) and is buried in the Church of Sant'Onofrio. It is probable that papal rule was not particularly conducive to the development of secular literature and poetry. It was not until the 19th century, in fact, that a major Roman poet appeared, Giovanni Gioacchino Belli, whose 2,000 sonnets in Roman dialect, for the most part composed around 1830, present a vivid and satirical picture of life in contemporary Rome.

By the late Renaissance, however, Rome had become a magnet for many foreign writers. Well-known early visitors include the French essayist Montaigne and the English poet John Milton. In the 18th and 19th centuries, inspired visitors included the German poet Goethe, the French writer Stendhal, the American writers Nathaniel Hawthorne, Mark Twain, and later Theodore Dreiser, and the English poets Percy Bysshe Shelley, George Gordon Byron, and John Keats as well as Robert and Elizabeth Browning. George Eliot sent her *Middlemarch* protagonist, Dorothea Brooke, on an eye-opening trip to Rome with her parson husband, and much of Henry James's *Daisy Miller* is set here.

In the 20th century, several major writers emerged in Rome. Alberto Moravia, who died in 1990, started out as a journalist and wrote of alienation in modern society. His first novel, *Gli Indifferenti* (Time of Indifference), was published when he was only 21. Other major works, most of which have been translated into English, include *Agostino* (*Two Adolescents*, 1944), *La Romana* (*The Woman of Rome*, 1947), *Il conformista* (*The Conformist*, 1951), and *La ciociara* (*Two Women*, 1957), which became a prize-winning movie with Sophia Loren. Moravia was married for a while to the writer Elsa Morante, who died in 1985. Her best-known work, remarkable for its epic quality, is the 1974 *La Storia*, published in English as *History: A Novel*.

Another well-known writer, poet, and movie director was Pier Paolo Pasolini, a northern Italian born in 1922 who came to Rome after the war and used the material from his contacts among the city's down-and-outs for two novels: *Ragazzi di vita* (*The Ragazzi*, 1955) and *Una vita violenta* (*A Violent Life*, 1959). Like his first film, *Accattone*, they deal with the lives of thieves, prostitutes, and other denizens of the Roman underworld. In 1975 Pasolini was murdered by a young man who could have been one of his characters.

THE MUSEUM REVOLUTION

In classic terms, Rome is not a cultural center. It is not a city you would visit for a chance to see opera or ballet. The theater, such that it is, is limited to Italian speakers. With a few exceptions, such as the Auditorium of Santa Cecilia, classical music programs leave much to be desired although there are many small chamber music concerts and recitals held in picturesque churches and palaces.

Nor are the city's art galleries generally on the international circuit. However, the city has incomparable riches to offer an art lover. Itself an open-air museum where city squares contain Roman temples, Renaissance palaces, and fountains designed by master sculptors, Rome also has a large number of well-endowed museums. The Vatican Museums are known the world over. Many of Rome's museums

have been renovated, reorganized, and reopened to become far more user-friendly. A case in point is the Borghese Gallery. Now on everyone's A list (and justly so), it was closed for over a decade while its poorly displayed masterpieces stood alone and ignored. Now, after a glorious restoration, it has a modern museum structure (although the internal organization is still far from perfect) to show off its incomparable collections.

The Museo Nazionale Romano, housed in the Baths of Diocletian near the station, for years was forced by lack of space to keep most of its ancient treasures in storerooms and cellars. Now, under the direction of the Superintendent of Archaeology, a former high school, Palazzo Massimo alle Terme, and a Renaissance cardinal's palace, Palazzo Altemps, have been made into parallel sections, wonderfully receptive structures where some of the best statuary and mosaic work—often organized along thematic lines—is on display.

Another new museum is the Montemartini, established in an obsolete power plant outside the downtown area to host many of the artworks of the Capitoline Museums, which in 1998–99 was closed for renovation, but has now taken on a life of its own. Other museums such as Villa Giulia (the Etruscan Museum) and the National Gallery in the Palazzo Barberini have also been somewhat refurbished, although the latter, despite a grand new entranceway and bookshop, still leaves a lot to be desired in arrangement, display, and labeling of works. Still, in a society that does not count efficiency and organization among its top priorities, the changes are really revolutionary.

And it doesn't end there. In 1827, Stendhal complained in his *Promenades dans Rome* that "the small-minded brains which currently hold power permit us to visit these museums [the Capitoline and the Pio Clementino at the Vatican] only once a week." That was, of course, a long time ago, but until only a few years back the visiting hours at Rome's museums were frustratingly short (most closed at 1 or 2 p.m.) and differed notably one from the other. Now all this has changed. Except for Mondays, when most public museums are closed, museums are open all day long and, in summer and in other holiday periods, until late in the evening. Services have become far more efficient, better qualified personnel have been hired, and reservation systems and information offices have been put in place, representing the creativity, flare, and style which the Italians are so good at—when they wish to be.

Rome also has a series of smaller, lesser-known museums that are worth a visit if there is time. The Museo di Roma, soon to be reopened, has art and artifacts related to Rome's history since the Middle Ages. The Colonna family collection goes on view only once a week on Saturday mornings but gives you the chance to step inside this massive patrician palace (entrance at Via della Pilotta 17). And, although the Palazzo delle Esposizioni in Via Nazionale is very large, other much needed exhibition spaces have recently been added such as the Museo del Corso (Via del Corso), the Compesso del Vittoriano (Via San Pietro in Carcere), and the magnificent, newly restored Scuderie or stables in Piazza del Quirinale.

"HOLLYWOOD ON THE TIBER" & AFTER

In the beginning there was Cinecittà, the giant film studio founded in 1937 by Italian dictator Benito Mussolini, who had decided to take on Hollywood and to make Italian film production into a source of national prestige. Ironically, Mussolini's project was to bear its best fruit only once the Fascist regime had been roundly defeated in World War II and superseded by a young democratic republic. As early as the 1950s Neorealism and post Neorealism had put the Italian film industry on the map, and the names of the best directors, actors, and actresses were known throughout the intellectual world. The success of Cinecittà was brought home to all in 1963 on the set of *Cleopatra*, which became the stage setting for a major love story between the film's two principal stars, Elizabeth Taylor and Richard Burton. By the end of that decade, the Italian film industry was churning out between 200 and 250 films a year, some of which, over 40 years later, are still considered masterpieces. "Hollywood on the Tiber" it was called at the height of its prominence.

Today, all this has changed. Most of the major directors who made their names in that period—Roberto Rossellini (*Roma Citta' Aperta*), Lucchino Visconti (*Obsession, Senso, The Earth Trembles*), Vittorio De Sica (*The Bicycle Thief* and *Sciuscià*), Giuseppe De Sanctis (*Bitter Rice*), Pietro Germi (*Divorce Italian Style, Seduced and Abandoned*), Federico Fellini (*La Strada, La Dolce Vita, Roma, Amarcord*, etc.)—have died or, like Ettore Scola (*A Particular Day, C'Eravamo Tanto Amati*), and Michelangelo Antonioni (*Blow Up, L'Avventura*) are very old. Pier Paolo Pasolini (*The Gospel According to St. Matthew, The Hawks and the Sparrows, Theorem*, and *The Decameron*) was murdered. Major actors such as Marcello Mastroianni and Ugo Tognazzi have passed away or, like Sophia Loren, spend most of their time abroad. Producer Dino De Laurentiis has been in Hollywood since the 1970s and the aging Gillo Pontecorvo (*The Battle of Algiers*) has left artistic direction for management and is currently president of Cinecittà Holding, which rents out the once bustling studios. Symbolically, Studio 5, that preferred by Fellini and Antonioni, is now leased by Rai (Italian state television) and Mediaset (Silvio Berlusconi's film production company). In fact, other well-known directors such as Bernardo Bertolucci (*Last Tango in Paris*), Carlo Lizzani, the Taviani Brothers, and Francesco Rosi (*Salvatore Giuliano*) and younger personalities such as Nanni Moretti, Gianni Amelio, and Marco Risi now work mostly for television or for TV-financed movies. Nowadays, only between 60 and 70 films a year are produced in Italy and only about 20, mostly comedies with a strong local flavor, are shown in first-run theaters.

Decidedly, American films are among the most popular in Italy, although French and other European films have a following among Roman intellectuals. There are, however, a few native bright stars on the horizon. Ricky Tognazzi's film *Ultras* won top prize at the Berlin Film Festival a few years ago. Giuseppe Tornatore (*Nuovo Cinema Paradiso*) has a following both in the U.S. and France. Massimo Troisi's *Il Postino* was well received in the U.S. and was nominated for an Oscar shortly after the Neapolitan actor-director died of heart disease at the age of 42. In March

In *Roman Holiday* (1953) Audrey Hepburn and Gregory Peck use a favorite form of Italian transport.

1999, the Tuscan comedian Roberto Benigni won three Oscars for the touching *Life is Beautiful* about an Italian Jew in a German concentration camp, who wants his young son to believe it is all a game.

L'ESTATE ROMANO (THE ROMAN SUMMER)

The concept of *L'Estate Romano* first surfaced in the mid-1970s, when city culture commissioner Renato Nicolini set it in motion, turning the city into an outdoor festival with a something-for-everyone flavor. Parks become ballet stages, piazzas are turned into concert halls, basilicas into auditoriums, riverbanks into bookstalls. In 1976 there was a film festival at the Basilica of Massenzio (later venues have included the Circus Maximus and Tiber Island as well as the area facing the Arch of Constantine where, in September 1981, thousands turned up for the historic screening of Abel Gance's *Napoleon*). At its height in the

early 1980s the Massenzio Festival scheduled as many as 180 films (four a night) over a seven-week period, attracting more than 200,000 paying customers. There was ballet in Villa Ada, concerts in Villa Pamphili, jazz at the Villa Borghese lake (these days jazz is available at Villa Celimontana and Testaccio), and prose near what remains of Tasso's Oak. Symphonic music was also played at Massenzio, while mimes, Sicilian puppet troupes, majorettes, and so forth, fanned out through less central neighborhoods.

In 1994, after a period of reduced activity, the festival was relaunched and in recent summers has attracted some five million spectators with poetry readings, films showing in nine different venues, theater, music, and dance. Critics contend that the quality is not what it once was, but nonetheless the city "Kultur-market" is alive and well, and makes sure no one has an excuse to be bored (see p. 260). ∎

Food

DORMOUSE GLAZED WITH HONEY, ROLLED IN POPPY SEEDS, AND BAKED (a favorite of Trimalchio, Petronius' intemperate gourmet in *Satyricon*) or, alternatively, stuffed with minced meat, pepper, and nuts, and then roasted or boiled. Sow udders stuffed with oysters, gourds with popular fish sauce made from salted and fermented fish intestines, crushed boiled brains with pepper, milk, and eggs, and then to finish off (after a minimum of seven courses) a roast pig stuffed with live quail (Trimalchio again). But not to worry. Although food, and the eating of it, is as important today as it was in ancient times, some things have changed, and happily dormice and fish sauce are off the menu.

Other things have changed for the better. In fact, if you look through Apicius's *De Re Coquinaria*, the first thing you'll realize is that many of the staple products that we associate with Italian cuisine today were unknown in ancient Rome. Tomatoes, eggplant, and zucchini to name just a few, arrived later from the New World. Instead of durum wheat—not used to make pasta in Naples until the 17th century—the Romans imported a type of

A viable alternative to a pasta meal can be a spread of starters or antipasti followed by a second meat or fish course.

grain called *faro adoreum*, and this was used to make *puls*, a boiled cereal that may have been similar to polenta. The unleavened bread of those days was sometimes cut into strips but it was far different from ours. What the two eras have in common, however, is gastronomic enthusiasm. Although the crowded sandwich

bars and the proliferation of fast-food outlets confirm that the three-hour lunch has more or less disappeared (and multicourse dinners are, also, increasingly infrequent)—food is still a top priority. In fact, if there is anything a Roman likes to do more than eat, it is to regale his dinner parties with tales of what he ate yesterday, or on some more remote occasion.

Rome has never been cited for the delicacy or the refinement of its cuisine, which is instead hearty and robust, a collection of dishes, often washed down with a bottle of Castelli white, that represent real comfort food but which the wise will ingest only infrequently. The pasta dishes most basic to the Roman cuisine are probably *rigatoni all'amatriciana* (with smoked pancetta, tomato, and onion), *spaghetti alla carbonara* (pancetta, beaten egg, and onion), *spaghetti alla gricia* (the same but without the egg), or the rudimentary *aglio, olio, peperoncino* (oil, garlic, and chili pepper). Best vegetables include artichokes, Roman style (*carciofi alla romana*) or fried, Jewish style (*carciofi alla giudea*). Also typical are *puntarelle in salsa d'alici* (raw chicory with anchovy sauce), *peperoni alla Romana* (red and green peppers sautéed with onion), lima beans with pancetta, or wild chicory with oil and lemon.

Another favorite is fried zucchini flowers, often part of a *misto fritto* (mixed fry) of *mozzarella*, artichokes, olives, and sometimes brains. As far as meat goes, the most characteristic dishes are roast pork (*maialino arrosto*), baby lamb (*abbacchio*), and tripe. In fact, innards are an important part of the city's traditional *cucina povera*. In the old days *rigatoni alla pajata* (lamb's intestine) was popular, and some people still swear by lamb heart (*coratella*), served with artichokes, and *coda alla vaccinara* (oxtail stew). ∎

Ave Caesar (Hail Caesar). Once the Roman Forum's temples echoed with these words. Today, the heart of ancient Rome is largely silent. But its splendid ruins testify loudly to the magnificent past when Roma was *caput mondi*.

Ancient Rome

Emperor Marcus Aurelius astride his mount at the Campidoglio

Ancient Rome

FROM THE BACK OF THE CAPITOLINE HILL, PROBABLY THE BEST PLACE TO take your first look at the Roman Forum, you are in the true sense of the term, a witness to centuries of history. In front of you, stretching for almost half a mile, is the Roman Forum and alongside it, flanking the Via dei Fori Imperiali, the excavated portions of the later imperial *fora* that were built by Julius Caesar, and a series of first-century emperors, to enlarge and beautify what had become an increasingly cramped downtown area. This small valley, tucked among several hills (the Palatine, the Capitoline, the Quirinal, and the Esquiline) is the heart of ancient Rome, in effect its birthplace.

The first Iron Age settlements, dating back to the ninth and eighth centuries B.C., were on the hilltops, specifically on the Palatine, which later became a prized site for imperial residences. Down below, where a somewhat marshy enclave was crisscrossed by a road or two, the foundations were laid for the development of an embryonic forum, an open space that could and would be used for everything from town meetings to commerce. In 753 B.C., or so they say, Romulus became the first king of Rome, performing the sacred ceremony (with a plow drawn by a snow white ox) of tracing the *pomerium* (perimeter) of the city, and (but this was not part of the ceremony) slaying his twin, Remus, for his irreverence. As the city grew, the forum was gradually transformed into a bona fide civic and religious center, a site for everything from protests and funerals to gladiatorial fights and theatrical presentations. The first monuments made their appearance during the monarchy. The Comitium, the circular open space in front of the Senate building, quickly became institutionalized as a place for discussion and debate. As Rome's wealth and power grew, and as conquering rulers returned from their first encounters with the more advanced Hellenistic world, the forum was to be further transformed, and increasingly embellished, to more adequately represent the grandeur of what was becoming a far-flung empire. From the fifth century A.D. on, however, it began declining in importance. Until the excavations of the 1800s, for most Romans it was of little interest: They called it Campo Vaccino, the cow pasture.

From your vantage point on the Capitoline Hill, you can easily identify the major sites. In the foreground is the Arch of Septimius Severus, to its left Diocletian's massive brick Curia, or Senate building, where Cicero declaimed against the would-be traitor, Cataline. The large, open space in front of the arch is the original Roman Forum, for centuries kept cleared of anything but Rome's three traditional food staples: the olive, the fig, and the grape. The eight large columns belonged to the portico of the Temple of Saturn. The long, rectangle beyond is all that's left of the Basilica Julia courthouse. Winding its way toward the Arch of Titus is the famous Via Sacra, believe it or not then considered a major thoroughfare, because there was room for two carts to drive abreast. Opposite you, toward the right, is the Palatine Hill, where Romulus and Remus may have lived, and farther away, to the left, you can just make out the top of the Colosseum.

Here on the hill, just to your right, you can see the grey blocks of peperino marble, now the foundation of the Palazzo Senatorio (see p. 39), that were once part of the Tabularium, the archives of ancient Rome. Nearby, atop a column, is a copy of the Capitoline wolf suckling Romulus and Remus. The original wolf, in the Capitoline Museum, is Etruscan: The infants were added later. In front of the Palazzo Senatorio is the Campidoglio, the magnificent Renaissance complex designed by Michelangelo to bring renewed glory to a site that for kings, tribunes, tyrants, and emperors was the heart of political and religious Rome. The smallest of the city's seven fabled hills, it is the most famous, giving us our word "capitol." The Capitoline Museums (see p. 40–41) are here, with famed statues such as that of Marcus Aurelius, the *Dying Gaul* and the *Boy with a Thorn,* as well as the sculpted faces of the elite of ancient Rome. ∎

Campidoglio

THE COMBINATION OF ARCHITECTURE AND HISTORY associated with the Campidoglio, or Capitol (Capitoline Hill), makes it an absolute must for any and every visitor. You should make it your business to come here at least twice, once during the day, preferably in the late afternoon, for the astonishing view of the sun-kissed Roman Forum below, and again at night, when marvelous lighting (for which the Italians have a real genius) turns the piazza designed by Michelangelo and the Roman ruins below into pure magic.

Campidoglio

Map p. 37

Bus: 56, 60, 62, 64, 70, 81, 87, 117, 170, 492 to Piazza Venezia or Teatro Marcello

The best way to reach the piazza is from the gradually ascending flight of stairs, called the *Cordonata,* designed by Michelangelo in 1536 to provide easy access to the square and flanked at the bottom by two black, basalt Egyptian lions. At the top of the staircase are the giant marbles statues of Castor and Pollux, which date back to Roman

times. Before you, in all its splendor (Pope Paul III commissioned it for a planned visit to Rome by the Holy Roman Emperor, Charles V) is **Piazza del Campidoglio,** set in what ancient times could clearly be seen to be a hollow between two hill crests. You might also want to note the statues of the Emperor Constantine and his son, ancient times was the temple to Jupiter Optimus Maximus, reported to be the largest of its kind ever constructed. Built in the 6th century B.C., we know that parts of it were still standing a thousand years later. Although excavations are in progress, all that you can see of it now is the podium, a wall of tufa blocks at the end of the long, second-floor corridor. Today, the two buildings house different sections of what are called the Musei Capitolini (see pp. 40–41).

Facing you from the bottom of the Cordonata is the **Palazzo Senatorio,** built in various stages in the 13th and 14th centuries on the remains of the Roman *tabularium,* and today the seat of Rome's municipal government.

Michelangelo designed the double ramp of stairs at the front, which is embellished by a fountain sporting two enormous reclining river gods, the Tiber on the right and the Nile on the left. In the niche in between is the "Dea Roma," a red-and-white stone composite of two earlier statues of Minerva, the goddess of wisdom and war. The bell tower, designed by Martin Longhi the Elder, was built between 1578 and 1582. The rest of the facade was added a bit later by architects Giacomo della Porta and Girolamo Rainaldi.

But at this point you'll probably only have eyes for the equestrian statue of the emperor **Marcus Aurelius** that stands in the center of the square. Actually, what you are looking at is a copy (the original, removed in 1981 for restoration, is now in the Palazzo Nuovo). But the copy manages to convey the same sense of history and drama. You might want to keep in mind when you're viewing the original that this is one of the rare surviving equestrian statues from classical Rome, possibly because for

Every April 21 a candlelit nighttime concert is performed in this piazza to celebrate the founding of Rome in 754 or 753 B.C.

Constantius, as well as two Roman milestones from the Appian Way. The modern statue halfway up the hill, to the left of the Cordonata, marks the spot where Cola di Rienzo, the 14th-century tribune who dreamed of restoring the Roman Republic, was executed.

The two identical buildings on your left and right are, respectively, the **Palazzo Nuovo** (built from scratch in 1655 to Michelangelo's design), and the older **Palazzo dei Conservatori,** the facade of which was redesigned by the Florentine sculptor and further modified by later Renaissance and baroque architects. You should know that, although few visible traces remain, the back portion of the Palazzo dei Conservatori (originally called Palazzo Caffarelli) stands on the site of what in centuries it was believed to be a statue of Constantine, the emperor who converted to Christianity. It was brought to the Campidoglio in 1538 on the recommendation of Michelangelo who created the pedestal. The bearded emperor has his right hand raised in a gesture of clemency. But don't be fooled! Historians tell us that the horse's raised hoof originally rested on the head of a vanquished barbarian. The bronze statue was originally covered in gold, and Romans used to say that if the gilt coating were to reappear it would be a sign that the day of judgment had arrived.

Walking up the Cordonata, you will have noticed a second, much steeper flight of stairs on the left leading to **Santa Maria in Aracoeli** (pronounced A-ra-CHEY-li. See p. 139), which translates into "St. Mary of the Altar of Heaven." Don't miss the only partly concealed remains of a multistory, second-century *insula,* on the far side of the steeper staircase. The 122 steps up to the church (not to worry, you can also get in from Piazza del Campidoglio), are said to have been built in 1348 in gratitude for God's deliverance from the plague, and provide a telling contrast to the Cordonata. The Aracoeli staircase reflects the medieval view that to achieve salvation life must be painful and arduous. Michelangelo's design, conceived 200 years later, embodied the concepts of Renaissance humanism; life's final destination is the same—death and salvation— but why not make the intervening voyage more enjoyable?

As you now know, the Palazzo Senatorio rests on the ancient tabularium and if you take the road to the left of the building (which leads to a lovely lookout point over the Roman Forum), you will see the blocks of peperino marble from the tabularium that have been incorporated into the sides of the newer building (as well as the medieval corner towers added later). ■

Musei Capitolini

THE TWO BUILDINGS (ON THE RIGHT AND LEFT OF THE Piazza del Campidoglio) are identical, even though the one on the right is older and larger; in fact, it includes another building (not visible from the square) called Palazzo Caffarelli, also part of the museum compound. Together, they constitute the Musei Capitolini, or Capitoline Museums, the city's sculpture and painting gallery which happens to be one of the oldest public museums in the world.

Start in the delightful courtyard of the **Palazzo dei Conservatori,** the building on the right; on view here are marble body parts from the colossal statue of Constantine which originally stood in the huge basilica of Constantine (or Maxentius) in the Forum. The marble fragments embedded on the upper portion of the opposite wall are also interesting. Look for the word "brit" on one of the larger pieces, a relic of the triumphal arch celebrating the Emperor Claudius' military campaigns in Britain. The large marble reliefs below probably come from Hadrian's temple in the Piazza di Pietra (see p. 134).

The first floor of the Palazzo dei Conservatori contains magnificent statuary, including several celebrated pieces such as the "Boy with a

Musei Capitolini

◪ Map p. 37

✉ Piazza del Campidoglio

☎ 06 6710 2071 or 06 6710 2475

🕐 Closed Sun. p.m. & Mon.

$ $ (Tickets sold until 30 minutes before closing. Free last Sun. of every month)

🚌 Bus: 56, 60, 62, 64, 70, 81, 87, 117, 170, 492 to Piazza Venezia or Teatro Marcello

Thorn," the Capitoline wolf, and Bernini's statue of Pope Urban VIII. The latter is in the Horatii and Curatii room, which contains frescoes depicting episodes from the days of the earliest Roman kings. Arnolfo di Cambio's wonderful statue of Charles of Anjou is unfortunately stuck in an out-of-the-way spot on the landing to the left of the entrance to this room. The **Pinacoteca** (painting gallery) on the second floor includes works by Velázquez, Dosso Dossi, Titian, Antonio Van Dyck, Reni, Annibale Caracci, and Caravaggio. There is also a porcelain collection. On the staircase landings you will find rectangular reliefs showing Marcus Aurelius making sacrifices to the gods. And you should keep in mind that these may be part of the same series that Constantine "borrowed"

to decorate the upper portion of the Arch of Constantine.

The **Palazzo Nuovo** (on the left) was built in 1655, primarily to give balance to the piazza and to hide the towering flank of the Aracoeli. It was opened to the public in 1734. The collection includes much of the city's best-known statuary. "Marforio," one of Rome's famous talking statues (see p. 145), reclines in the courtyard. The original bronze statue of Marcus Aurelius is on display here behind a protective glass wall. The **Sala dei Filosofi** (Philosophers' Room) and the **Sala degli Imperatori** (Emperors' Room) contain innumerable Roman busts and heads. Upstairs is the poignant "Dying Gaul," the "Capitoline Venus," and the "Marble Faun" of Nathaniel Hawthorne's last novel. ∎

The torso of this giant statue of Constantine was made of wood and bronze and has been lost. The remaining marble pieces are in the courtyard of the Palazzo dei Conservatori.

Foro Romano

FOR PURPOSES OF PRACTICALITY, THE FORO ROMANO, OR
Roman Forum, can be divided into two sections. If, as we suggest, you
enter the Forum through the Via dei Fori Imperiali entrance, it will be
easier for you to tackle this complex of monuments. You can visit the
older, western section first and then continue along the middle and
upper section of the Via Sacra to see the rest. Therefore, when you get
to the end of the entrance ramp, you'd best turn to your right. The
rectangular open space on your left, surrounded by a low iron railing,
is the Forum proper. Each of its long sides is flanked by the remains
of a basilica and, on its short sides, you can see on the western end
the only remaining arch of the four that stood at the Forum's corners,
the high *Rostra*, or speakers' platform and, opposite, the Temple of
Julius Caesar. You cannot miss the Arch of Septimius Severus, nor can
you mistake the eight surviving columns of the portico of the Temple
of Saturn.

Foro Romano
- Map p. 37
- Largo Romolo e Remo 5/6 (Via dei Fori Imperiali)
- 06 699 0110
- Closed Sun. p.m. during winter
- Bus: 75, 81, 85, 87. Metro: Linea B (Colosseo or Circo Massimo) to Via San Gregorio entrance

Illustration: Foro Romano reconstruction

WESTERN SECTION

The **Basilica Aemilia,** to the
right of the Forum proper, was built
originally in 179 B.C., and like all
basilicas (which, you should
remember, were primarily tribunals
or meeting halls, not churches) had
one wide central nave and two narrower side aisles. On the other side
of a tiny street at its far end you'll
find the **Curia,** or Senate, built by
Julius Caesar and reconstructed by
Diocletian after a fire in A.D. 283. If
you are surprised by its fine state of
preservation, thank the Christians
for converting it into a church in the
seventh century. Amazingly enough
the original doors have survived,
although they are now at San
Giovanni in Laterano. The curia's
marble pavement is a stunning
example of what is called *opus
sectile*, a repetitive geometric pattern
of different colors. The wide steps
on the right and left sides are the
platforms where the senators sat in
their portable curile chairs (Julius
Caesar's was reportedly made of
gold), moving to the "aye" or "nay"
side as necessity dictated. The two
marble reliefs or *plutei* (note the
Roman buildings in the back-

ground) probably came from the
Rostra outside. If you're wonder-
ing about the holes on the latter's
base, remember it was the custom
to insert here the iron "beaks," or
"rostra," of captured warships.

The triple **Arco di Settimio
Severo** (Arch of Septimius
Severus), which stands just beyond
the Curia, was erected in A.D. 203 to
commemorate the tenth anniversary of Septimius's reign and was
dedicated to his (and his sons')
victories over the Arabs and the
Parthians. It is considered to be a
superb example of the genre due to
the harmony of its proportions.
Note the barbarians on the column
pedestals, who appear (as was
intended) to support the weight of
the entire arch. Nearby is the **Lapis
Niger** (literally, the black stone)
which marked the location of an
important early grave, possibly that
of Romulus himself.

On the other side of the Forum,
and just across the Via Sacra, was
the **Basilica Giulia,** another tri-
bunal or courthouse. On the steps
you can still see some carved-in-
stone game boards which may have
provided diversion to those waiting

Colosseo

Arco di Costantino

Tempio di
Venere e Roma

Via Sacra

Arco di Tito

Regia

Atrium Vestae

Tempio di
Vesta

Tempio di
Cesare

Via
Sacra

Statue
of Nero

Basilica di
Massenzio

Tempio del
Divo Romolo

Tempio di
Antonino e
Faustina

Curia

Basilica
Aemilia

Basilica
Giulia

Arco di Settimio
Severo

Rostra

Tempio di Saturno

Julius Caesar's funeral was held in the Roman Forum, and a temple (the low building in the central foreground) was built over the spot where his body was cremated.

patiently for the wheels of justice to turn. One game resembles Chinese checkers, another is a circle divided into wedge-shaped sections.

The eight towering Ionic columns farther along toward the Capitoline are what remain of the *pronaos* or porch of the **Tempio di Saturno** (Temple of Saturn). Saturnus was originally the god of seed or sowing and the Saturnalia festival was the Romans' favorite holiday. It lasted seven days and can be compared to a mix of Christmas and Mardi Gras. The temple also served as the state treasury. Note the top line of the inscription on the architrave, "*Senatus Popolusque Romanus*" ("the Senate and People of Rome"). The initials SPQR, a once famous acronym, is nowadays seen mainly on manhole covers and buses.

As for the Forum proper, measuring approximately 394 by 164 feet (120 by 50 m), and originally paved in travertine by Augustus, it was deliberately left clear and unencumbered to symbolize the openness of democracy. For centuries its only occupants were the three Mediterranean plants par excellence, the fig, the olive, and the grape. Only later, under the emperors, did other constructions make their appearance around and on it. In later centuries, to the chagrin of traditionalists, the Forum's open space began to get really crowded, with commemorative columns and triumphal arches springing up everywhere. The Emperor Domitian went so far as to erect an equestrian statue of himself here (you can still see the pedestal) and so infuriated everyone that after his death it was torn down and he was erased, in "*dannatio memoriae,*" from official history. The lone **Colonna di Foca** (Column of Phocas), put up in 608 to honor the Byzantine emperor of the same name, was the last monument erected here.

Looking eastward, that is toward the Palatine Hill, on the right are the three lovely Corinthian columns that were part of the temple to the twin semigods **Castore** and **Polluce** (Castor and Pollux), and the focal point of another ancient Roman cult. Legend has it that in the early fifth century B.C. the brothers helped the Romans defeat the Latins in the battle of Lake Regillus and were then seen later the same day at the nearby Fountain of Juturna, touting their victory and watering their mighty, white steeds. The **Tempio di Cesare** (Temple of Julius Caesar) was built (but not immediately) on the spot where Julius Caesar was cremated after being assassinated in 44 B.C. His body had lain in state on the rostra in a gilded shrine. Mark Antony's funeral oration so moved the crowd that it was decided to forgo the traditional funeral on the Campus Martius and to cremate him in front of the **Regia.** Today the latter is little more than a pile of rubble, but in Caesar's day it was the headquarters of the chief priest or Pontifex Maximus (a title, by the way, that the Roman Catholic Church still uses for the pope). Although controversial, Caesar's deification soon followed, initiating a practice that would be followed by many of the later emperors, some of whom actually became divine even before death! The remains of his temple, built in 29 B.C., are rather insignificant, but standing in front of it you'll get a nice view of the western Forum with the imposing tabularium in the background.

EASTERN SECTION

Visiting the second part of the Forum, the eastern section, means you'll be going in the opposite direction from that you took at the start. In other words, now you'll walk towards the Arch of Titus, following the middle and upper portions of the Via Sacra under cypress trees and through laurel groves. On your left as you start your walk is the **Tempio di Antonino e Faustina,** erected by the Emperor Antoninus in A.D. 141 when his beloved wife, Faustina, died. At his own death 20 years later, the temple was dedicated to him as well and you can see on the entabulature above the columns where "*Divo Antonino,*" "Divine Antoninus," was added above the original inscription. This temple, too, was later turned into a church. On your right, behind what remains of the Regia, you'll find the intriguing Vestal Virgin complex, composed of a circular **Tempio di Vesta,** goddess of the sacred fire, and the **Atrium Vestae.** This was the home of the Vestal Virgins where six priestesses, guardians of the sacred fire, lived in splendid isolation. This cult was of major importance in ancient Rome. Indeed, it survived until the end of the fourth century, which was even after Christianity had practically become the state religion. The Vestal Virgins, chosen when they were between six and ten years of age and required to serve for 30 years, may well have been the most important women in Roman society with the exception, of course, of the females of the imperial family. The size of their second-century residence gives you an idea of how cosseted and pampered they were. The enormous atrium, with three large pools, was surrounded by a colonnade and a multistoried building. The priestesses enjoyed all sorts of privileges, but there was a downside: If it was discovered they were no longer virgins, they were walled up alive.

The small **Tempio del Divo Romolo** across the Via Sacra is also round and may have served as a vestibule to Vespasian's Temple of Peace, today occupied in part by the church of **Santi Cosma e Damiano** *(Tel 06 699 1540, closed 1–3 p.m.).* The temple's original bronze doors, which still open and shut perfectly, date back to Roman times. The church, the entrance to which is outside the Forum in Via dei Fori Imperiali 1,

The Arch of Titus, built in A.D. 81 by Emperor Domitian to commemorate his brother and his father, Vespasian, spans the Via Sacra, which leads from the Roman Forum to the Colosseum.

has a magnificent sixth-century mosaic in its apse; you shouldn't leave Rome without seeing it as it is one of the few mosaic works in the late classical Roman style to have survived. Its stylized layout—Jesus, his arm raised in benediction, is flanked by saints while, below, between the two holy cities, Bethlehem and Jerusalem, 12 sheep represent the Apostles—was used as a model for later mosaics in many Roman churches.

Next is the huge **Basilica di Massenzio** (Costantino). The building was begun by Maxentius (A.D. 306–312), but before he

finished he was killed by his brother-in-law, Constantine, over the throne at the battle of the Milvian Bridge. The giant statue of Constantine you saw (in pieces) in the Palazzo dei Conservatori originally stood here. As the Via Sacra continues uphill, you come to a wide flight of steps leading up to what appears to be a large open space. The steps are all that remain of the western entrance of the enormous double temple complex erected by the Emperor Hadrian in the second century A.D. and rebuilt later, after a fire, by Maxentius. The **Tempio di Roma** faced the Forum and the **Tempio di Venere** faced the Colosseum, and the two were joined at their apses. **Santa Francesca Romana** *(Tel 06 679 5528, closed 12–3:30 p.m.),* also called Santa Maria Nova, was built on the temple's remains. Its lovely cloister has been turned into the **Antiquarium Forense,** which contains a jumble of marble fragments found in various excavations. The rooms inside exhibit funeral urns, glass, and ceramic pieces, as well as several Roman skeletons. This church, too, is accessible from Via dei Fori Imperiali.

Back on the Via Sacra, you'll find yourself at the **Arco di Tito** (Arch of Titus), completed in A.D. 81 after Titus's early death. This triumphal arch was built to commemorate the victory over the Jews and the destruction of the Jerusalem Temple in A.D. 70. The reliefs inside the archway are particularly interesting. The south side, that closest to the Palatine, depicts the triumphal procession on its return from the campaign in Palestine. Jewish slaves, money, and the trumpets and menorah from the temple are depicted amid the booty, one reason why, until the foundation of Israel in 1948, no Roman Jew would walk under it. ■

Palatino

IF YOU'RE NOT TOO TIRED, THIS IS THE TIME TO GO UP TO THE Palatino (or Palatine Hill), the site of both Rome's original paleolithic settlements and, later, of many of its ancient imperial palaces. This is one of the loveliest spots in Rome and definitely not to be missed, although you'd be wise to save this visit for a sunny day, preferably in the afternoon. Lush and green, often breezy, and endowed with a couple of drinking fountains and a reasonable number of park benches, this hill, one of Rome's seven, is a place tailor-made for dreaming and contemplation, rather than for scholarly nit-picking.

In fact, none of the structures are intact and most of the ruins are hard for the average visitor to identify, but because of their extent and intricacy (there are massive substructures beneath these buildings, many of which housed workshops, warehouses, and underground passages), they are imposing. So arm yourself with imagination, and keep in mind that this is where it all started!

This area, in fact, has always been associated with Rome's founder, Romulus, and his twin, Remus. Supposedly, the two brothers were brought up somewhere on this hill by Faustulus, the shepherd, who had found them after they washed up onto the river bank.

Paradoxically, then, this area was the site of both humble, early Iron Age settlements and—as time went by—a residential neighborhood reserved for the elite. During the late Republican period (the second and first centuries B.C.) notables, such as Cicero, the politicians Crassus and Catulus, and the orator Hortensius lived here. Once Octavius (later Augustus) chose to forsake his residence near the Forum for the Palatine house he had bought (from Hortensius), it became the "in" place to live, especially if you were a Roman emperor. It remained the site of the imperial residences until Constantine moved to his new capital in the fourth century in what is today

An extremely desirable address in ancient Rome, in the Renaissance the shaded Palatine Hill was turned into a Cardinal's private park.

Palatino

Map p. 37

There are two entrances, one from within the Forum (just after Titus's Arch at Piazza di Santa Maria Nova), the other outside, Via di San Gregorio 30 (near Constantine's Arch)

06 481 5576

$$

Bus: 64, 75, 81, 85, 87, 117 to Piazza Venezia. Metro: Linea B (Colosseo)

Colosseo

Tempio di Apollo

Domus Flavia

Casa di Livia

In the shadow of the Palatine Hill are the scanty remains of the Circus Maximus, probably the largest racecourse ever.

Turkey. But if Octavius's lifestyle was fairly austere, he found few imitators among his successors (in particular Nero, Domitian, and Septimius Severus), whose unchecked taste for opulence made the Palatine synonymous with luxury. No wonder it is the root of our word "palace."

As we see it today, the Palatine can be divided into three sections. The first includes the ruins from the imperial residences, particularly that of the Flavian emperor Domitian (A.D. 81–96), which is divided into two sections, a private area (Domus Augustana) and the

public, or ceremonial part (Domus Flavia). Coming from the Arch of Titus, walk straight up the path (Via di San Bonaventura) and follow it as it turns left, all the time keeping in mind that much of the Palatine has yet to be excavated.

When you turn left, you will be skirting ruins of the Domus Flavia, including a basilica and an audience hall. This part of Domitian's palace was dedicated to official business and includes the audience hall, or *aula regia*, a basilica for court cases that required the emperor's personal attention, and the enormous *triclinium* for state dining. This must have been impressive. It was decorated in different colored marbles and flanked by courtyards, each containing a fountain. Domitian and his architect, Rabirius, built over earlier buildings constructed by Tiberius and Nero, among others. In fact, you should be aware that despite all the greenery, the ground level has been artificially pumped up (some scholars say by as much as 50 foot/15 m) by layers and layers of used and discarded building materials.

Domitian's Stadio

Domus Augustana

Imperial box

Circo Massimo

Keep on and you will come to **Domitian's Stadio** (or hippodrome), an impressive, large sunken area generally assumed to have been a racecourse or stadium. The ruins directly to the right of the stadio are part of the **Domus Augustana,** a sprawling structure of which lots of bits and pieces—archways, sunken rooms, some of which may have been pools or fountains, and courtyards—are there to explore even if they are not easily identifiable. Gradually work your way toward the terrace from where there is a fantastic view of the Circus Maximus below and the Aventine.

Antiquarium del Palatino, located in an ex-convent, is small but displays archaeological finds from the area. Immediately in front

of and to the left of the museum are the remains of the Domus Flavia.

At the southwestern end of the hill are the sites of those Iron Age settlements from the time of Romulus and Remus. There is a temple to Apollo and another to a goddess, Magna Mater. There are also two houses from the late Republican period, the so-called **Casa di Livia** and **Casa di Augusto,** both of which are usually closed to the general public.

The **Orti Farnesiani,** a Renaissance garden once full of rare botanical species was created in the 16th century. Two pavilions afford a fine view of the Forum below. Steps to the right and the left lead down to another landing with a stupendous, fern-draped nymphaeum. ■

Illustration: Palatino reconstruction

The emperors: the good...the bad, & the ugly

The Roman emperors personified the best and the worst of Roman culture. One of the best was Octavius (27 B.C.–A.D. 14), who assumed the title of Augustus in 27 B.C. and is generally considered to be the first true emperor in the Julian-Claudian dynasty started by Julius Caesar. Born in 63 B.C. to a niece of Caesar's and later adopted by his great-uncle, Octavius (Octavian in English) was only 19 in 44 B.C. when his uncle was assassinated. He allied with Mark Antony to punish Caesar's assassins and divided up the empire with him. That alliance ended when Octavian trounced Antony and Cleopatra at the naval Battle of Actium (Greece) in 31 B.C.

Although he always made sure to maintain a facade of republicanism, the rest of Octavius's life was dedicated to the process, begun by his uncle, of concentrating power in the hands of one person, himself. But his accomplishments were such that his imperial proclivities can be forgiven. Shrewd, astute, and an able administrator, he reformed the Roman bureaucracy, overhauled the fiscal system, and reorganized the military. Above all, he extended and secured the empire's borders giving rise to what was known as the Pax Romana, a 200-year period of stability and security. It was of course under this same stable and secure regime that the new Christian religion was born. As we know, the solidity of the Augustean Empire proved to be conducive to the new cult's rapid expansion.

Several other good" emperors have also left important legacies: Vespasian (A.D. 69–79) restored stability after the Neronian chaos. And Trajan (98–117) extended the empire to its furthest limits of expansion. Even more important was his successor, Hadrian (117–138), who is often referred to as the philosopher-emperor because of his devotion to the arts, literature, and architecture. Hadrian enormously embellished the city of Rome: He built a magnificent mausoleum which today we call Castel Sant'Angelo (see p. 177–78), the sprawling villa in Tivoli that bears his name (see p. 232–33), and rebuilt the Pantheon (see pp. 126-29). He put into effect a policy of containment that had a far-reaching impact throughout the empire. Military contingents became fixed rather than mobile. Civilian settlements near military installations thus grew in size, and commerce exploded. Fortification became increasingly important, with defensive architecture reaching new heights as in Hadrian's Wall (in England). Hadrian traveled widely during his reign, both for his own pleasure and because of his unusual concept of the Roman Empire: a single, political entity rather than a series of subject states to exploit.

There is no dearth of bad guys in the annals of the empire, and you've probably heard of many of them: Caligula, tall, pale, ungainly with a wide but sinister forehead and clearly mentally unstable, or Caracalla, who had his younger brother, Geta, killed. But it is Nero who most frequently is seen to personify the worst in Roman imperial rule (among other things he murdered his mother). Nero was born into the imperial family in A.D. 37. Adopted by Claudius after the emperor had married his mother, Agrippina the Younger (Caligula's sister), he became emperor in A.D. 54. During the first ten years of his reign, Nero had a good record. He promoted legal and bureaucratic reform and demonstrated interest for the well-being of his population. All of this changed with the raging, nine-day fire of A.D. 64 during which the emperor did not actually fiddle, but simply took his own sweet time in leaving his villa in Anzio to come to Rome. Later, he put the blame on the new Christian religious sect, setting off a series of persecutions during which both Peter and Paul were probably martyred. Although after the fire he rebuilt much of the city, Nero gave precedence to his own personal interests, expropriating large tracts of terrain to build the vast and sumptuous Domus Aurea (see p. 64–65). The populace seethed and rebellion threatened. In A.D. 68, Nero committed suicide thus bringing the Julian-Claudian dynasty to a premature and inglorious end. ∎

This French painting shows the "good" emperor, Augustus, and the Sibyl interpreting his vision of the Virgin and Child.

Above: Like most emperors, Nero minted his own coins. This one is gold and carries his name.

Right: A bust of Julius Caesar on display in the Vatican Museum. Founder of the first imperial dynasty, he never accepted the title of emperor. After his assassination, the term Caesar was given to all emperors.

Fori Imperiali

IT IS NOT EASY TO COMPREHEND THE LAYOUT OF THE FIVE Fori Imperiali, or Imperial Forums, because the modern Via dei Fori Imperiali (built for military parades by the Fascist regime in the early 1930s) cuts directly through them, covering over much of the area. Ceremonial areas built between the first century B.C. and the start of the second century A.D., the Imperial Forums were attempts by Rome's highest leaders both to glorify themselves and to create additional space for the political, religious, and institutional needs of the expanding Roman Empire. Today they are still only partially excavated although work is now underway. The long-term plan is to significantly narrow the avenue, but presently the wide Via dei Fori Imperiali makes the forums of Augustus, Nerva, Vespasian, and Trajan appear to be totally separate from the Roman Forum (of which, instead, they formed an integral part).

EARLIER IMPERIAL FORUMS

Julius Caesar was the first to construct his own forum (Foro di Cesare) which, begun in 54 B.C., stands between the Curia or Senate building and Via dei Fori Imperiali. He even rebuilt the Senate to bring it into proper alignment. Measuring 147 by 406 feet (45 by 124 m), the forum was surrounded by a double portico of which a small portion is still visible, as is the base of the Tempio di Venere Genitrix, the goddess to whom the Julian-Claudian dynasty traced its descent. Augustus, Caesar's political heir, followed suit. The **Foro di Augusto,** near that of his adopted father, ends at the high fire wall he erected to protect the civic center from the frequent fires in the densely populated residential Suburra area on the other side. It took 20 years to complete and was mostly taken up by the Tempio di Marte Ultare, which the young emperor built after killing Caesar's assassins at the battle of Philippi in 42 B.C. Three of its 24 tall Corinthian marble columns are more or less all that remain, but try to imagine it as it was: The porticoes were dotted with statuary;

floors and walls were done in colored marbles—pure white, Phrygian purple, Numidian yellow, Lucullan red or black; there was even a separate room for a colossus in precious metal, possibly Caesar or Augustus himself, and presumably some 33 feet (10 m) tall.

Most of the **Foro di Vespasiano** (built between A.D. 71 and 75 to mark the defeat of the Jews), is hidden underneath the Via dei Fori Imperiali–Via Cavour intersection. What remains of the Temple of Peace, as it was called, is incorporated into the monastery and church of **Santi Cosma e Damiano.** In between Augustus's and Vespasian's forums is Nerva's Forum (**Foro di Nerva**), which actually was built by Domitian, Nerva's predecessor. Long and narrow, flanked by colonnades, it was often called the Forum Transitorium. It transformed the Argiletum, the route from the Suburra to the Roman Forum, into a decorated passageway. All that remains are two massive Corinthian columns (the Italians call them the "*colonnacce,*" the ugly columns) in the corner near Via dei Fori Imperiali and the podium of a

Fori Imperiali
Map p. 37
Bus: 64, 75, 81, 85, 87, 117 to Piazza Venezia. Metro: Linea B (Colosseo)

Opposite: A fluted column in Trajan's Forum where excavations are in progress. Behind, in Trajan's Market, a new museum contains reconstructions of the Imperial Forum's most important monuments.

temple dedicated to Minerva. The entablature between the columns has a lovely frieze depicting scenes from domestic activity like spinning and weaving, while a statue until recently identified as Minerva keeps watch. Last spring a second, sister statue was found, leading archaeologists to wonder if they might instead have represented two imperial provinces.

FORO TRAIANO

The major attraction of the Imperial Forums is the magnificent complex—forum and markets—built by the Emperor Trajan and dedicated in A.D 112. This was the last of the forums to be built and undoubtedly the grandest and the most splendid; at the time it was considered to be one of the architectural wonders of

Detail of the relief sculptures on the towering column in Trajan's Forum. The story unfolds in a 219-feet (67-m) sequence.

the world. To enter the Forum you passed through a large, rectangular courtyard flanked by two long porticoes, 367 feet (112 m) in length, and closed off at the northern end by the gigantic two-story **Basilica Ulpia.** The latter, richly decorated in sumptuous colors, marble work, and precious metals, had five aisles separated by columns, with a semicircular apse at each end. Beyond

Mercati Traianei
- 🅰 Map p. 37
- ✉ Via IV Novembre 94
- ☎ 06 6790 0048
- 🕐 Closed Mon.
- 💲 $
- 🚍 Bus: 64, 70, 170 to Piazza Venezia and walk

the basilica was a second, smaller courtyard. Here rises **Colonna Traiana** (Trajan's Column), which tells the story of his military campaigns against the Dacians in magnificent relief work involving 2,600 carved figures that spirals up for about 100 feet (30 m). Made of 29 cylindrical blocks, it has a staircase inside lit by 40 small windows. A giant statue of the emperor was replaced in the 16th century with one of St. Peter. After Trajan's unexpected death in A.D. 117 his remains were placed inside in a gold urn which was placed in the column's hollow base. Flanking the courtyard were two libraries, one Greek and one Latin.

But wait, there's more. In building the markets, Trajan and his court architect, Apollodorus of Damascus, effected what was for the time a technological miracle. They hollowed out much of the high ridge (which was about the same height as the column), linking the Capitoline and the Quirinal Hills that had impeded access to the Campus Martius. Then there are the **Mercati Traianei** (Trajan's Markets). This three- or four-story semicircular structure was also built by Apollodorus, and was essentially a reconstruction of the neighborhood removed by the forum's construction. An ancient Roman street (Via Biberatica) runs through it, and wandering from shop to shop (there are about 150), gives an idea of what life was like in the second century A.D. The alcove-like shops on the ground floor probably sold dry goods (flour and sugar), flowers, and vegetables. Those off the gallery were probably storehouses for wine and oil. There were also special shops for eastern spices, and there were fishponds. But the world's first mall, with its impressive vaulting, also housed some administrative offices, such as the *congiaria*, the public aid agency for the poor. ∎

The massive Colosseum has always been Rome's best-known landmark. But only a short distance away you will find other marvels. Imperial monuments alternate with early Christian churches and their glorious frescoes and mosaics.

Colosseo to San Clemente

Detail from the 12th-century apse mosaic in San Clemente

Colosseo to San Clemente

SET IN A VALLEY BETWEEN THREE OF THE SEVEN HILLS (THE PALATINE, THE Esquiline, and the Caelian), the Colosseo (Colosseum) is undoubtedly the Roman landmark that has been most closely identified with the city for the longest time. As the Venerable Bede put it in the eighth century: "*Quandiu stat Colisaeus, stat et Roma; quando cadet Colisaeus, cadet et Roma. Quando cadet Roma, cadet et mundus*" ("As long as the Colosseum stands, Rome stands; when the Colosseum falls, Rome will fall. When Rome falls, so falls the world"). Beyond a doubt, the single best-known site of the Eternal City, it has inspired travelers, historians, and men of letters. "You must look to the East, among the ruins of Palmyra, Balbek, and Petra, to find buildings comparable in grandiosity to the Colosseum," wrote Stendahl in his *Roman Promenades* in the early 1800s. For the French writer, who was of the opinion that the best time to visit the monument was after midnight, "in the company of the woman you love,…these walls, blackened by time, have the same effect on one's soul as the music of Cimarosa, who knew how to render sublime even the words of a vulgar libretto".

Two thousand years after it was built by the Emperor Vespasian, on the site of the artificial lake that Nero had built for his magnificent pleasure house, the Domus Aurea (Golden House), the Colosseum is still standing. It looms over one of the most extensive archaeological areas in the world, to remind us of both man's achievements and his cruelty. It cannot be forgotten after all, that while this was a place of celebration it was also a site of unchecked (human and animal) slaughter.

Not far away is the Arch of Constantine built in A.D. 315 to celebrate the emperor's victory at Ponte Milvio over his brother-in-law and predecessor, Maxentius. But for all its size (it is the largest of the triumphal arches to have survived) and apparent splendor, the arch, decorated mostly with derivative art, is generally considered to be an indication of Rome's incipient decline.

On the other side of the Colosseum are the remains of the first-century Domus Aurea which, with the exception of Diocletian's Palace in Split (Croatia), is the only floor-to-ceiling Roman imperial structure to have survived. Nero's extensive pleasure palace, which reflects the vast wealth and architectural prowess of imperial Rome, was built in the aftermath of the terrible fire of A.D. 64 which totally destroyed three of Rome's 14 neighborhoods. Its exact dimensions are as yet unknown (excavations are still going on) but 150 rooms have already been unearthed.

The surrounding area has many important early churches. San Pietro in Vincoli, the location of Michelangelo's imposing "Moses," was originally named the Basilica Eudoxiana after the empress who built it to hold St. Peter's Chains. The multilevel San Clemente, which lies between the Colosseum and San Giovanni in Laterano, was built in the fourth century to commemorate Clement, martyred in the Crimea sometime during the reign of Trajan (A.D. 98–117). In the 11th century invading Norman armies destroyed the original church, but important treasures from the new church survive, such as the wonderful 12th-century apse mosaic. San Clemente is also a prime example of Rome's architectural stratification, concealing the remains of a fourth-century church as well as older, first-century structures.

The quiet Caelian Hill facing the Palatine, on the opposite side of Via di San Gregorio, offers other jewels of both early Christian culture and Renaissance design. St. Gregory (San Gregorio Magno) built his church and monastery here in the sixth century, although both the church and the three frescoed chapels near it were rebuilt in the 17th century. The Basilica of Santi Giovanni e Paolo has medieval buttresses and a Romanesque campanile, but the church, which incorporates the house of the two martyred Roman soldiers, dates back to the fourth (or possibly fifth) century. Villa Celimontana, whose grounds today are a lovely park, testifies to the quality of Renaissance

LARGO
VENOSTA

Ⓜ Cavour

VIA   GIOVANNI   LANZA

PIAZZA
SAN MARTINO
AI MONTI

San Pietro
in Vincoli

VIA

CAVOUR

PIAZZA DI
SAN PIETRO
IN VINCOLI

VIA   MERULANA

OPPIO

PARCO

DI

ESQUILINO

MONTE   DEL   MONTE   TRAIANO

Terme
di Traiano

VIALE

Domus
Aurea

FORI   IMPERIALI

Ⓜ
Colosseo

COLLE

PARCO

OPPIO

OPPIO

VIA

San
Clemente

PIAZZA
DEL
COLOSSEO

VIA DI SAN

LABICANA

Arco di
Costantino

Colosseo

VIA CELIO VIBENNA

GIOVANNI IN LATERANO

MERULANA

PARCO
DEL
CELIO

VIA

CLAUDIA

Santi
Quattro
Coronati

PIAZZA
SAN GIOVANNI
IN LATERANO

VIA DI SAN GREGORIO

PIAZZA CELIMONTANA

Santi Giovanni
e Paolo

VIA   DI   SANTO   STEFANO   ROTONDO

San Gregorio
Magno

VIA   DI   SANTO

ZZA
ORTA
PENA

MONTE

VILLA

Santa Maria
in Domnica

Santo Stefano
Rotondo

VIA   DELL'AMBA   ARADAM

VIA DEL LATERANI

CELIO

Villa
Celimontana

VIA DELLA NAVICELLA

CELIMONTANA

VIA DELLE TERME DI CARACALLA

PIAZZA
DI PORTA
METRONIA

0   250 yards
0   250 meters

design. Santa
Maria in Domnica
has marvelous ninth-
century mosaics. The
fifth-century Santo Stefano
Rotondo (the first of the few
circular churches to be built in
Rome) retains its aura of mystery, and
Santi Quattro Coronati has interesting frescoes and one of Rome's oldest, and loveliest
cloisters. Its fortresslike appearance dates from
the Middle Ages when the monastery was fortified to serve as a refuge for the popes. ■

PIAZZALE
NUMA
POMPILIO

VIA DRUSO

Rome

Tevere

Area of map detail

Colosseo

THE COLOSSEO, OR COLOSSEUM, WAS BUILT BY THE THREE
Flavian emperors, and its proper name is the Flavian Amphitheater. Its
construction was part of the new imperial family's campaign to
promote a good public image. Vespasian (A.D. 69–79), the founder of
the dynasty, was not of noble birth; he became emperor a year after
Nero's suicide, stepping in after the reigns of three short-lived and
unsuccessful emperors. Nero was not missed; his vast land expropria-
tions and other excesses had angered most of the populace. So almost
no one minded when Vespasian decided to drain the artificial lake that
had formed part of Nero's extravagant Domus Aurea complex (see
p. 64) and transform the site into a place for public entertainment.

Probably built with the spoils of the
Temple of Jerusalem at the end of
the so-called Jewish campaign,
waged and won by his son Titus in
A.D. 70, the amphitheater was inaugurated in A.D. 80 by which time
Titus had ascended to the throne.

Made from travertine (130,800
cu yards/100,000 cu m, were
hewn from quarries near Tivoli
and hauled to Rome along a specially built road), the stone oval
(620 feet/189 m long; 512 feet/
156 m wide; and 157 feet/48 m

high) was the largest amphitheater in the Roman world. Some 300 tons of iron are believed to have been used for the grapples that held the stones together.

It is generally assumed that the name, Colosseum, came into being because of the structure's super size. But many historians believe that the term is derived from the giant, or colossal, bronze statue that stood nearby. Its base, today planted with five trees, is still visible between the arena and the Temple of Venus and Rome. The original statue was of Nero, but political correctness of the time dictated a change and the Flavians very pragmatically added sunbeams around the statue's head, changed the inscription, and came up with an image dedicated to the sun god. The statue remained standing until sometime in the early Middle Ages when it was removed and probably melted down.

Externally, the Colosseum is composed of a series of three **arcades,** topped by a fourth story, or attic. The columns are disposed on three levels according to classical canons (starting from the ground up, Doric, Ionic, and Corinthian). Running below the fourth-story cornice are 240 small ledges with holes in them used to hold the tall wooden poles that supported the *velarium,* the canvas awning that sailors from the imperial fleet would raise to protect spectators from the summer heat, the rain, or the winter cold, turning it into a first-century Astrodome.

Estimates of crowd capacity in the Colosseum range from 50,000 to almost 90,000. There were three tiers of seats: the *ima* (lowest), the *media,* and the *summa,* plus a standing-room-only balcony at the top for the least important members of society: women, slaves, and the poor. Even on the other levels

Most of the holes in the Colosseum, the largest Roman amphitheater anywhere, held the iron grapples that were plundered and reused during the Middle Ages.

seating was arranged according to social status and profession: Members of the imperial family and Vestal Virgins had special boxes. The senators, in their red-bordered white togas, sat on the same level, in the "orchestra" section; then came the knights *(equites)* followed by the *plebs* (ordinary citizens). Special sections were set aside for various professions, such as soldiers, scribes, students with tutors, and foreign dignitaries. Spectators poured into the arena through the 80 arched entrances on the ground floor. They poured in and out through the 160 exits, called *vomitoria,* distributed throughout the tiers on the various levels, allowing for quick exit (some say it could be emptied in 10 minutes) by the often unruly and rambunctious crowds.

The arena had a wood floor that was covered with sand to absorb the blood and stench of the spectacles involving human beings fighting for their lives *(munera).* Now that this floor has gone, you can see the **corridors and tunnels** that ran underneath the arena to allow celebrities to avoid the crowds and to bring in animals and gladiators. Vertical shafts were used to hold the caged animals (which were brought up to the arena level along ramps or in pulley-system elevators). And we're not just talking about the lions and tigers dear to Hollywood. The thousands of animals killed in the festivities, which on special occasions could last for three to four months, included hyenas, elephants, hippopotamuses, wild horses, elk, giraffes, and zebras. The program was divided into various parts: Animal hunts *(venationes)* in the morning, public executions at noon, and gladiatorial contests in the afternoon.

There was also a tunnel connecting this understage section with

Vomitoria, or exits

Internal corridor

Wood floor of arena, covered in sand

Understage corridors and tunnels

Illustration: Colosseum reconstruction

the Ludus Magnus, the gladiatorial barracks and training area located between the Colosseum and San Clemente. The gladiators—who were chosen from among condemned criminals, slaves, and prisoners of war—were divided into different categories. There were those who fought heavily armed, with sword and shield; those lightly armed with dagger and arm buckler; and those armed only with nets and tridents as you saw in the Roman floor mosaics in the Galleria Borghese. "*Ave, Imperator,*

muratori te salutant" ("Hail, Emperor, we who are about to die, salute you"), the gladiators scheduled to fight that day would intone during the pre-games parade. Naturally, they all hoped to survive and enjoy the booty they were awarded in the case of victory. But, except for rare cases, survival (or the thumbs up sign from the crowd) generally meant only having to fight again. The lucky few were awarded the laurel crown and allowed to retire. As Christian influence grew in Rome, the Colosseum

Velarium, a canvas awning for all-weather protection

Above: Mosaic displaying gladiatorial combat, Galleria Borghese

Top right: A view of the Colosseum interior showing the substructure below its wooden floor.

declined in importance. The last recorded gladiatorial games were in the early fifth century, whereas the staged animal hunts lasted another hundred years.

After the decline of Rome, the Colosseum was utilized for a variety of purposes. It was used by the Frangipane family in the Middle Ages, and its southern side collapsed in a major earthquake in 1349. However, time and natural calamity were not the structure's only enemies. Much of the responsibility for its deterioration goes to the Romans themselves. For about 400 years, from the mid-14th to 18th century, it was used as a quarry for marble and travertine building blocks to be used in other city structures, for example the Palazzo Venezia and even the new St. Peter's. This practice stopped when Pope Benedict (1740–1758) declared the Colosseum a sacred place because of the Christian martyrs' blood that reportedly had been shed there. In effect, historians are not agreed on this. Since the 19th century, a Way of the Cross ceremony involving the direct participation of the pope has been held here every year on the evening of Good Friday before Easter. ■

Arco di Costantino

CONSTANTINE IS OFTEN REFERRED TO AS THE FIRST Christian emperor, but you won't find any Christian images on the arch built in his honor in A.D. 315. His baptism, such that it was, only took place on his deathbed 22 years later. And, impressive as it seems, the Arch of Constantine is untypical.

Constantine built this arch to mark his tenth year in power. He placed it near the end of the Via Triumphalis, the route taken by triumphal processions.

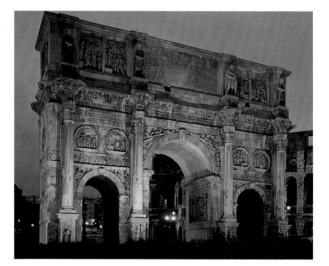

Arco di Costantino
⬛ Map p. 57
✉ Between Via di San Gregorio and Piazza del Colosseo
🚌 Bus: 75, 81, 85, 87, 117, 175, 186, 204, 810, 850. Tram: 30B from Circus Maximus or San Lorenzo. Metro: Linea B (Colosseo)

Most of the Arch's decorative work was, in fact, taken from structures built by previous emperors, suggesting that Roman art had entered a phase of decline. Thus, the eight **rectangular reliefs** on both sides of the upper portion (the attic) originally adorned a structure dedicated to Marcus Aurelius (A.D. 161–180) and the portrait of the emperor was recut with Constantine's likeness. (The narrative content of three other reliefs from the same series, now in the Capitoline Museums, clearly shows the Emperor Marcus Aurelius.) Also plundered from other monuments were the round medallions over the lateral arches (four on each side). These hunting and sacrificial scenes date from the first half of the second century, a period coinciding not with the

reign of Constantine but with that of Hadrian. Eight **statues of barbarians** (the ones wearing trousers, of course!) on top of the columns were also derivative. Naturally, some of the work was original but, even to the untrained eye, it appears clearly inferior workmanship. The four **panel friezes** underneath the above-mentioned medallions, on both sides, were sculpted specifically for the arch. Note the one on the south side (toward the Circus Maximus), over the leftmost arch, showing Constantine and his army besieging the city of Verona: The figure of the centurion who is scaling the walls is dwarfish, and there is a general lack of perspective. Compare the body proportions in this relief with the ones directly above, sculpted about 180 years before. ■

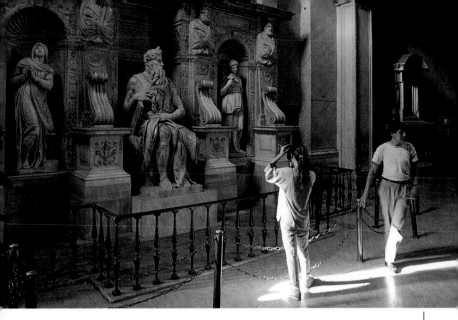

San Pietro in Vincoli

TRY TO SCHEDULE YOUR VISIT TO SAN PIETRO IN VINCOLI (also known as the Basilica Eudoxiana) early in the day, in the hopes that you can beat the crush of tourists coming here to see Michelangelo's "Moses." Situated at the end of the right transept, this is the pièce de résistance of the unfinished tomb of Pope Julius II (1503–1513), the pontiff who built the Sistine Chapel.

Michelangelo's original design for a mammoth, freestanding structure with some 40 statues destined for St. Peter's was never to be. Nevertheless, the **statue of Moses,** shown returning from Mount Sinai with God's Commandments under his arm, is incredibly powerful. Clearly annoyed with his idolatrous brethren for flirting with the Golden Calf, he is scowling (the profile under his lower lip is said to be a Michelangelo self-portrait). The striking statues of Jacob's two wives, Leah and Rachel (symbols of active and contemplative life) were probably finished by one of Michelangelo's pupils, Raffaele da Montelupo.

But for Christians there is a precious relic to see: The chains from St. Peter's two imprisonments (in Jerusalem and Rome) which, when placed side by side, are said to have miraculously fused. The church was built by the Empress Eudoxia to host the chains, displayed under the altar. Also, if you ignore the baroque ceiling, you'll get a good idea of the stark and simple basilica structure that so appealed to the ancient Romans and which was later adopted by many Christian churches. Despite repeated remakes, seen from inside the church the brickwork over the windows of the Renaissance facade still reveals the outline of the five arches of the original fifth-century entrances.

To the left of the main entrance is a lovely 15th-century fresco depicting a 1476 procession against the plague. ∎

A gash on Moses's knee is said to have been caused when Michelangelo threw a tool at it.

San Pietro in Vincoli

🗺 Map p. 57
✉ Piazza di San Pietro in Vincoli
☎ 06 488 2865
🕐 Closed 12:30–3:30 p.m.
🚌 Bus: 75, 87 (lets you off on Via dei Fori Imperiali), 117. Metro: Linea B Colosseo or Cavour

Domus Aurea

INACCESSIBLE SINCE 1983, THIS JEWEL OF WHAT MANY would call imperial folly has now been reopened to the public, although excavation and restoration is still going on. On the lower slopes of the Colle Oppio, the Domus Aurea (Golden House) was so-called because of the extensive use of gold leaf in the decorations.

The Emperor Trajan sought to obliterate Nero's Golden Palace, but ironically more remains than of his own Imperial Baths.

Domus Aurea

🅰 Map p. 57

✉ Via della Domus Aurea (inside the park)

☎ 06 397 49907

💲 $$ for self-guided tour, $$$ with archaeologist (reservations necessary)

🚌 Bus: 75, 81, 85, 87, 117. Metro: Linea B (Colosseo)

This structure was built by Nero as a vast pleasure palace, and was a complex of reception and banquet halls, courtyards, porticoes, gardens, and pools which extended beyond the artificial lake he created in the valley below to connect up with the older imperial residences on the Palatine. Part of this vast estate was demolished when Vespasian, the first of the Flavians, came to the throne in A.D. 69 and built the Colosseum on the lake-site.

Half a century later, Trajan completed the job, systematically removing all precious materials (including the marble on the walls), and the statuary, which may have included famous pieces such as the "Dying Gaul" (see p. 41) and the "Laocoön" (see pp. 170, 176). Trajan built massive supporting walls and filled the spaces with rubble to make a foundation for his imperial baths. Paradoxically, his attempts to wipe out all traces of Nero backfired because he unwittingly created the conditions for the Domus Aurea's preservations through the centuries.

The existence of the Domus Aurea, written about by Roman writers such as Tacitus, Pliny, and Suetonius, has long been known. But it was only during the Renaissance that the collapse of part of the baths structure above led to its rediscovery. Famous artists including Michelangelo, Raphael, and Pinturicchio visited what seemed caves, or grottoes (sometimes leaving their signatures) to examine the unusual decorations on what we now know were the upper portion of high-ceilinged rooms. This type of decoration is similar to that used on the walls and ceilings of many buildings in Pompei. The Renaissance artists copied the fantastic motives—small winged creatures, dragons, floral and leaf patterns—that were probably the work of the famous Roman artist Fabullus, and created a "new" art form. These "grotesques" (from "grotto") were used to decorate many new structures including the Vatican Loggias and the Villa Farnesina. Several 18th-century artists visited the ruins, then erroneously identified as the Baths of Titus, making engravings that today are essential for the understanding of first-century imperial art.

It was only later that archaeologists identified the underground structure as part of Nero's famous domain. So far Italian archaeologists have excavated close to 150 rooms, although only about 30 underground rooms are currently open to the public. In summer, bring a sweater because once inside the temperature plummets.

Naturally, the Domus Aurea today is only a shadow of its former self when it was a riot of colored marbles, stuccos, and gold leaf. Another major change is that Trajan closed in all the terraces that in Roman times exploited the palace's vast southern exposure. But it is still overwhelming, as you will see in the 45-minute tour (choose between guided visits with an Italian archaeologist or "accompanied" visits for which audiocassettes in English can be rented).

Access to the palace is through one of Trajan's massive galleries, and the tour itself starts in **Room 35** and heads eastward. The highlights include **Rooms 44** and **45,** where you will see a *nymphaeum,* an area decorated to resemble a grotto with the remains of a fountain and

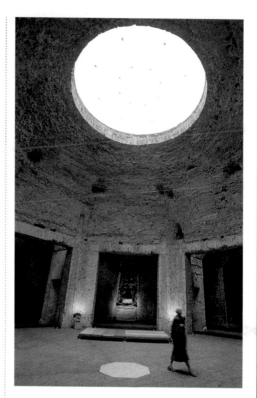

a mosaic decoration depicting Polyphemus (the Cyclops) and Ulysses. There are colorful wall decorations in **Room 70** and **Room 79,** where some of the Renaissance signatures are located. In Nero's day, visitors to **Room 80,** the Room of the Gilded Vault, could look out onto a five-sided courtyard and the valley beyond with its artificial lake, later drained for construction of the Colosseum. You should remember that although these rooms are now underground, in Nero's time they were filled with sunlight and most looked out on magnificent views. **Rooms 123** and **125** contain the first examples of groined vaults in Roman architecture. **Room 128** may have been the famous dining room with the rotating dining room of which Suetonius wrote. ■

The Octagonal Room (Room 128) complex is the focal point of the Domus's eastern pavilion. Light entered through an oculus in the ceiling. The apse in the rear wall had a waterfall, and all the rooms are paneled in marble.

Monks, mosaics, & martyrs walk

Only a short distance from the hue and cry of the Colosseum, the Caelian (Celio) Hill has always been one of the quieter and less populated areas of Rome. Right from the earliest centuries of Christian Rome it was therefore a perfect setting for monastic life and spiritual contemplation.

From the Colosseum, walk along Via di San Gregorio on the left-hand sidewalk, noting the brick arch across the street, part of an aqueduct built by Nero to supply the imperial residences on the Palatine with water. Just past the arch, steps (on your left) lead up to the imposing facade of **San Gregorio Magno ❶**. (Be careful crossing the tram tracks!) The church *(Closed 12:30–1:45 p.m.)* was built by Pope Gregory the Great (590–604)—later St. Gregory—on the grounds of his family home. Its baroque facade, added in the 17th century, belies its antiquity.

The atrium, on the other hand, is typical of the city's early churches, especially those built in sparsely inhabited areas like the Caelian Hill. Note the fresco in the rightmost lunette which shows Gregory in 590, on his way to St. Peter's at the head of a procession (to pray for deliverance from the plague) when he sees the archangel Michael above Hadrian's Mausoleum. The angel is sheathing his sword, a clear sign that the Black Death is over, and the reason why a statue of the archangel stands atop Castel Sant'Angelo. To see the interior, ring the bell on the wall of the atrium's right portico. By the way, it was from here that Pope Gregory, himself a monk, dispatched St. Augustine of Canterbury and 40 Benedictine monks to the British Isles to convert the heathen Angles and Saxons to Christianity and to bring that distant isle back into contact with the classical world. All ties with Rome had been cut in the early fifth century when the last Roman garrisons were withdrawn.

To the left of the church there are three small chapels. The chapel of **Santa Barbara,** farthest to the left, is frescoed with scenes from

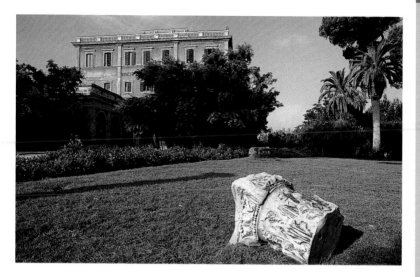

Like many Roman parks, Villa Celimontana was the home and gardens of a nobleman.

the life of St. Gregory, including one showing the pope sending Augustine off on his mission. In it is the stone table at which Gregory usually served meals to 12 paupers. Once, a 13th diner turned out to be an angel. The other two chapels, dedicated to St. Andrew and St. Sylvia (Gregory's mother), contain frescoes by Domenichino and Guido Reni. To arrange a visit to the chapel, call 06 512 2992 (mornings) or the adjacent shop *(Tel 06 700 051)*, which also sells honey and other natural products made by the monks.

From San Gregorio, walk up the steep Clivo di Scauro on the left, from where you will have a fine view of the apse of the church of **Santi Giovanni e Paolo 2**. Having walked under its medieval flying buttresses, unusual for this city, you will find yourself in Piazza dei Santi Giovanni e Paolo. This church was dedicated to John and Paul, two Roman soldiers who suffered martyrdom after refusing to worship pagan idols. Directly ahead, you will see the back entrance to the **Villa Celimontana 3** (see p. 118). If closed, a small door on the right on Via San Paolo della Croce will let you into the park, once the gardens to the Renaissance Villa Mattei. After a pleasant stroll past the fountains and ferns, leave the park from its main entrance. You'll find yourself on **Via della Navicella,** named for a Roman votive

boat now placed atop a fountain in the middle of the street to your left on exiting. The fountain stands in front of **Santa Maria in Domnica 4** with its superb ninth-century apse mosaic of the "Virgin Enthroned with the Christ Child." Across the street (beyond more remnants from Nero's aqueduct) begins Via di Santo Stefano Rotondo. At No. 7 is the round church of **Santo Stefano Rotondo 5** (see p. 72). Continue along Via di Santo Stefano Rotondo until you come to a Romanesque portico made with recycled Roman columns. Turn left onto Via dei Santi Quattro, which leads to the medieval fortress that encloses **Santi Quattro Coronati 6** (Four Crowned Saints church and its monastery, see p. 72). ■

🗺 Also see area map, p. 57
▶ Colosseo
↔ 1.5 miles (2.5 km)
🕐 2.5 hours
▶ Santi Quattro Coronati

NOT TO BE MISSED
- Chapel of Santa Barbara
- Santa Maria in Domnica
- Santo Stefano Rotondo
- Santi Quattro Coronati

San Clemente

THIS MULTILEVEL CHURCH, FOUNDED IN THE FOURTH
century to commemorate the martyr Clement, Christianity's fourth
pope, is one of the most fascinating in the city. Clement, who had
been banished to the Crimea sometime during the reign of Trajan
(A.D. 98–117), continued to make converts there until he was
weighted down with an anchor (his saint's symbol) and thrown into
the sea. Destroyed by the Norman invading armies in 1084, the
church was rebuilt (over the rubble of the preexisting church) by
Pope Paschal II in the early 12th century.

It has a baroque veneer (primarily
the out-of-place gilded ceiling and
the pilasters that encase several of
the original columns). But these
fortunately do not overwhelm the
older treasures such as the reconstructed sixth-century *schola cantorum*, the marble barrier defining
the monks' choir stall, the colorful
pre-cosmatesque (see p. 206) pavement, the porticoed atrium (con-
ceptually part of the main entrance
from Piazza San Clemente), and the
wonderful 12th-century **apse
mosaic.** This has a triumphal
cross in the center (with twelve
doves symbolizing the Twelve
Apostles) between Mary and St.
John. From the base of the cross a
luxuriant Tree of Life sends out spirals of foliage, each of which
encloses images of the learned
Doctors of the Church, exotic
birds, flowers, and other Christian
symbols. The waters of life flow at
the base of the mosaic, and if
you've brought your binoculars be
sure to note the tiny figures performing daily farmyard activities,
a return to the classical style that
by the fifth century had largely
disappeared. Farther below is the
Lamb of God, Agnus Dei, in the
standard format: the lamb in the
center with six sheep on each side.
The external arch around the apse
is just as interestingly decorated.
Jesus is center top, flanked by symbols of the Four Evangelists. Just
below, Paul and St. Lawrence are

San Clemente

- Map p. 57
- Via di San Giovanni
  in Laterano (oppo-
  site the pharmacy
  at No. 108)
- 06 704 51018
- Closed 12:30–3 p.m.
- Bus: 75 (to
  Colosseo), 81, 85,
  87, 117. Metro:
  Linea B (Colosseo)
  & walk

Saints & their symbols

In Roman Catholic iconography,
many saints—especially those
who were martyred—have a
symbol that represents them, often
the instrument of their death. Thus
St. Bartholomew is represented by
a knife because he was skinned
alive, St. Cecilia's symbol is a musical
instrument because she sang while
her persecutors tried to steam her
to death, whereas St. Jerome—who
was not martyred, but exiled himself in the desert to resist temptation and translate the holy
scriptures—is shown as a scantily
clad old man with a lion. The
church of San Clemente is notable
in that you can find the symbols of
three saints here. First, of course, is
Clement himself, whose symbol, the
anchor, is on the canopy over the
main altar in both the upper and
lower church. The frescoes in the
Chapel of St. Catherine show the
torture wheel on which she was
martyred. And on the arch outside
the apse, St. Lawrence is shown
with his foot over a flame and grill,
his symbol because he was slowly
roasted to death. ∎

shown on the left while Peter and Clement are shown in the corresponding spot on the right.

Another must in the main church is the **Chapel of St. Catherine of Alexandria,** immediately to the right of the Via di San Giovanni in Laterano entrance. This chapel contains a series of very celebrated frescoes dating from about 1430 painted by Masolino da Panicale, who was probably helped by his assistant, Masaccio. The far wall is completely covered by a Crucifixion scene, while the ceiling vaults show the Four Evangelists and their symbols as well as the Doctors of the Church. The most interesting frescoes, however, are on the side walls. Those on the right depict scenes from the life of St. Ambrose. Those on the left are scenes from the life of St. Catherine, including, in the middle scene in the lower order, the unsuccessful attempt to murder her on a spiked wheel. Note the 15th-century St. Christopher painted on the outside left wall of the chapel (protected by a glass panel) with some ancient graffiti etched into its lower right-hand section.

But there is more. San Clemente is a microcosmic example of the architectural stratification that is a prime characteristic of Rome. It is an odyssey back through time. You enter, from street level, a 12th-century church, descend to the excavated fourth-century church below, and eventually go down a further level to the remains of several first-century structures. Access (for a small fee) is from the sacristy, and there are generally guides on hand if you want a guided tour.

The subject matter of this 12th-century apse mosaic is unusual. It represents a tree of life, its swirling branches growing out of an acanthus plant at the base of the Crucifix.

Above: Much of the decoration of San Clemente, as well as the facade, is baroque in style, but this hasn't altered its 12th-century essence.

Right: There are two versions of this Mithraic altar in San Clemente. The first you come to is a copy. The original is on the lowest level.

How did all the stratification come about? The explanation is simple enough. When Pope Paschal II (1099–1118) decided to build the present church, the rubble from the fourth-century church was simply packed in to form a foundation. The new church was built directly over the old one, which was more or less forgotten. It was rediscovered by accident in 1857. Excavations were begun that led to the discovery of the even earlier Mithraic shrine.

From the sacristy you descend a staircase (note the plaster cast of the Mithraic altar) to find yourself in what was once the entrance portico. In front of you are three doorways, corresponding to the standard three aisles. Note the two frescoes (like the others on this level from the 9th to the 11th century) flanking the middle door. The one on the right narrates one of Clement's miracles. Allegedly, every year the waters of the Black Sea would part to allow the faithful to pray at the spot where Clement drowned. One year an apparently absentminded mother forgot her child and he was submerged. When

she returned the next year, she found him safe and sound (note the fish painted around the border to represent the encroaching sea). Now step inside this door and walk until you are almost parallel with a door leading off to the right aisle. To get an idea of the dimensions of this church, look through the door at a column embedded in a retaining wall. Now look, to your left, at the wall where other columns are embedded. The distance between the columns indicates the width of the central nave of the fourth-century church (which was bigger than the present one), laid out in a

- 12th-century church
- Apse mosaic
- 18th-century portico and facade
- High altar
- Atrium, with 18th-century additions
- Schola cantorum, or choir area
- Chapel of St. Catherine of Alexandra
- Nave supports (mid-19th century)
- Sisinnus fresco
- 4th-century church
- Wall of original nave
- Frescoes
- 1st–3rd-century buildings
- Altar of Mithras in triclinium, or dining area, of temple
- Courtyard (not excavated)
- Catacomb with wall tombs

typical basilica plan. There are other interesting frescoes here. One (on the left wall of the nave, just before the altar) tells the story of a Roman prefect named Sisinnus. Note the inscription on the bottom half. It is believed to be one of the earliest written examples of the vernacular, the language that eventually evolved into Italian.

The third and **lowest level** of the site is reached by another staircase at the far end of the left aisle. Down you go, by another 200 years. At the bottom, where you'll hear the gurgling of an underground spring, follow the path until you can look into the ancient **Mithraeum,** a temple to the Eastern god, Mithras. Dating from around the end of the second century, or the beginning of the third, it has a ceiling decorated to simulate a grotto (Mithras was reportedly born in one), and the original of the altar you saw upstairs. The barrel-vaulted room opposite, with traces of stucco work on the ceiling,

was probably a vestibule of the temple. The Mithraeum was opposite the house where the original first-century Christian place of worship (possibly Clement's house) existed. On the labyrinthine way to the exit, as amazing as it seems, you'll be passing through a series of first-century rooms. ∎

More places to visit

SANTI QUATTRO CORONATI

Nine, not four, martyred saints are commem-
orated in the Church of the Four Crowned
Saints. The four soldiers and five sculptors
were killed for refusing either to pray to the
Greek god Aesculapius or to sculpt his image.
The story of their demise is shown in the
early 17th-century apse fresco. (The soldiers
are on the top level, the sculptors down
below.) But if something seems odd, it is.
The apse is too large for so short a nave. What
happened? Partially damaged during the 1084
Norman invasion, the church was rebuilt and
foreshortened by Pope Paschal II (1099–1118).
Indeed, the second of the two outdoor courtyards you walked through was once part of
the interior. Ring the bell near the door in
the left aisle and an Augustinian nun will
admit you to the beautiful, tiny, 13th-century
cloister, one of the first in Rome. A small
offering is expected. To see the frescoes in the
chapel of St. Sylvester *(open 4:30–6:00 p.m.)*,
on exiting head for the vestibule marked Suore
Agostiniane, ring the bell, pay, and get the
key from the nun who will answer your ring.
The chapel's frescoes depict Constantine's supposed "donation" to Sylvester of the western
Roman Empire.
🗺 Map p. 57 ✉ Via dei Santi Quattro 20
☎ 06 7047 5427 🕐 Closed 12–4 p.m.
🚌 Bus: 81, 85, 87. Metro: Linea B (Colosseo)

SANTO STEFANO ROTONDO

One of the rare circular churches to be found
in Rome, this one is extremely picturesque. In
the first place, you enter the grounds of the
church through a portion of the sustaining
wall for Nero's aqueduct. The church itself is
probably fifth century and is dedicated to St.
Stephen, the first of the many early Christian
martyrs. In the 12th century the three arches
inside were built for support. Originally, there
were two ambulatories or circular porticoes
running around it, but one of these was eliminated during a 15th-century remake (check
the outer walls where you can still see the
embedded columns).

The best time for a visit is mid-morning
when the sunlight streams in through the
22 clerestory windows. But don't let your
mood of serenity be marred by looking too
closely at the 34 frescoes that line the surviving ambulatory. Painted by Pomarancio and
Antonio Tempesta, and commissioned by
Pope Gregory XIII, the frescoes chronological-
ly depict the various methods of torture that
were used by the Romans on the early
Christian martyrs.
🗺 Map p. 57 ✉ Via di Santo Stefano
Rotondo 7 ☎ 06 7049 3717 🕐 Closed
12:30–3:30 p.m., Mon. a.m., & Sun. 🚌 Bus: 81
(from downtown and Circus Maximus), 117.
Metro: Linea B (Colosseo) then 117 bus ∎

Underground Rome

More often than not you can't see it, sometimes you need special permission to get
to it, but never forget that it's there. In fact, the
two older structures tucked away in the underground recesses of San Clemente are only a
tiny part of the ancient hidden city concealed
below the surface of Rome. Subterranean
structures nestle everywhere, often protected
(and obscured) by the tons of dirt and rubble
used to construct the foundations of later
buildings and by the more or less deliberate
landfills that, as you can best see looking down
into the Roman Forum, have raised the ground
level by several meters. The Domus Aurea was
hidden for centuries below the ruins of Trajan's
Baths. Under the Colosseum is a network of
tunnels. Below many Roman monuments,
including Caracalla and the Circus Maximus, are
more Mithraea (some bearing traces of animal
sacrifices) dedicated to that Eastern god. San
Lorenzo in Lucina, a lovely church off Via del
Corso, conceals below its marble floor part of
the remains of the giant sundial Augustus built
in the Campo Marzio. Portions of Pompey's
Theater are visible in the cellars of a downtown restaurant, while beneath the Palazzo
della Cancelleria water still runs in an ancient
canal that once crossed that part of the city. ∎

Early Christian churches, Byzantine mosaics, and relics from the Holy Land are some of the gems found in this slice of the city—along with a treasure trove of antiquities in a major museum complex.

Laterano to Terme di Diocleziano

An angel in Santa Maria Maggiore

Laterano to Terme di Diocleziano

AFTER ST. PETER'S, SAN GIOVANNI IN LATERANO IS THE most important Roman Catholic church in the world; along with the Baptistery and Santa Croce, it was one of the few Christian structures built by the Emperor Constantine inside the walls of Rome. And it is, after all, the episcopal seat of the bishop of Rome, that is the pope. "*Omnium urbis et orbis ecclesiarum mater et caput*" ("Mother and head of every church of the city and of the world") is written on the facade and on several of the columns inside.

Before you begin your visit, make sure you realize that the term "in Lateran" means that the Basilica is part of a loosely knit complex of structures that also includes some of Christianity's most important monuments: the Scala Santa, the Sancta Sanctorum, the Baptistery, and the Lateran Palace. The area takes its name from the Roman family, the Laterani, whose pater familias, Plautius, participated in a plot against Nero thus losing both his life and the family estate. The land was confiscated by the emperor and later Constantine chose it for San Giovanni since the location was less likely to prove offensive to the city's pagan majority. For centuries, the original Lateran Palace would be the official residence of the popes, who moved to St. Peter's only after their return from a self-imposed exile in Avignon in 1377. In the postwar period, the area has also had a more modern political resonance: It is traditionally the site of the annual May Day rally organized by Italy's unions, and of demonstrations by left-wing political parties.

The area that lies between the Lateran and the Esquiline and Viminale Hills contains other important Christian churches, most notably Santa Pudenziana and Santa Prassede, both known for their mosaics. Here, too, is the imposing Basilica of Santa Maria Maggiore, one of Rome's seven pilgrim churches, dedicated to the Virgin Mary and filled with mosaics celebrating her life. Several popes are buried in this church, which, unusually, has two imposing domes. Also buried here, with surprisingly little ostentation, is the baroque sculptor and architect Gian Lorenzo Bernini. The most famous of Bernini's three "Ecstasies," "St. Teresa in Ecstasy," is nearby in the church of Santa Maria della Vittoria.

In recent years the Museo Nazionale Romano (National Museum of Rome), originally confined within the walls of Diocletian's Baths, has been renovated, refurbished, and decentralized. One of several new branch sites is the Palazzo Massimo alle Terme, across the street from the baths and a stone's throw from the bustling Termini train station, a key junction for Rome's still embryonic but nevertheless useful subway system. Unlike Palazzo Altemps, near Piazza Navona, Palazzo Massimo as a building is of little interest, but it may well be the best organized museum in the city and its exhibition of ancient Roman frescoes and mosaics is unique. The museum's collection of Greek and Roman statues and sculpture is equally magnificent and is effectively organized along thematic, iconographic, and historical lines.

Facing Diocletian's Baths is Piazza della Repubblica, another area that illustrates the architectural stratification of Rome. Built shortly before World War I, the piazza's design follows the outlines of the external perimeter and the *exhedra* (a hemicycle enclosure) of the ancient baths. This busy traffic circle, which the Romans call Piazza Esedra, coincides in fact with what was once the open-air *palestra* or gym of Diocletian's complex. At the break in the exhedra is the onset of Via Nazionale, a major thoroughfare and shopping street which passes by the Palazzo delle Esposizioni, a giant exhibition space, as well as Trajan's Market, to end in Piazza Venezia. The modern fountain in the center of the piazza (Fountain of the Naiads) raised eyebrows when it was unveiled at the beginning of this century because of the generously endowed female statues. ■

San Giovanni in Laterano

FOUNDED BY THE EMPEROR CONSTANTINE IN THE FOURTH century B.C., San Giovanni in Laterano (St. John Lateran), like most Roman churches, has been rebuilt several times over the centuries. In fact, the pope's church—the Cathedral of Rome—only assumed its modern appearance in the 17th century when major overhauls of the interior and the facade took place. The last important architectural change was fairly recent: an enlargement of the presbytery in the 1880s.

The travertine **facade,** divided into a ground-floor portico with a loggia above, was designed by Alessandro Galilei in 1735. It is crowned by 15 giant statues, each about 23 feet (7 m) tall, which can be seen from miles away. The three central statues—Jesus with St. John the Baptist and St. John the Evangelist—are flanked, six on each side, by 12 Doctors of the Church, men or women elevated to this post by the pope for the profundity of their theological thinking. Five doors lead into the barrel-vaulted portico, one for each of the aisles within. The central bronze doors open onto the wide central nave. Originals from the Curia (or Senate) in the Roman Forum, they

were brought here in 1660. The door farthest to the right is the Holy Door which, like that in St. Peter's, is only opened during the Holy Years—generally falling every 25 years.

The interior, in some ways rather cold and unwelcoming (although this is less true of the warmly hued transept), betrays nothing of the church's ancient past. But there is significant grandeur, not surprising since the popes were crowned here until 1870, the year pontifical Rome, until then an independent state, fell to the armies of the Savoy monarchy. But the basilica's monumental magnificence reflects, above all, the creative genius of Francesco Borromini, commissioned by Pope Innocent X in 1646 to do a total renovation for the 1650 Holy Year.

Borromini created the 12 niches flanking the central nave, later transformed into a parade of giant baroque **statues of the Apostles.** If you are not well versed in Apostolic lore, not to worry, the statues are labeled. If you are, you'll be able to identify them by their trademarks: for example, St. Matthew's bag of money (he had been a tax collector), or St. Bartholomew's knife, the symbol of his martyrdom. Artistically, the most interesting are the four sculpted by Camillo Rusconi: Matthew, James the Elder, Andrew, and John. But Borromini's contribution did

**San Giovanni
in Laterano**

⬛ Map pp. 74–75

✉ Piazza di Porta
San Giovanni 4

☎ 06 6988 6433

💲 Basilica: free.
Cloister: $

🚍 Bus: 81, 85, 87,
117, 186, 714.
Metro: Linea A
(San Giovanni)

**Left: The Scala
Santa is the most
impressive of
the many relics
brought to Rome
from the Holy
Land by St. Helen,
the emperor
Constantine's
mother.**

**Right: The Gothic
canopy and the
end of the nave in
St. John's contains
a wooden table
that St. Peter may
have used to
celebrate Mass.**

not end here. To preserve something (but not too much) of the church's former style, he selected pieces of medieval monuments or artworks housed in the church, enclosed them in elaborate baroque frames, and created the **funerary monuments** against the pilasters in the outer aisles. The cosmatesque-style pavement (see p. 206) in the central aisle was made during the reign of Pope Martin V (1417–1431), whose bronze floor tomb is in the sunken *confessio*.

The transept of the church was renovated in the late 16th century by Giacomo della Porta and the frescoes (the "Baptism of Constantine," the "Foundation of the Basilica") were painted under the direction of Cavalier d'Arpino, who was responsible for the Ascension over the altar at the end of the left transept. The beautiful frescoed Gothic canopy over the main altar (where only the pope is allowed to say Mass) dates from 1367. Above the frescoes, a grill safeguards two silver bust-shaped reliquaries that contain the **heads of St. Peter and St. Paul,** the two founders of the Church of Rome. Although reconstructed, the **apse mosaic** is striking, and portions of this panoply of figures of varying sizes (depending on their importance) may date from the original fourth-century basilica. The tiny figure kneeling at the feet of the Virgin is Pope Nicholas IV (1288–1292), who commissioned the mosaic's restoration. The even smaller kneeling figures inserted into the row of Apostles on the bottom are the mosaicists, Jacopo Torriti and Jacopo da Camerino.

A door in the left-hand wall, just before the transept, leads to the **cloister** and its accompanying mini-museum. Fashioned between 1215 and 1223 by cosmati Maestro Pietro Vassalletto and his son, the cloister has a lovely mosaic frieze running around the garden side of the portico and a number of attractive cosmatesque colonettes. The walls are decorated with monuments from the original basilica, including what may be one of the oldest surviving papal thrones.

Leaving the church by the side door (in the right transept), you will be in Piazza San Giovanni in Laterano, with the tallest and oldest obelisk in Rome facing you (see p. 80), the Battistero on your left and, to the right, the Lateran Palace. Note the double brick arch on the other side of the piazza. It was part of the Claudian aqueduct lengthened by Nero to furnish his Domus Aurea with water. If you cross the street, you get an excellent look at the Lateran complex. The basilica's side facade has a portico, surmounted by a loggia designed by Domenico Fontana in 1586. The twin, triangle-topped bell towers of an older 13th-century version of the church are visible above it.

The **Battistero** (Baptistery) also dates back to Constantine and was built into a previous structure that formed part of an imperial residence. In the earliest days of Christianity, only the pope could baptize new converts, usually on Easter, and this was where it was done. With the spread of the new religion, however, this became impractical and parish priests were authorized to perform baptisms. Restored many times, the Baptistery has retained its fourth-century octagonal shape. The circular center space is surrounded by eight porphyry columns surmounted by an architrave with eight smaller white marble columns above. A green basalt urn (for baptisms) stands in the center. The 17th-century frescoes on the outer walls depict scenes from the life of Constantine, and the medallions encompass

The Emperor Constantine was baptized on his deathbed in 337. He built this Baptistery earlier, and it quickly became a model for future churches.

Battistero
🕑 Closed 12:30–4 p.m.

Scala Santa
🕑 Closed winter 12–3 p.m., summer 12–3:30 p.m.

views of Roman churches somehow connected to him. The chapel to St. Venantius, on the left, has magnificent seventh-century Byzantine-style mosaics, although the altar partially obstructs them. Perhaps the most interesting mosaics are in the chapel opposite the door, which until the 12th century was the original narthex (entrance) into the Baptistery. Their classical motifs—acanthus or vine leaves on a blue background—confirm that in the fifth century a real Christian iconography had not yet emerged.

The **Palazzo Lateranense** (Lateran Palace), also built by Fontana, replaced the original papal residence (the Patriarchate), which after a thousand years was reduced to a pitiful state. Fontana salvaged the **Sancta Sanctorum,** the private chapel of the early pontiffs, by moving it to a new though somewhat uninspiring structure across the street. Because of the many relics accumulated there, this chapel was known in the Middle Ages as the holiest site on earth. Renovated in the 13th century, it, too, is a cosmatesque marvel. Above the altar is an *acheiropoieton* image of the Redeemer, meaning it was (supposedly) not painted by human hands.

Also moved there was the **Scala Santa,** the ceremonial staircase, composed of 28 marble steps sheltered by a wooden covering, believed to be the one in Pontius Pilate's Jerusalem palace that Jesus had ascended. The Sancta Sanctorum is at the top of the staircase. Even today the highly religious climb it on their knees. Lateral staircases are available for non-believers and the less energetic. ■

Obelisks

Hieroglyphics? Obelisks? No, you are not in Egypt. But many of ancient Rome's emperors, or their emissaries, were there, and one of the most popular trophies for a conquering Roman leader was an Egyptian obelisk (*obelisco*). Symbols of divinity and immortality for the pharaohs, they were rated back in Rome as plunder of the highest order and were used as decorative elements for temples, circuses, and mausoleums. After the fall of Rome they lay buried under rubble for centuries. Unearthed during the Renaissance, they were then—paradoxically—given over to the glory of the city's Christian rulers, the popes.

Today, 13 of these stone giants can be found in modern Rome. They embellish some of the city's most beautiful squares and are now as much a part of the Romans' cultural heritage as triumphal columns or arches. Pope Sixtus V (1585–1590), known for his urban planning schemes, obviously had a thing about obelisks: He converted four of them to Christian usage. The Vatican Obelisk in St. Peter's Square was brought to Rome by either Caligula or Nero, and from A.D. 40 on it beautified a nearby circus. It was, amazingly, still standing in 1585, when Sixtus ordered architect Domenico Fortuna to move it to its current location, a feat requiring 900 men, 140 horses, and several dozen giant winches. The pontiff's campaign to Christianize Rome's pagan monuments proceeded with the erection on the Esquiline Hill (behind Santa Maria Maggiore and, incidentally, in front of Sixtus' private villa) of the almost 50-foot (15 m) tall Esquiline Obelisk. Once it had graced the entrance to the Emperor Augustus's Mausoleum but now, says

the inscription, it is "serving the Lord Christ." The Lateran Obelisk (see p. 78) was retrieved from the Circus Maximus along with another erected in Piazza del Popolo, and the Flaminio Obelisk was now "prouder and happier" to be dedicated to Mary.

The obelisks have been so well integrated into Rome's decor that you may almost miss them. Bernini incorporated the Agonale Obelisk into his imposing baroque Fountain of the Four Rivers (see pp. 96, 145) in Piazza Navona, and the Minerva Obelisk, a relative dwarf at only 17 feet (5 m), rides on the back of the whimsical marble elephant in front of Santa Maria sopra Minerva (see pp. 132–33). Renaissance nobleman Ciriaco Mattei placed his in the gardens of Villa Celimontana. The Macuteo Obelisk stands atop Giacomo della Porta's fountain in Piazza della Rotonda.

Sixtus V was not the only obelisk-minded pontiff. Two centuries later, Pope Pius VI (1775–1799) also had a go at relocating them. He put the red granite Quirinale Obelisk in between Castor and Pollux in front of the Quirinal Palace. A similar monument was erected at the top of the Spanish Steps. And in 1792, the obelisk Augustus had used as the needle for his giant Campus Martius sundial was raised in Piazza Montecitorio. Two other obelisks were repositioned in the 19th century: The Antinous Obelisk, originally erected by Emperor Hadrian to honor the memory of his dazzlingly handsome friend and lover, Antinous, was put on the Pincian Hill by Pius VII in 1822. The Termini Obelisk dates from the reign of Rameses II. Excavated in 1883, it has been relegated to a small, somewhat neglected park near the Termini train station. ■

Erected in Piazza del Popolo by Pope Sixtus V in the 1580s, this obelisk dates from the 13th century B.C. and is the second oldest in Rome.

Right: Pope Pius VI placed this obelisk before the Italian parliament. He gave it a pointer like the one it had when it was the needle in Augustus's giant sundial.

Santa Croce in Gerusalemme

SANTA CROCE, A SHORT WALK FROM SAN GIOVANNI DOWN Viale Carlo Felice, was originally part of the palace of St. Helena, Constantine's mother. Its baroque appearance belies its classical origins. Redecorated in the 18th century, the facade's concave and convex movement reveals a strong Borromini influence.

Santa Croce in Gerusalemme

 Map pp. 74–75

Piazza di Santa Croce in Gerusalemme 12

06 7014 779

Bus: 9 (from Termini), 81, 87 to San Giovanni and walk. Tram: Line 30b from Circus Maximus or Colosseum. Metro: Linea A (San Giovanni)

It is topped by an array of statues, including St. Helen (holding the cross) on the left and her son, Constantine, on the right. The name (Holy Cross in Jerusalem) derives from the church's foundation as a home for the important relics Helen brought back from the Holy Land. Around the back of the church to the right, just through the arches in the Aurelian Wall, and on the left, you can see the outlines of the Castrense amphitheater, used for court performances.

It's hard to discern the original basilica's layout. Only eight of the original granite columns remain: the others are encased in concrete piers. Fortunately, the marvelous cosmatesque pavement (see p. 206) has survived, as has the wonderful fresco in the apse, sometimes attributed to Antoniazzo Romano (ca 1492), showing Jesus and scenes relating to the discovery of the cross. Downstairs are two chapels; the chapel of St. Helen is built over soil that she brought back from the Holy Land. From the left aisle in the church, stairs lead up to the Chapel of the Relics. Here you'll find what are said to be parts of the True Cross, parts of its inscription, two thorns from the Crown of Thorns, a nail from the Cross, and the finger of (the Doubting) St. Thomas. ■

Like the Lateran, this church was built on the outskirts of the city (on land owned by the imperial family) to avoid offending the pagan majority.

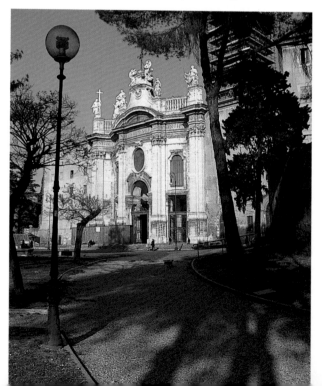

Santa Pudenziana

It is unclear whether Santa Pudenziana, who was supposed to be Santa Prassede's sister (see box below), ever really existed. The name may stem from an erroneous translation of her father's name (Ecclesia Pudenziana), an early Christian who welcomed St. Peter into his home. In any event, this is believed to be one of the oldest churches in Rome although frequent restorations have undermined much of its charm. A notable exception is the fourth-century apse mosaic. Classical in style, rather than Byzantine, it shows Jesus seated on a jewel-encrusted throne surrounded by ten Apostles (the two others were cut off during a 16th-century restoration). The women standing behind the Apostles (one on each side) with crowns in their hands have been variously identified as Prassede and Pudenziana, or as symbols of the early church composed of the ex-circumcized and the ex-Gentiles, as in Santa Sabina (see p. 208–209). What is significant, is that they are all dressed as Romans and the architectural background—with temples and basilicas—is unmistakably classical. ■

Santa Pudenziana
Map pp. 74–75
Via Urbana 160
06 481 4622
Closed 12–3 p.m.
Bus: 70 (Argentina, Venezia), 75 (from Colosseum), 714 (from Caracalla or Termini). Metro: Linea B (Cavour) or Linea A (Termini)

Santa Prassede

The present church was built by Pope Paschal I (817–824) in the early 9th century and was later restored several times, most recently in the 19th century. A typical basilica structure with a restored cosmatesque pavement (see p. 206), it is known for the ninth-century Byzantine mosaics in the apse. The Redeemer is flanked by saints: on the right, St. Peter, Santa Pudenziana (see above), and St. Zeno, with St. Paul, Santa Prassede, and Pope Paschal, holding a model of the church and whose square halo shows he was alive at the time, on the left. These mosaics are Byzantine in character (the two sisters are dressed like Byzantine princesses). A second mosaic masterpiece, one of the most important Byzantine monuments in Rome, is the decoration in the Chapel of St. Zeno. The figures are placed against a gold background, which in Eastern iconography symbolized heaven. ■

Santa Prassede
Map pp. 74–75
Via S. Prassede 9A
06 488 2456
Closed 12–4 p.m.
Bus: 70 (Argentina, Venezia), 75 (from Colosseum), 714 (from Caracalla or Termini). Metro: Linea B (Cavour) or Linea A (Termini)

The Seven Pilgrim Churches

All related to Jesus' Passion, its relics made Santa Croce one of Rome's seven pilgrim churches, Christian places of worship of particular note thanks to their association with important saints or their relics. In medieval and Renaissance times, pilgrims who managed to visit all seven were granted a special indulgence known as a plenary indulgence. A formal itinerary helped them better navigate the distances. The grand tour included the four patriarchal basilicas (St. Peter's, San Giovanni in Laterano, Santa Maria Maggiore, and San Paolo fuori le Mura) plus San Lorenzo fuori le Mura, Santa Croce, and San Sebastiano on the Appian Way. ■

Santa Maria Maggiore

LEGEND HAS IT THAT IN A.D. 352 POPE LIBERIUS HAD A vision: The Virgin Mary commanded him to build a church dedicated to her on a snow-covered spot. This was quite a presumptuous command because it hardly ever snows in Rome, much less in the summer. Nonetheless, on August 5 it supposedly snowed on the Esquiline Hill, and it was there that Liberius built what was to become one of the four major basilicas of Rome.

Ferdinando Fuga's 17th-century facade belies the early Christian origins of this church, the largest, and the oldest, of the Roman churches dedicated to the Madonna.

Santa Maria Maggiore

- Map pp. 74–75
- Piazza Santa Maria Maggiore
- 06 483 195 (Sacristy)
- Sistine Chapel closed p.m.
- Bus: 70 (Argentina, Venezia), 75 (from Colosseo), 714 (from Caracalla or Termini). Metro: Linea A (Termini) or Linea B (Cavour)

Every August a ceremony is held inside Santa Maria Maggiore to re-enact that miracle, with thousands of white flower petals (the snow) fluttering down from the ceiling. Naturally, the church you see is a later version, built by Pope Sixtus III in the early fifth century, at the tail end of a raging battle among Christian dogmatists over Mary's status: Was she only the mother of Christ the human being (Christokos)? Or was she the mother of Christ in both his human and divine natures (Theotokos)? At the Council of Ephesus in 431 the second view prevailed, giving impetus to the Marian cult. So it shouldn't surprise you that Jacopo Torriti's 13th-century **mosaic in the apse** depicts Mary as a Byzantine princess being crowned by Jesus. By

the way, if you have binoculars, you're going to need them here. The 36 fifth-century mosaic panels in the nave, illustrating scenes from the Old and New Testaments, have recently been cleaned, but they are high up and hard to see.

Many additions have been made to this church throughout the centuries, but its basic form—a basilica with three wide aisles divided by 40 massive Ionic columns—faithfully reflects fifth-century canons. The beautiful, coffered ceiling was gilded with gold from the New World donated by Ferdinand and Isabella of Spain. The sunken *confessio* holds an 1802 gold and silver relic case said to contain pieces of Jesus' cradle. The giant statue is of Pope Pius IX (1846–1878), who enlarged the confessio.

The two richly decorated, domed chapels on the ends of the transept were added in the 16th and 17th centuries. The one on the left was built by Pope Paul V, who is buried in the Borghese family crypt below. (Another occupant is Paolina Borghese who was sculpted in the nude by Canova, see pp. 120, 122.) The other, commissioned by Pope Sixtus V is, like its cousin in St. Peter's, called the **Sistine Chapel.** It is decorated with colored marbles from the Septizodium (a pagan structure which stood below the Palatine Hill) and contains Sixtus's tomb. An underground crypt (open only between Christmas and Epiphany) contains a nearly complete set of magnificent medieval manger figures by Arnolfo di Cambio. (To see them, apply mornings at the church office at Via Liberiana 27.) Near the chapel entrance, in front of the side presbytery banister, a marble slab on the floor marks the **grave of sculptor Gian Lorenzo Bernini** and his ancestors. How peculiar so lavishly baroque an artist should have such a simple, nondescript tomb!

The 18th-century front facade partially covers the early 14th-century mosaics in the loggia. These are worth a visit, anyway, since they tell the story of that miraculous August snowfall. Stop by the piazza at night when, thanks to the Italian genius at artificial lighting, the mosaics glow much as they must have by candlelight. The 14th-century bell tower is the tallest in Rome. The giant marble column in front of the church comes from the Roman forum. ∎

The canopy, or *baldacchino,* over the altar covers a sunken *confessio* containing a fragment of the infant Jesus' crib.

Palazzo Massimo alle Terme

THE NATIONAL MUSEUM OF ROME'S ENTIRE COLLECTION was originally housed in a portion of Diocletian's Baths but is now divided among four sites: the beautiful Palazzo Altemps near Piazza Navona and in this area, the Aula Ottagona, the Baths, and Palazzo Massimo alle Terme, now the linchpin of the newly decentralized system. In fact, if you only have time to see one museum (other than the Vatican), this would be a top contender. It plays host to some of the museum's finest pieces of Roman sculpture, displayed in an intelligent, articulate, and happily instructive fashion (in English, too) that belies this city's reputation for chaos and confusion.

Decorative mosaic panels from the Basilica of Junius Bassus. The charioteer depicted here is probably Giunio Basso.

The museum has four display floors, including the basement where a massive coin collection dating back to Roman times is enhanced by a charming audio-visual presentation in several languages and a splendid mechanical device: an automated magnifying glass for every one of the vertical display cases that allows you to study in detail any coin you select.

But this is only the beginning. The first thing to do when you get to the museum ticket office is to sign up for the next available accompanied visit to the top floor (the second floor, Italian style) which is dedicated to ancient Roman interior decoration, primarily wall frescoes, and wall and floor mosaics. Entire rooms from first-century to late-Roman Empire villas have been reconstructed with their original parietal decoration. While the museum's own guidebook will tell you that the frescoes here do not compare in number with those from Pompeii "nonetheless, Rome and its suburbs preserved pictorial cycles of exceptional importance and quality." To avoid any security risks, the National Roman Museum's authorities have decided not to allow visitors to wander freely on this floor, and to make sure everyone gets a chance to visit, they have—unfortunately—set a rather draconian time limit: 45 minutes on weekdays, which should thus take preference over Sundays and holidays when only 30 minutes are allowed. These are not exactly guided visits as we know them and there is no extra charge. But the *accompagnatori*, all of whom speak English, lead you though the area, stopping at the major points of interest to give a brief description of

Statue of
the Emperor
Augustus as
Pontifex Maximus

what you are to see. They are knowledgeable and courteous and will also answer questions.

Whether or not you've been to Pompeii, however, you probably won't be prepared for the beauty of the summer *triclinium* (dining room) with the garden wall frescoes from the House of Livia. This lady was not just anyone: She was married to Augustus and was the mother of the future emperor, Tiberius. And she had taste. The walls of this room, transported here from a site on the Via Flaminia outside Rome were frescoed to create an imaginary walled garden with trees, plants, flowers, and fruits of all types as well as with exotic birds and animals. Incredibly, experts were able to remove the frescoes from each of the long side walls in a single piece. And take notice of the

grotesques—smallish painted decorations on walls and ceilings in which leaves, spirals, and mythological figures generally alternate— and the stucco work on the ceiling. Another set of staggeringly beautiful frescoes come from a first-century villa discovered in 1879 on the grounds of the Villa Farnesina in Trastevere (see pp. 186–87). These frescoes have black backgrounds with friezes and decorative motifs. The mosaics displayed on this floor of the museum are equally enthralling. The four charioteers from a third-century villa belonging to the imperial Severi family show the delicacy of pictorial design. The marble inlay decorations from the Basilica of Junius Bassus are disturbingly modern.

Whether it's before your accompanied tour or after, you won't want

Palazzo Massimo alle Terme

🅰 Map pp. 74–75

✉ Largo di Villa Peretti 1

☎ 06 4890 3501

🕐 Closed Mon.

💲 $$. Audio cassettes available. Guided tours in Italian with an archaeologist four times a day; cost under $4

🚌 Bus: 64, 115, 492, 640. Metro: Linea A (Repubblica or Termini) or Linea B (Termini)

to miss the other two floors (ground floor and first floor) dedicated to the sculpture and statuary that make up the bulk of the Museo Nazionale Romano's ancient art section. The museum has sought, quite successfully it must be said, to organize the sculptures thematically

Subiaco), and include the Anzio Apollo and a magnificent Crouching Aphrodite. The Lancellotti "Discobolus" (Room VI), the bronze "Dionysus," the amazingly beautiful "Reclining Hermaphrodite," the "Wounded Niobid" (all in Room VII), and the

The "Reclining Hermaphrodite," a popular statue found in the ruins of a private garden

and by historical periods. It would be impossible to mention all the pieces but the ground floor, which deals primarily with the images and accoutrements of power, mainly from the second and first centuries B.C., contains a variety of treasures, some of which are Greek and many of which bear clear Hellenistic influences. Most notable are the multicolored giant cult statue of Minerva (the head is a modern plaster cast of another statue), and the various portraits of Augustus in Room V, which also contains the beautiful Ostia altar, dedicated to Mars. The frescoes from the Esquiline *colombarium* or dovecote tomb and the mosaic floor from a suburban villa (Galleria I) are particularly lovely.

One flight up on the first floor there's more. Much more. Here the emphasis is on the iconographic trends in official Roman art, again many with considerable Greek input. The collection is extremely rich. Room V, for example, contains marvelous pieces from suburban imperial villas (Anzio, Tivoli,

not-to-be-missed Portonaccio Sarcophagus (Room XII), with its battle scenes between Roman and barbarian soldiers, are all simply thrilling. You'll be amused to note the juxtaposition of the statues in Room II: The busts of the Emperor Hadrian, his wife Sabina, and Hadrian's lover, Antinous (the one to whom he dedicated an obelisk), are grouped here together. The busts of the emperors will give you a good idea of what these men really looked like. Another gallery is dedicated to women's head portraits. Room XIV is also memorable. Grouped under the title "Iconography and celebration from the Severi to the Constantine," the pieces here include several commemorative sarcophagi, the artwork on some of which (for example that of Marcus Claudianus with its scenes from the Old and New Testaments) indicates that influential Romans were beginning to forsake paganism for Christianity. In general, however, there is only one word for the carved reliefs on these stone coffins: breathtaking. ∎

Terme di Diocleziano

THE BATHS OF DIOCLETIAN (A.D. 284–305), INAUGURATED in A.D. 306, could accommodate about 3,000 bathers. They were built so well that much of the complex's outer structure is still standing. As in Trajan and Caracalla's baths the *natatio, frigidarium, tepidarium,* and *calidarium* were laid out along a central axis.

In 1561, Michelangelo (age 86) was commissioned by Pope Pius IV (1559–1565) to design a church utilizing part of the structure. The result was **Santa Maria degli Angeli,** the imposing entrance to which was built into an apse of the *caldarium* (the hot room), while the vestibule corresponded to the ancient *tepidarium*. In the 18th century, Michelangelo's design was somewhat altered; architect Luigi Vanvitelli changed the axis of the church by creating a new main altar opposite the entranceway and transforming Michelangelo's nave into a transept (which is just a bit too large even for a church of this size). The proportions are awe inspiring. The eight massive granite columns are 45 feet (14 m) high.

The transept is 298 feet (90 m) long, 88 feet (26 m) wide, and over 90 feet (27m) high—and overwhelming.

Another portion of the baths was later (in 1889) transformed into the **Museo Nazionale Romano,** which has its entrance on Viale Enrico de Nicola. Much of the original collection of the museum has now been transferred to other, decentralized sites such as nearby Palazzo Massimo and Palazzo Altemps, near Piazza Navona. But this is no rump museum. Its major sections deal with prehistoric Rome, Roman inscriptions, and funerary monuments (the collection of sarcophagi is enormous). Also to be seen here is the inner courtyard, designed by Michelangelo. ■

The Great Cloister of Santa Maria degli Angeli, part of a Carthusian monastery, was built into a portion of Diocletian's sprawling thermal complex.

Terme di Diocleziano

🅜 Map pp. 74–75
✉ Piazza della Repubblica
☎ 06 488 0812
🕐 Closed 12–4 p.m.
🚌 Bus: 60, 61, 62, 64, 115, 492, 640. Metro: Linea A (Repubblica)

More places to visit

AULA OTTAGONA

This octagonal structure between Via Cernaia and Via Parigi was originally the western corner of the central baths complex. Its concrete dome has remained intact and for this reason in the 1920s it was turned into a planetarium. Since 1986 it has been an annex of the Museo Nazionale Romano and houses statuary from the Baths of Diocletian, the Baths of Caracalla, and the remains of Constantine's Baths on the Quirinal Hill. The 12 pieces shown here are all lovely. Note the wonderful first-century bronze statue of a boxer whose fatigued expression alone is well worth the visit. Also worthy of mention is the marble statue of Aphrodite, a copy of a Greek original dating back to the second or third century.

🗺 Map pp. 74–75 ✉ Via Romita 8 🕐 Closed p.m. & Mon. 💲 $$ 🚌 Bus: 60, 61, 62, 64, 115, 492, 640. Metro: Linea A (Repubblica)

played in the giant sunburst over the altar is a copy of one found near the scene of the battle to which the victory was attributed. The facade was paid for by Cardinal Scipione Borghese (1576–1633) in exchange for a Greek sculpture found on the premises when laying the foundation.

The decoration is the epitome of baroque opulence: Marble, gilded stucco work, sculptures, and paintings abound. This is high baroque at its best, or in any event at its most. Despite the works of artists such as Guercino and Domenichino, the main attraction is Gian Lorenzo Bernini's "The Ecstasy of St. Teresa" in the Cornaro Chapel at the left end of the transept. St. Theresa, enveloped in the folds of marble drapery, wounded by an arrow shot by the cherubic angel to her left, lies in the throes of a mystical ecstasy. Members of the Cornaro family are sculpted into what appear to be

The opulent, baroque Santa Maria della Vittoria contains carvings by Bernini.

SANTA MARIA DELLA VITTORIA

Built between 1608 and 1620, this church is later than most in Rome. Designed by Carlo Maderno, it was originally dedicated to St. Paul. But in 1622, in commemoration of a victory over Protestant forces in the Battle of the White Mountain near Prague, it was renamed Santa Maria della Vittoria (St. Mary of Victory). The image of the Madonna dis-

theater boxes on the right and left walls of the chapel. This emphasizes the dramatic, theatrical effect so often achieved by Bernini, and is enhanced by the indirect lighting, in this case from above, favored by the artist.

🗺 Map pp. 74–75 ✉ Via XX Settembre 17 ☎ 06 482 6190 🕐 Closed 12–4 p.m. daily & p.m. in Aug. 🚌 Bus: 60, 61, 62, 175, 492. Metro: Linea A (Repubblica or Barberini) ∎

The Trevi Fountain is one of the biggest crowd-drawers in Rome. But this area also includes other Renaissance and baroque masterpieces, a major museum, and the once glamorous Via Veneto with its luxurious hotels and cafés.

Fontana di Trevi to Via Veneto

Detail from the Fontana del Moro in Piazza Navona

Fontana di Trevi to Via Veneto

TOGETHER WITH THE COLOSSEUM AND THE SPANISH STEPS, THE TREVI Fountain is the other monument that the entire world associates with the Eternal City. It is instantly recognized by travelers from every part of the globe and it, too, has overwhelming, monumental proportions. But the Trevi, hidden away among secondary side streets like St. Peter's was once, gives you a special feeling. Rounding a corner, you almost accidentally discover this travertine giant tucked among narrow, city streets. Even in a city like Rome, where fountains abound, you will find it hard not to be overwhelmed, or at least impressed, by Nicola Salvi's dramatic, late baroque masterpiece, cunningly built into the side of a (contemporary) princely palace.

Even though it is right downtown and contains more than one example of Roman majesty, the area around the Trevi has retained much of its traditional character, and you will find simple artisans' shops and boutiques mixed in with baroque masterpieces. The Colonna Palace (with its private art gallery, open only on Saturday mornings) is nearby. Walking uphill along Via della Dataria you will come to the Quirinal Hill and, atop it, the Quirinal Palace. This was once the summer residence of the popes and is now the home of the president of the Italian Republic, where at 4:00 p.m. on Sundays you can see the changing of the guard.

After the late Renaissance popes made this their summer getaway (today's pontiffs head instead to Castelgandolfo on Lake Albano), the surrounding neighborhood became more desirable and several important churches, such as the Jesuit Sant'Andrea al Quirinale and San Carlo alle Quattro Fontane, were built here by major architects such as Bernini and Borromini. These two masters of Italian architecture were thrown together repeatedly; in fact, in the beginning Borromini worked for the older Bernini as a draftsman. They had already collaborated on Palazzo Barberini, the huge baroque palace that Maffeo Barberini, recently elected Urban VIII, had decided to refurbish and expand to make it worthy of the Barberinis' newly exalted status. Decorated by some of the major artists of the 17th century—the ceiling of the great hall of the palace bears the remarkable frescoes of Pietro da Cortona—it is now the principal seat of the National Gallery. The museum is still in the

process of reorganization and hopefully, in the near future, will improve its didactic accoutrements. Its collection includes a series of masterpiece paintings ranging from a Fra Filippo Lippi "Annunciation" to Caravaggio's "Judith Beheading Holofernes."

Near the Palazzo is Piazza Barberini. Today this is both a busy traffic circle and the center of a major shopping area, with the result that despite the repaved traffic island most passersby probably don't even notice Bernini's charming Triton Fountain, one of the first he designed. The Fontana delle Api, which enshrines the Barberini family's bee symbol, is now located across the street. Today, Romans don't pay much attention to it either, but when it was erected in the 17th century things were different. An inscription stated that the fountain had been put up in the 22nd year of the papacy of the Barberini pope, Urban VIII. Unfortunately, it was unveiled a few weeks before the anniversary, making the superstitious Romans nervous.

Rightly so, it would seem. Urban died eight days before his 22nd year would have begun.

The Bee Fountain is located at the start of Via Veneto, the long winding avenue that for decades was this city's "great white way" as well as the location of the most elegant hotels and cafés. Once (both in Roman times as well as much later, in the 16th and 17th centuries) a neighborhood of sprawling residential villas, after 1870 this area was wantonly subdivided in a frenzy of real estate speculation. After World War II, the Via Veneto became known for the dolce vita, an era of glamour and glitter, now vanished, that was depicted in many movies of the time, in particular, Federico Fellini's *La Dolce Vita* (1960). ■

Fontana di Trevi

BY ROMAN STANDARDS, THE FONTANA DI TREVI, OR TREVI Fountain is almost new; it was, after all, built only some 240 years ago. The water that flows over and through it was brought to Rome by the Aqua Virgo, a largely underground aqueduct originally built by Marcus Vipsanio Agrippa (Augustus's right-hand man) in 19 B.C. to supply water to the baths he constructed in the Campus Martius near the Pantheon. The Aqua Virgo got its name because the spring from which it comes was reputedly revealed to Agrippa's soldiers by a young virgin. You can see her in the relief on the right side of the fountain's upper portion (the attic) as she points to the spring. The other relief shows Agrippa approving the plans for the aqueduct's construction. Damaged by the Goths in 537, it was repaired several times and continued to supply the Campus Martius section of town all through the Middle Ages.

Fontana di Trevi

- Map pp. 92–93
- Piazza Fontana di Trevi
- Bus: 56, 60, 61, 62, 71, 95, 116, 175 to Via del Tritone

Opposite: Rome's fussiest English residents used to send their servants here to get water for their afternoon tea. The Acqua Vergine spring (Italian for Aqua Virgo) is reputed to have the best water in Rome.

A succession of popes thought about building a monumental fountain on this spot, and various projects, including one by Bernini, were presented. It was only in 1732 that Pope Clement XII (whose papal crest is seen at the top of the fountain) approved the design submitted by Nicola Salvi. The project, which took 30 years to complete emphasizes the central portion of the fountain, dominated by Neptune, while below, among the rocks, two Tritons struggle with two horses (one calm, one bucking to represent the sea in its various moods), while the bubbling and gushing water re-creates the ocean's power and turbulence. These central figures were begun by the little known Giovanbattista Maini but were finished by Pietro Bracci.

The figures in the niches on the right and left represent Abundance (left) and Health (right) and are both by Filippo Valle. The four figures set against the attic, all by different sculptors, represent the beneficial and fertilizing effect of water in the different seasons. As the terminus of the Aqua Virgo aqueduct, the Trevi Fountain is also one of Rome's several *mostre d'acqua*, a term meant to denote a monumental fountain with enough pressure to push water on to other outlets.

Where and when the custom began of throwing a coin (over your shoulder, if you please!) into the Trevi Fountain in order to guarantee a return trip to Rome is not really known, but to judge from the amount and type of coins pitched in here daily, the practice has become generally accepted by tourists and was, of course, immortalized in the 1954 film, *Three Coins in the Fountain.* Don't miss the beautiful late 18th-century *aedicola* (niche) on the building at the corner of the piazza with Via del Lavatore. Facing it is the high baroque church of **Santi Vincenzo e Anastasio,** parish church for the popes while they lived on the Quirinal. In the crypt are the hearts and other innards of almost all the popes of the 17th, 18th, and 19th centuries. The practice was discontinued by Pius X (1903–1914). The surrounding streets, Via del Lavatore (where there is a morning food market), Via Panettieria, and Via in Arcione, have grocery and artisans' shops. ∎

Fountains & aqueducts

Immortalized in two films, *Three Coins in the Fountain* (1954) and Fellini's *La Dolce Vita* (1960), the Trevi Fountain is certainly the best known in Rome, but it is hardly alone. In effect, fountains (or *fontane*)—small and large, sculpted and plain—are everywhere in the Eternal City. Water spouts from lions' heads, stone tiaras, gargoyles, nymphs, sea gods, masks, barrels, seahorses, a pile of amphorae, and even a heap of stone cannonballs. It trickles, too, from the small neighborhood *fontanelle* from which many Romans once drew their drinking water and today use to wash their cars or quench a summer thirst.

Romans swear by their fontanelle, learning at a tender age that a finger placed over the spigot opening turns a small hole in the top into a drinking spout. It gushes from the *mostre d'acqua* (monumental fonts) that help circulate water throughout the fountain network.

"Nothing can be more agreeable to the eyes of a stranger, especially in the heats of summer, than the great number of public fountains that appear in every part of Rome, embellished with all the ornaments of sculpture, and pouring forth prodigious quantities of cool, delicious water," wrote British writer Tobias Smollett in 1765. In fact, the fountains are omnipresent, testifying both to the grandiosity of the city's ruling class, and to the special relationship that Romans have always had with this life-giving liquid. Historically, Rome had few nearby sources of water, and its

engineers built aqueducts (*aquedotti*) to bring enough of it into the urban area, from as far as 31 miles (50 km) away.

For a fountain lover, Rome is a dream. In the Trident area, on the same aqueduct line as the Trevi, are the Barcaccia, (the "old boat" fountain at the foot of the Spanish Steps), the Pantheon Fountain, and the magnificent 16th-century fountains of Piazza Navona, designed by Gian Lorenzo Bernini. The star attraction in Piazza Navona is Bernini's Fontana dei Quattro Fiumi (Fountain of the Four Rivers), inaugurated in 1651 and financed to the tune of 29,000 scudi by a highly unpopular bread tax. Its four stone giants represent the great rivers of the then known world: the Ganges, the Plate, the Danube, and the Nile, whose veiled countenance stood for the mystery of its (then) uncharted source.

Bernini also designed Il Tritone (the Triton Fountain) and the Fountain of the Bees in downtown Piazza Barberini (see p. 104). These fountains are fed by another mostra d'acqua, the oversize fountain in Piazza San Bernardo near the Grand Hotel. Commonly called the Moses Fountain because of its large central figure, its real name is the Fontana dell'Acqua Felice, after the modern aqueduct built in 1586 by Pope Sixtus V to bring running water to that area. It also sends water to the four charming corner fountains on the intersection of Via delle Quattro Fontane with Via Venti Settembre and to the beautiful Bernini Triton Fountain in the courtyard at Via della Panetteria 15 (near the Trevi).

A third mostra d'acqua is Fontana dell'Acqua Paola (see p. 189) on the Janiculum Hill, built to commemorate the reopening in 1612 of Trajan's aqueduct, built in A.D. 109 to bring water from Lake Bracciano. Probably one of the most beautiful fountains in Rome is the Fontana delle Tartarughe (Tortoises) in tiny Piazza Mattei, a small square tucked away behind the Ghetto (see p. 203). In 1581 Giacomo della Porta's design was executed by Taddeo Landini, who sculpted the four boys and dolphins that make up this lyrical bronze composition. The tortoises, by an unknown artist, were added a century later. ■

Opposite: Detail from Fontana del Moro
Top left: The Barberini family's bees grace a
fountain in their piazza.
Above: This Neptune group was added to a
Piazza Navona fountain in 1878.
Left: A bronze tortoise from the Turtle
Fountain in Piazza Mattei
Below: Roman aqueduct

Quirinale

This obelisk, like its twin behind Santa Maria Maggiore, originally embellished the entrance to the Emperor Augustus's Mausoleum.

THE QUIRINAL HILL (MONTE QUIRINALE), THE HIGHEST OF Rome's famous seven, and just up the street from the Trevi Fountain, is another sight you shouldn't miss, if only because of the magnificent view over the city as far as St. Peter's. Probably named after the ancient Temple of Quirinus which once stood here, it was a site greatly appreciated by Emperor Constantine who chose it for his Imperial Baths. This was probably the source of the enormous statues of the semigods Castor and Pollux and their heavenly steeds that for centuries have graced this piazza (the obelisk and fountain were added later). In fact, in the Middle Ages the hill was called Monte Cavallo.

Palazzo del Quirinale

- Map pp. 92–93
- Piazza del Quirinale
- 06 69991
- Open 2nd & 4th Sun. of the month 8:30 a.m.–12:30 p.m. Changing of the Guard 3:15 p.m. daily (4 p.m. Sun.)
- $$
- Bus: 64, 70, 170 to Via Nazionale or 56, 95, 116, 175, 492 to Piazza Barberini. Metro: Linea A (Barberini)

As far back as the first century B.C., this area had a particular residential cachet. The writer Martial lived here, as did Cicero's good friend, Pomponius Atticus. In the late 1500s Pope Gregory XIII decided to build a summer residence here where it was somewhat cooler than at the Vatican. Over the decades many important artists—Ponzio, Fontana, Bernini, Maderno, Fuga—worked on the **palazzo,** which has a Renaissance facade facing onto the piazza and a secondary entrance on the wing known as the *manica lunga* (the sleeve) on the Via del Quirinale.

Also on the piazza are several other important palazzi. The **Consulta,** on the far side looking toward St. Peter's, was built by Pope Clement XII in the 1730s to house a papal tribunal (today it is the site of Italy's Constitutional Court). Next door is **Palazzo Pallavicini-Rospigliosi,** constructed in 1603 for the Borghese family, while across from the Quirinale are the stables, renovated and now used for temporary exhibits. After Italian unification in 1870, Italy's Savoy kings moved into the Quirinale. Since 1947, it has been the residence of the president of Italy. ■

Sant'Andrea al Quirinale

When in 1658 the Jesuits decided to build a new church to serve its novices, they chose the "Strada Pia" (today's XX Settembre), the road designed a century earlier by Michelangelo to connect the Quirinal Palace—which in the time being had become the summer residence of the popes—to the Porta Pia gate. The man in charge was Cardinal Camillo Pamphili and his choice fell on Gian Lorenzo Bernini who had already designed the Piazza Navona fountains for the family. Generally considered Bernini's masterpiece in ecclesiastical architecture, the church is oval in shape while the interior embodies his theory that the visual arts, combined with the effective use of lighting and color, should aim at the creation of an intensely emotional, even theatrical, experience. For Bernini lovers, this is a site not to be missed. Note the colored marbles, the gilded ceiling, and the stucco cherubs on it tumbling down from the small, elliptical dome in a swirl of frenetic activity. ■

Sant'Andrea al Quirinale
- Map pp. 92–93
- Via del Quirinale 29
- 06 4890 3187
- Closed 12–4 p.m. daily & Tues.
- Bus: 60, 61, 62, 175, or 492 to Piazza Barberini; 64, 70, 170 to Via Nazionale. Metro: Linea A (Barberini)

Bernini's unusually simple facade gives no clue to the opulence of this church's baroque interior.

San Carlo alle Quattro Fontane

How fitting that the architect of San Carlo alle Quattro Fontane down the street from Bernini's masterpiece should be none other than his archrival, Carlo Borromini, who in his first solo commission seems to have created an antithesis (note the monochromatic off-white interior) to Bernini's opulence. Completed in 1667, the church is so small that it could fit into one of the four supporting pilasters of St. Peter's. Borromini's genius is exemplified by his sublimely beautiful dome, a beehive of geometric design (crosses, octagons, and hexagons in relief), its windows ingeniously hidden by stucco decorations.

Outside, note the four late 16th-century fountains (two river gods and two virtues, Fidelity and Strength) at the intersection with **Via delle Quattro Fontane.** From the intersection's center you can see three of Rome's obelisks. ■

San Carlo alle Quattro Fontane
- Map pp. 92–93
- Via del Quirinale 23
- 06 488 3261
- Closed 1–4 p.m.
- Bus: 60, 61, 62, 175, or 492 to Piazza Barberini; 64, 70, 170 to Via Nazionale. Metro: Linea A (Barberini)

Palazzo Barberini & Galleria Nazionale d'Arte Antica

DESPITE SOME REORGANIZATION, THE WAVE OF RENEWAL that has swept Rome's museum system seems to have bypassed the National Gallery, located downtown in Rome's monumental Palazzo Barberini. True, there is a new entrance (you can still use the Via della Quattro Fontane gate but head downstairs to the ticket booth), and a new reservation system for special exhibits and the Barberini apartment. Otherwise, the organization of the regular collection is not worthy of its paintings.

Palazzo Barberini & Galleria Nazionale d'Arte Antica

- Map pp. 92–93
- Via Barberini 18
- 06 32810
- Closed Tues.
- Gallery & Apartment: $$
  Special exhibits: $$$
- Bus: 56, 60, 61, 62, 95, 116, 175, 492.
  Metro: Linea A (Barberini)

Inexplicably, the numbers of the rooms are not displayed, the meager explanatory information is exclusively in Italian, and the map available to visitors is outdated. However, the collection includes several priceless masterpieces, and the Palazzo itself is a work of decorative and architectural genius.

The permanent collection is currently displayed on two floors. On the first floor (Italian-style) the first rooms to your left contain some lovely primitives (mostly on wood). Paintings from the 15th and 16th centuries are in the next rooms and among these, in Room 3, are Fra Filippo Lippi's "Annunciation" and a "Madonna and Child," and "Mary Maddalena" by Piero di Cosimo. In Room 4 you will find several important works by Antioniazzo Romano and Perugino. Room 6 contains Raphael's famous "La Fornarina" (the baker's daughter said to have been his mistress), although others attribute it to his pupil, Giulio Romano. Note Raphael's name on her bracelet. Also here are Giovan

Antonio (Il Sodoma) Bazzi's "Rape of the Sabine Women," and Andrea del Sarto's "Sacred Family" and "Madonna and Child." The ceiling vault displays Andrea Camassei's "Creation of the Angels." In contrast, the vast ceiling of Room 7 is a "Divine Providence" painted by Andrea Sacchi. In Room 8, there are several masterpieces: Tintoretto's "St. Jerome," Titian's "Venus and Adonis," Lorenzo Lotto's "Sacred Conversation," and Bronzino's striking "Portrait of Stefano Colonna." Room 9 has an interesting "Pietà" by a follower of Michelangelo as well as Jacopo Zucchi's "Bath of Bathsheba."

The rest of the exhibition continues up the staircase designed by Bernini. In the first room you will find several paintings of Guido Reni, including his "Beatrice Cenci," and a "Pietà" by Giovan Battista Gaulli (Il Baccicia). The room down a few steps on the left from this central room has Hans Holbein's "Henry VIII" and leads to yet another room where you will find the museum's three Caravaggios ("Judith Beheading Holofernes," "Narcissus," and "St. Francis"). Back in the central room, but on the other side, is a door from which tours of the small but really lovely, 18th-century apartment designed for Princess Cornelia Costanza Barberini start.

What you really want to take note of is the building itself, considered a prime example of baroque Roman patrician architecture. It is also another structure to which both Bernini and Borromini contributed, although the original design is attributed to Carlo Maderno, Borromini's uncle, who died only a year after construction began. Commissioned by the Barberini in 1625, that is shortly after their scion, Maffeo Barberini, became Pope Urban VIII, it epitomizes the level of

noble life in 17th-century Rome. Borromini, who began the job as Bernini's assistant, is believed to have designed the oval staircase in the right wing viewed from Via delle Quattro Fontane. At some point you'll want to walk outside to the front garden to get a good look at Bernini's impressive central portico and the original facade. But the pièce de résistance of Palazzo Barberini is without a doubt Pietro da Cortona's magnificent ceiling in the Salone, the "Triumph of Divine Providence over Time," in which you can see a more than queen-size version of the three Barberini bees. The room also includes several of Da Cortona's cartoons.

Unfortunately, if a special exhibit is on, you may have to buy a ticket to it in order to see this exceptional masterpiece. ∎

Jacques de Backer's "Dead Christ Supported by an Angel" is just one of the non-Italian paintings here. The most famous is Hans Holbein's "Henry the Eighth."

Via Veneto

IN ANCIENT TIMES, THIS WAS A RESIDENTIAL SUBURB where the wealthy had their landscaped villas. There are next to no traces of those first-century buildings or of the extensive gardens which surrounded most of of them.

In the 1950s and 1960s Roman paparazzi (photographers) would stalk the famous habitués of the Via Veneto cafés as they sipped their *aperativi* or downed their nightcaps.

Via Veneto

Map pp. 92–93

Bus: 52, 53, 95, 116, 119

The best known were the Horti Sallustiani, the gardens that surrounded the magnificent home of Sallust, a Roman general and scholar who was a contemporary of Julius Caesar. After the turmoil of the fifth and sixth centuries A.D. (barbarian invasions and wars resulted in an interruption of the water supply), the area was abandoned in favor of more central zones. But the suburban tradition was reborn in the 17th century when much of this area was occupied by the sprawling Villa Ludovisi. This was sold in the late 19th century when real estate speculation opened the way for modern urban development.

By the early 20th century the Via Veneto (officially the Via Vittorio Veneto) had become Rome's most elegant street, the site of the city's best hotels and restaurants. In the 1950s its upper portion became the undisputed hub of la dolce vita (the sweet life), a term used during the economic boom of the 1950s and 1960s to describe the gossip and glitter of Roman night life, the comings and goings of the Eternal City's international galaxy of stars, and the unrelenting assault of its tabloid photographers or paparazzi on the city's beautiful people.

The era was depicted in many movies of the time, in particular *La Dolce Vita* (1960), one of the finest works of Federico Fellini. The movie includes the unforgettable scene of a voluptuous Anita Ekberg, the prey of the cynical reporter Paolo Rubini (Marcello Mastroianni), immersing herself in the waters of the Trevi Fountain (see pp. 94–95). The most memorable character was Paparazzo, Rubini's photographer sidekick. By then the street's most famous bars and cafés—Doney's, Café de Paris, and Harry's Bar—had become hangouts for actors and directors such as Sophia Loren, Gina Lollobrigida, Vittorio De Sica, Roberto Rossellini, Ingrid Bergman, Liz Taylor, Richard Burton, Burt Lancaster, and many more who went there to see and to be seen.

Today, however, it is simply one of Rome's broader avenues, pleasingly lined with charming (and very expensive) sidewalk cafés, elegant shops, and luxury hotels such as the Excelsior and the Flora. At the upper end is **Porta Pinciana,** the fortified gateway built into the Aurelian walls in A.D. 403 by the Emperor Honorius, leading to Villa Borghese and the Galleria Borghese. Its lower end, where you'll find banks, ministries, and other hotels, ends in **Piazza Barberini,** one of the center's major traffic junctions and the site of two famous Bernini statues (see p. 104). ■

More places to visit

GALLERIA DELL'ACCADEMIA DI SAN LUCA

This is a delightful but mostly unknown treat for people keen to see the less visible parts of Rome. Since the 1930s, when its headquarters near the Roman Forum were transferred because Mussolini razed much of that old neighborhood, the Academy of St. Luke has been housed in Palazzo Carpegna, around the corner from the Trevi Fountain and built originally by Giacomo della Porta (or one of his disciples) in the late 16th century. The building was subsequently modified by Borromini, who built the spiral staircase, ingeniously masked by stucco decoration until you are right upon it. This was another of those little optical diversions that Borromini and his rival Bernini liked to create to trick the eye of the beholder. The staircase is reached after passing through the tiny open garden on the right with sculptures dating from the end of the 19th and beginning of the 20th centuries.

The academy was founded in the late 16th century by a group of artists whose gifts, along with bequests by nonmembers, make up the interesting collection. It was named for St. Luke because the Apostle was supposed to have had artistic inclinations. The collection includes works by Raphael, Titian, Poussin, Bronzino, Barocci, Giovanni Paolo Pannini, Rubens, Van Dyck, Canova, and many more. It also includes examples of work by several of the rare female artists who managed to make a name for themselves, including Lavinia Fontana, Angelika Kauffmann, and Elisabeth Vigee-Lebrun.

Nearby, on Via della Stamperia, is the **Calcografia Nazionale,** with what may be the largest collection of copperplate engravings in the world. It has more than 20,000 plates including over 1,400 by G.B. Piranesi and is generally open to the public.

🅰 Map pp. 92–93   ✉ Piazza dell'Accademia di San Luca 77   ☎ 06 679 8850   🕐 Closed p.m. & Tues., Thurs., Sat. Open last Sun. of the month 10 a.m.–1 p.m.   💲 Free   🚌 Bus: 56, 62, 71, 116. Metro: Linea A (Spagna or Barberini)

PIAZZA BARBERINI

Today this piazza is both the center of a busy traffic circle and in the middle of a major shopping area, with the result that, despite the repaved island, for most passersby Bernini's magnificent Triton Fountain (circa 1643), the **Fontana del Tritone,** is kind of an afterthought. A good look at the Tritone seated on a shell balanced by four dolphins while blowing water through a conch shell will, however, remind you of the sculptor's genius. The statue, made of travertine rather than marble, was Bernini's first fountain. The whimsical **Fontana delle Api** across the street bears three stone bees (the Barberini symbol) and an inscription says that its water is for the public and its animals.

🅰 Map pp. 92–93   🚌 Bus: 56, 60, 61, 62, 95, 116, 175, 492. Metro: Linea A (Barberini)

SANTA MARIA DELLA CONCEZIONE (DELL'IMMACOLATA)

From an architectural point of view the Church of the Cappuccini, as it is generally called after the Franciscan monks that run it, is simple and unprepossessing, an attempt by its founder, Cardinal Antonio Barberini (the younger brother of Pope Urban—he is buried there), to run counter to the then (1626) baroque tide. Inside, however, there is rich decoration. The first chapel on the right has Guido Reni's "St. Michael Trampling on the Devil" and was decorated by Pietro da Cortona; the second has works by Lanfranco; the third by Domenichino; and the fifth by Andrea Sacchi. Most of the church's visitors, however, have something else in mind. In fact, the church conceals several somewhat macabre but nonetheless fascinating underground burial chapels lined with the skeletons (or loose bones) of some 4,000 Capuchins. Take a sweater.

🅰 Map pp. 92–93   ✉ Via Veneto 27   ☎ 06 487 1185   🕐 Closed 12–3 p.m. Crypt closed 12–3 p.m. & Thurs.   🚌 Bus: 60, 62, 95, 116, 175, 492. Metro: Linea A (Barberini) ∎

W ith its magnificent Spanish Steps and elegant shops, Piazza di Spagna is the *salotto,* or living room, of Rome. But nearby Piazza del Popolo is also impressive, as is the Villa Borghese park.

Piazza di Spagna to Villa Borghese

Detail of a funerary monument in Santa Maria del Popolo

Museo Nazionale
di Villa Giulia

Galleria
Nazionale d'Arte
Moderna

GIARDINO
ZOOLOGICO

VILLA
STROHL-
FERN

VILLA

PIAZZA
GIARDI
ZOOLOGIC

ZOOLOGIC

PIAZZALE
DEL FIOCCO

GIARDINO
DEL
LAGO

PIAZZA DI
SIENA

PIAZZALE
DEL FLAMINIO

Flaminio

BORGHESE

Porta del
Popolo

MONTE

PIAZZALE
DEL
CANESTRE

Santa Maria
del Popolo

Piazzale
Napoleone I

Obelisco

Obelisco

Piazza del
Popolo

PINCIO

GALOPPATOIO

Santa Maria
di Montesanto

MURO

TORTO

PIAZZA
BRASILE

Santa Maria
dei Miracoli

Porta
Pinciana

Tevere

Villa
Medici

Spagna

Trinità
dei Monti

Scalinata
della Trinità
dei Monti

Babington's
Tea Room
PIAZZA
DI SPAGNA
Fontana
della Barcaccia

Ara Pacis
Augustae

Mausoleo
di
Augusto

Caffè
Greco

Museo
Keats-Shelley

Palazzo
di Spagna

V. TOMACELLI

Palazzo di
Propaganda Fide

Rome

Area of map detail

LARGO
CHIGI

0   400 yards
0   400 meters

Piazza di Spagna to Villa Borghese

WHEN ITALIANS TALK ABOUT A CITY, THEY OFTEN USE the word *salotto*, living room, to describe an area that is both central and welcoming. In that sense the Trident, and, in particular, Piazza di Spagna, is the salotto of Rome, the neighborhood that best plays host to the city's myriad visitors, those who come to dine and shop and those eager to revisit Rome's architectural, artistic, and archaeological past.

PARCO DEI DAINI

Galleria Borghese

The original design (later dropped) for Piazza del Popolo included a matching tiered garden opposite this one.

The area begins just inside the Porta del Popolo, the gateway in the Aurelian walls (once called Porta Flaminia) that was the terminus of the Via Flaminia, the Roman road built to connect the capital to Rimini on the Adriatic Sea. It includes important archaeological monuments such as Augustus's Mausoleum and the Ara Pacis, Renaissance palaces such as Villa Medici, and innumerable churches, including Trinità dei Monti, with its splendid view of the city. The name, "il Tridente," literally something with three teeth, takes its cue from the street plan developed in the 1500s by the popes of the era, then the city's temporal rulers. In fact, there are three major streets fanning out from Piazza del Popolo: Via Ripetta, which ran to the ancient river port; Via del Babuino, which runs through Piazza di Spagna and on to the Quirinal Hill (then the site of a papal

residence); and Via del Corso, which cuts straight through downtown Rome ending at Piazza Venezia and on which important horse races, la Corsa dei Barbari, were held.

For centuries, the area stretching from the Pincio Hill (see p. 112) to the Tiber had been uninhabited: rumored to be haunted by evil spirits, this was a weak point in the city's defenses. With the construction of Santa Maria del Popolo and the other churches of Piazza del Popolo all this was to change, and Via del Babuino's route through Piazza di Spagna would transform the latter, into an all-important tourist and shopping center. The Spanish Steps linked the area to the Pincio Hill and, through the latter to the Villa Borghese, a magnificent park that embraces several major museums such as Villa Giulia and, in particular, the magnificently renovated Galleria Borghese. ■

Piazza di Spagna

FOR AT LEAST FOUR CENTURIES, THIS LONG, IRREGULARLY shaped piazza with its un-Italian palm trees has been the heart of nonarchaeological Rome. The elongated square, which boasts one of the city's major monumental attractions, the Scalinata (Spanish Steps), was fashioned into its current form by several important influences: The popes commissioned the best artists to design its major landmarks; the French financed the construction of the three-tiered staircase; and their competitors for the affections of the pope, the Spanish, built their impressive embassy to the Holy See, Palazzo di Spagna (1647), only a stone's throw from Propaganda Fide, the seat of the Vatican's missionary activities. And let's not forget the English, who early on made Rome an obligatory stop on the Grand Tour for poets and gentlemen alike.

Piazza di Spagna
- Map pp. 106–107
- Bus: 116. Metro: Linea A (Spagna)

The **Scalinata della Trinita dei Monti**, or "Spanish" Steps, is a misnomer. Prior to the inauguration of the Spanish Embassy (across from American Express), the area was known as Piazza di Francia. Designed by Francesco de Sanctis, the Scalinata was built in the 1720s to replace the footpath linking the piazza to the lovely French church of **Trinita dei Monti** with its double bell towers and the double flight of front stairs. The money to build the 138 travertine steps (24,000 scudi) was bequeathed by a 17th-century French diplomat in his will and then augmented by a contribution of the then king of France, Louis XV.

The steps, which have become a meeting place for young tourists, are particularly lovely in the spring when they have a magnificent display of flowering azaleas. At Christmas time, a life-size nativity scene is erected there, and every December 8 the pope pays a visit to the narrower, southern end of the piazza where a wreath is placed on the statue of the Virgin Mary atop a Roman column, erected in the last century to commemorate the 1854 dogma of the Immaculate Conception.

At the foot of the Spanish Steps is the **Fontana** (or fountain) **della Barcaccia** (see p. 96), attributed to Pietro Bernini (Gian Lorenzo's father) and commissioned almost a century before the staircase, in the 1620s, by Pope Urban VIII, a Barberini, as you can tell by the stone bees, the family's

symbol. Because of low pressure, the water does not spout forcefully from the top but rather trickles from nozzles located on the prow, stern, and sides of this marble version of an old, leaky boat. Was this a reference to St. Peter's role as a fisher of men? Or a commemoration of the 1598 flood? It's not clear. The street facing the Steps, **Via dei Condotti,** *the* shopping street of Rome (see p. 110), is named for the underground conduits that Pope Gregory XIII (1572–1585) built to supply the neighborhood with running water.

Beyond the Roman column you'll see, wedged between two streets, the 17th-century **Palazzo di Propaganda Fide,** which houses the Vatican's Congregation for the Propagation of the Faith. Considered an architectural masterpiece, the building combines the work of the two rival geniuses of the era, Gian Lorenzo Bernini and Francesco Borromini. Bernini designed the facade facing the piazza (look, more stone bees here!), while his artistic nemesis, Borromini, was commissioned to create the side facade on Via Propaganda Fide. ∎

In Charles Dickens's day, the Scalinata (Spanish Steps) was a meeting place for artists' models. The Keats-Shelley Memorial House (open to the public) is in the first building on the right. Babington's Tea Rooms is on the left.

The English Quarter

In the 18th century the foreign presence in the Piazza di Spagna area escalated with intellectuals and artists of many nationalities taking up residence in the surrounding streets. But there were so many English visitors that Italians began using the word *"inglesi"* to mean foreigners in general. The major hotels had names like Hotel de Londres and the Hotel des Anglais (even today, a favorite in the area is the Hotel d'Inghilterra). Tennyson and Thackeray had lodgings on Via dei Condotti across the street from the **Caffè Greco,** a famed meeting place for intellectuals. The young English poet, John Keats, was living at Piazza di Spagna 26 (the rose-colored building to the right of the steps) when he died in 1821, and his apartment now houses the small but interesting **Museo Keats-Shelley** (Keats and Shelley Museum and library). **Babington's Tea Rooms** on the other side of the Steps (great scones!) is an expensive but charming Victorian institution opened to cater to Rome's English-speaking community. ∎

Shopping & fashion

Piazza di Spagna is at the same time the heart of Rome's major shopping district and of the city's fashion world. These days its central position in the universe of Roman *alta moda* is dramatized by the Sotto le Stelle (Under the Stars) fashion show every July when the city's haute couteur designers exhibit their fabulous creations on the stone cascade that is the Spanish Steps. The piazza itself and the network of cross-streets that run from here to Via del Corso (the best known are Via dei Condotti, Via Frattina, Via Borgognona, Via delle Carozze e Via della Croce, Via Bocca di Leone, Via Mario dei Fiori, and Via Belsiana) are a fashion victim's delight. Armani, Balestra, Bulgari, Biagiotti, Fendi, Ferragamo, Ferré, Genny, Gucci, MaxMara, Missoni, Prada, Valentino, Versace—all the signature stores are here, as are countless other shops that sell elegant clothing, jewelry, housewares, and objets d'art.

The prices are not low, bargaining is rare, *saldi* (sales) are very often misleading, and tax rebates, while enticing, generally require enormous patience at the airport on your day of departure. (An exception is the Euro Free Tax stores that makes a stop at the airport customs office unnecessary.) The clothes are beautiful, eye-catching, and well made and, with some products, particularly leather goods—clothing, shoes, and bags—you may find a real bargain, a trophy to show off at home. Naturally, there are also apparel stores with lower prices. On tiny Via del Gambero you can find bargain blouses and sweaters. On Via del Corso, the long street connecting Piazza del Popolo and Piazza Venezia (adored by writers such as Stendhal for its 18th-century elegance), there are many shoe stores and casual-wear outlets. And the same goes for Via della Croce, which has some nice food stores as well.

Rinascente at Largo Chigi, one of Rome's oh-so-few department stores, has been totally refurbished in recent years and does a brisk trade in attractive clothing and accessories for both men and women. Like a growing number of stores in the center, it now stays open all day long. It is also one of only a very few that are open every single day, including Sundays and Monday mornings when clothing stores are generally closed (except in summer months when they close Saturday afternoons and remain open on Monday mornings).

The streets around the Spanish Steps are not the only important shopping district, however, merely the most elegant, fashionable and…expensive. There are two major alternatives. One is Via Nazionale, the broad cobblestone avenue that runs from Largo Magnanapoli to Piazza della Repubblica (or Esedra), where clothing and leather goods stores abound. Another is Via Cola di Rienzo, across the river in Prati, which is in a similar price range. If you are in this neighborhood, check out Franchi (pronounced FRANCK-ee), known for its expensive-but-worth-it takeout food. If you have a craving for something from home, Castroni, the specialty food shop next door, may well have it. In addition, the area around Campo dei Fiori and Piazza Navona is filled with interesting boutiques and specialty shops.

A few of the many specialty shops that once filled the center still survive and can generally be classified into two groups. They either sell items necessary for a specific clientele or else handmade articles requiring a great deal of time and qualified workmanship. A good example of the first category is the many shops (clustered in the streets behind the Pantheon) that satisfy the haberdashery needs of ecclesiastics. Of the second category, some survivors still sell knotted silk fringes, and tassels for the keys to antique armoires and drapery pull-ropes. One of these *passamanerie* shops is to be found on the Via d'Aracoeli just up the street from Il Gesù, another is near the Parliament.

Despite the overflow of clothing stores, Via del Babuino retains something of its former character as a center for antiques. Shops along here sell everything from silver spoons to antique, marble-topped tables and credenzas. ∎

valentino

Many people come to the Italian capital as much for the shopping as for sightseeing. "Made in Italy" has become a well-deserved synonym for excellence.

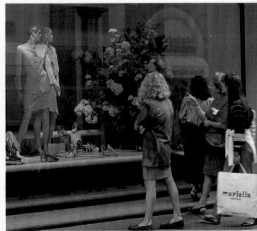

Pincio

Pincio

Map pp. 106–107

Bus: 95, 175/116, 116, 490, 910.
Metro: Linea A
(Flaminio)

Domes, bell towers, and terraces are the major components of the view from any of Rome's many hills.

HISTORIANS DISAGREE ABOUT THE ORIGINS OF THE Pincio (pronounced Pin-CHO) Hill, which, by the way, is not one of the famous seven (see p. 191). Was it the location of an imperial residence? The site of the Emperor Nero's tomb? Or simply a suburban residential area inhabited by ancient Rome's patrician families, including the Pinci to whom the hill owes its name? Whatever. At the beginning of the 19th century, the area was transformed into a charming park and promenade that was called the Bois de Boulogne of Rome and figured largely in writings by Stendhal and Henry James.

The French influence in the layout was inevitable since it was landscaped during a brief period of French administration. Circular ramps and terraced landings lead from the Piazza del Popolo to a lookout with a superb view—especially at sunset. The architect, Giuseppe Valadier, designed circular ramps and terraced landings that lead from the piazza to a lookout that affords a superb view (especially at sunset—as guidebooks never fail to point out). The cupolas of Rome, including that of St. Peter's, loom up at you through the gathering dusk, as does the impressive dome of the Pantheon and the all-too-white monument to Victor Emanuel II. The paths are lined with the busts of Italian patriots added several decades later at the instigation of Giuseppe Mazzini, the 19th-century Italian nationalist. The Egyptian **obelisk** (see p. 80), brought to Rome by the Emperor Hadrian, was placed on the Pincio in 1822 by Pope Pius VII.

Like the **Piazza del Popolo** below, a century ago the Pincio was considered to be the in place for a stroll. Today, however, on weekends there are far more children than lords and ladies, but the view is certainly worth a visit. For those in the mood for a long walk, remember that from the Pincio you can walk to Villa Medici, Trinità dei Monti, and the Spanish Steps or, in the other direction, to the Villa Borghese park (see p. 118). ■

Piazza & Porta del Popolo

THIS LARGE, OPEN SPACE ECHOES THE MONUMENTAL architectonic style of Paris, and is probably one of the most impressive piazzas in the city, especially now that Rome's municipal government has banned all traffic. Piazza del Popolo takes its name from the church of Santa Maria del Popolo (see p. 114), but it has always been a major landmark. Since Roman times it has been one of the principal entrances into the city. From an architectural point of view, however, it is primarily a product of the Renaissance, baroque, and neoclassic periods.

Blood once ran in this piazza, where the three streets of the Trident converge. Formerly used for public executions, it was also the starting point for the races held in Via del Corso.

In 1589, Pope Sixtus V moved the Egyptian **obelisk** that stood in the Circus Maximus (see p. 207) to the center of the piazza. The foundations for the two churches, whose presence so dramatically enhances the theatrical effect of the square for those entering the city by the Porta del Popolo, were laid in the second half of the 17th century. Although apparently identical, **Santa Maria di Montesanto,** on the left, has an oval dome whereas **Santa Maria dei Miracoli's** dome is round. In 1655, Alexander VII commissioned Bernini to redecorate the inside facade of the Porta to honor the arrival of Queen Christina of Sweden, whose conversion to Catholicism was regarded as a great propaganda coup for the Counter-Reformation. *"Felice faustoque ingressui"* reads the inscription, "For a happy and blessed entrance."

The credit for the piazza's final neoclassic layout, however, goes to Valadier who created the semicircular structures that enclose the oval piazza, as well as the fountains and the lions. It is a superb mix of French monumentality and Roman warmth. In fact, since the early 19th century, **Piazza del Popolo** has been considered a chic place to stop for a coffee at its cafés. ∎

Piazza & Porta del Popolo

🅼 Map pp. 106–107
🚌 Bus: 64/95, 95, 490, 926. Metro: Linea A (Flaminio)

Santa Maria del Popolo

Santa Maria del Popolo

- Map pp. 106–107
- Piazza del Popolo 12
- 06 361 0836
- Closed p.m.
- Bus: 64/95, 95, 490, 926. Metro: Linea A (Flaminio)

THE REMAINS OF THE EMPEROR NERO WERE SAID TO HAVE been buried on the site of this church, and as part of the medieval penchant for exorcising the remnants of paganism, Pope Paschal II (1099–1118) dug up the gravesite, burning the human remains he found there and throwing them into the Tiber. Then he built a chapel, dedicating it to the Virgin Mary. Subsequently, Santa Maria del Popolo was redone several times and what we see today—a church with three aisles and many side chapels—is basically the 15th-century Renaissance version. Subsequently, there were some other modifications. Bramante enlarged the apse and Bernini redecorated the interior and added some baroque touches to the facade. In the early 1500s, Martin Luther, the Augustinian monk who only a few years later was to trigger the Protestant Reformation, boarded in the adjoining monastery that then existed.

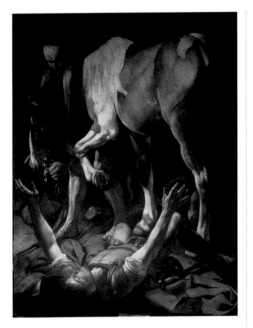

The "Conversion of St. Paul" is one of two dramatic Caravaggio paintings that decorate one of this church's magnificent chapels.

magnificent biblical scenes on the vaulted ceiling of the presbytery. The painting of the "Madonna del Popolo," set into the main altar, which is baroque in style, for centuries was believed to have been painted by the Apostle St. Luke, until art experts attributed it to the 13th-century Sienese school. The original marble altar designed by Andrea Bregno in 1473 now stands in the sacristy (go through the door at the end of the right transept and down the corridor within). Behind the main altar are the magnificent tombs of Cardinal Ascanio Sforza and Cardinal Girolamo Basso della Rovere, both by Andrea Sansovino.

However, the star attraction of the church is the **Cerasi Chapel** (to the left of the main altar) with Caravaggio's paintings, the "Conversion of St. Paul" and the "Crucifixion of St. Peter." Also not-to-be-missed is the **Chigi Chapel** by Raphael Sanzio, whose unusual pyramid-shaped marble tombs of the banker, Agostino Chigi, and his brother on the left and right walls of the chapel, may have been inspired by the Roman pyramid of Cestius. The mosaic decoration in the dome of the chapel is based on

But the enormous artistic value of the church lies in its interior decoration, to which some of the most talented artists in the 1500s and 1600s contributed. The Della Rovere Chapel, the first on the right, has frescoes by Pinturicchio, who also painted the "Adoration of the Child" above the altar and the

the designs (generally known as cartoons) of Raphael. Two of the four corner statues, "Habakkuk" (who in the Old Testament brought food to Daniel in the lion's den) and "Daniel and the Lion," are by Bernini. The "Birth of the Virgin" above the altar is by Sebastiano del Piombo. In the apse (behind the main altar) there are two stained-glass windows. Fairly unusual in Rome to begin with, these are surely among the first in the city. Before you leave, note the some-what gruesome skeleton sharing a cage with a butterfly (symbolizing rebirth or resurrection) to the right of the rightmost door. ■

Bernini designed the marble floor and hanging bronze lamp—three intertwined cherubs—in the gloriously appointed Chigi Chapel.

Ara Pacis Augustae

ONE OF THE MOST FAMOUS MONUMENTS IN ANCIENT Rome, the Ara Pacis was a ceremonial altar inaugurated in 9 B.C. to commemorate the Pax Romana that followed Augustus' conquest of Spain and Gaul (as France was then known). Dug up (in pieces) back in 1568 near Piazza San Lorenzo in Lucina, it was reassembled in the 1930s. Missing segments were reconstructed, and it was enclosed in a modern, glass-walled structure.

Made of white Italian (Luna) marble, the altar is set on a rectangular platform and surrounded by four walls with entrances on two sides. The reliefs are a stunning example of the highest quality classical sculpture and are also of great historical interest. The procession represented on the outside of the longer, lateral walls actually took place (on July 4, 13 B.C.). The half-figure on the side facing the nearby mausoleum is Augustus. He is followed by several priests (flavins) and family members, including his son-in-law Agrippa whose place as the second nobleman in the procession indicates he is the heir apparent. An inscription on the outer modern structure reads "Res gestae Divi Augusti," the title of the emperor's own account of his accomplishments.

Given its apparent state of neglect, it is hard to believe that the **Mausoleo di Augusto** next door was once a major monument of ancient Rome, the first of the city's two large circular tombs (the other is Castel Sant' Angelo). Two obelisks (now on the Quirinal and Esquiline Hills) flanked the entrance. It was built by Augustus as a family tomb, and upon his death in August A.D. 14, the emperor's ashes were interred there, as were those, later on, of his adored wife, Livia, and of most of the Julian-Claudian emperors—Augustus' stepson Tiberius, Claudius, and Nerva. ∎

Ara Pacis Augustae
- Map pp. 106–107
- Largo Augusto Imperatore
- 06 813 6071
- Currently closed. Expected to remain so until some time in late 2001
- $
- Bus: 115, 119, 926

Villa Giulia

WHAT MORE COULD YOU ASK FOR? NOT ONLY IS VILLA Giulia an absolutely superb example of Renaissance architecture, but since 1889 it has provided the backdrop for one of the most important collections of Etruscan and pre-Roman antiquities in the world. The villa itself was built between 1551 and 1553 by Pope Julius III (1550–55) who commissioned some of the most important architects of the time (Michelangelo, Vasari, Ammanati, and Vignola) to enlarge and ennoble an earlier structure. The resulting building is a consummate expression of the Renaissance architectural concept of exterior–interior "interpenetration" that began with the Villa Farnesina (see pp. 186–187) 40 years earlier.

The mysterious Etruscans dominated Central Italy until the sixth century B.C. when power in the peninsula began passing to the Romans who absorbed much of their culture.

Once past the entrance vestibule, you find yourself in a semicircular portico, its ceiling frescoed to create a pergola effect that is in perfect harmony with the courtyard and the gardens with, in the one on the right, a reconstruction of an Etruscan temple. At the other end of the courtyard is a loggia that leads down to a shady, sunken nymphaeum. The two-floor museum **(Museo Nazionale di Villa Giulia)** is housed in the right and left wings of the villa, initial access to which is from the far left-hand side of the portico. The first six rooms display artifacts primarily from the necropolis of Vulci and other digs. There is even a reconstruction of a tomb from Cerveteri, a town in the heart of what was once Etruria.

Not all of this will have general appeal, but who would want to miss **Room 7** with its compelling, life-size terra-cotta polychrome statues of Hercules, Apollo, and a goddess holding a young child, dating from the late 6th century B.C. They were probably done by Vulca, the master sculptor of Veio, who may also have decorated the giant temple to Jupiter that stood on the Capitoline Hill. **Room 9** on the left-hand side of the ground floor is an absolute must. It houses the magnificent

world-famous sarcophagus (also 6th century B.C.) of a young husband and wife reclining on a couch. Upstairs are countless objects—domestic implements, bronze utensils, armor, jewelry, and ceramics.

The other wing of the museum exhibits additional material from tombs or temples. The partially reconstructed pediment of the Temple of Apollo allo Scasato is intriguing, and the bust of Apollo is superb. His face, in deep concentration, is turned slightly to the right as if he were listening to a prophetic phrase. ∎

Villa Giulia
- Map pp. 106–107
- Piazzale di Villa Giulia 9
- 06 320 1951
- Closed Sun p.m. & Mon.
- $$
- Tram: 19, 30 (from Termini), 225

Villas & parks

Rome is one of Europe's greenest cities, and if it has an unusual number of parks it owes most to the city's aristocracy, and—it must be said—to the financial difficulties that forced them, in modern times, to turn over their former estates to the government. A major clue to the origins of these vast areas of rolling grassland, normally open from dawn to dusk and ideal for joggers, pensioners, and idlers of all types, is the word *villa*, a sign that the park was once a private house with land surrounding it. Interestingly enough, many of these suburban villas were not built as residences, but for pure enjoyment, as was often the case with the estates that ringed the city in ancient Roman times.

The building was called a *casina* or *casino*, literally, a little house, but the word "little" should be used advisedly. Starting in the Renaissance and continuing into the baroque era, as the nobility rushed to build elegant pleasure palaces steeped in verdant and contemplative surroundings, the houses grew ever greater and grander. What were they used for? A day trip for refuge from the summer heat, a picnic, a party, or, as in the case of Villa Borghese, the best known of them all, to house and display a magnificent art collection.

Not all have survived. Villa Ludovisi, which once occupied much of the Via Veneto area, has totally disappeared. The gardens of Villa Giulia, today the Etruscan Museum, have been swallowed up by urban encroachment, as have those of Villa Giustiniani near the Lateran. But fortunately for today's Romans, dozens remain. Villa Ada, Villa Torlonia, and Villa Sciarra are only some of the parks providing a fresh-air outlet for families, lovers, and fitness freaks. Naturally, there are other parks, including those built around ancient monuments, such as the Parco di Traiano (the Colle Oppio) around Trajan's Baths and the Parco degli Scipioni, near the Appian Way, extending around the remains of the tomb of the Cornelii Scipiones, built by that powerful family around the third or second century B.C.

Villa Borghese (pronounced Bor-GAY-zi), is the Roman equivalent of Central Park in New York or St. James's Park in London, and its 198 acres (80 ha) offer the city's residents a downtown escape hatch for strolling, biking, horseback riding, and jogging among extensive greenery, statuary, neoclassic temples, and fountains. There is an artificial lake, a zoo, and a grassy amphitheater shaded by graceful umbrella pines (Piazza di Siena) where the annual horse show is held every May. The Villa Borghese can be accessed from various points including Porta Pinciana, at the top end of Via Veneto, Piazzale Flaminio, just beyond Piazza del Popolo, and from the Galleria Borghese. Several major museums (Galleria Borghese, see pp. 120–22, the Modern Art Museum— Galleria Nazionale d'Arte Moderna— and Villa Giulia, see p. 117) are in the park.

Heading south from Villa Borghese, between the Pincio (see p. 112) and the Spanish Steps, is Villa Medici. Built for a Tuscan cardinal on the site of the gardens of Lucullus, the famed Roman gourmet and high-liver, this late Renaissance building's gardens were described by Henry James as "a fabled, haunted place." Today it houses the French Academy and guided tours are available from mid-March to June at 10:30 a.m. and 11:30 a.m. on Saturdays and Sundays (*Tel 06 67611*). If you have the time, this is a real treat.

Among the city's other parks, Villa Doria Pamphili on the Janiculum Hill was laid out in the 17th century for Prince Camillo Pamphili and has a beautiful casino, unfortunately not generally open to the public. With 445 acres (180 ha) and a 5.5-mile (9 km) perimeter, it is the city's largest park, a haven for joggers and other fresh-air enthusiasts. Princess Pamphili sold it to the state in the 1960s to settle an enormous tax bill. Villa Celimontana (see p. 67), originally called Villa Mattei after the family that built it in the 16th century, is situated on the Caelian Hill. It is a lovely place for a stroll amid lush greenery, pieces of ancient sculpture, and one of Rome's 13 obelisks (see pp. 80–81). ■

Right: Ornamental gardens inside the Vatican. Tours of Vatican City can be arranged at the information office in St. Peter's Square.

Above: The Villa Borghese park is a place to relax for Romans and visitors to the city. Below: The Janiculum park is one of the few places to see Harlequin and Pulcinella.

Galleria Borghese

CARDINAL SCIPIONE BORGHESE LIVED DOWNTOWN IN HIS princely Roman palace at Piazza Fontanella Borghese, but in the early 1600s he built himself a casino (summerhouse) on his vast estate on what was then the city's outskirts. It was a place to go for picnics, but above all it served to house the family's massive sculpture collection. In 1807 Scipione's descendent, Camillo, who was married to Napoleon's sister Pauline Bonaparte, was forced by his brother-in-law to cede a great chunk of this (374 pieces) to the Louvre. But the collection was later refurbished by new acquisitions and excavations on family-owned land. In 1891 the family painting collection was also moved here and subsequently, in 1902, financial problems forced Prince Paolo to sell the villa and park to the state.

Modified in the 18th century and restored again in recent years, the gleaming white, three-story building today has a facade composed of twin towers flanking a recessed central core or portico. A double ramped staircase (that deliberately imitates Michelangelo's entrance to the Palazzo del Senatore on the Campidoglio) leads up to the main entrance, which is nevertheless considered the ground floor. Stucco work and decorative niches embellish parts of the facade. Don't miss the newly relandscaped Renaissance-style Secret Garden.

The interior decoration of the villa also dates from this time and it must be said that if the outside appears attractive, the inside is simply remarkable. Frescoed ceilings, sumptuous wall coverings, faux marble wall decoration, porphyry mantelpieces, gilded moldings, and marble inlay all vie for our attention with even the most magnificent pieces of art. It is important to realize that every room has a theme, that the ceiling decorations (you mustn't forget to look up) and sculptures are displayed in tandem, and that wherever possible an attempt has been made to extend this thematic link to the paintings on the walls. You'll

want to buy a book in the basement bookshop or rent an audio guide.

The sculpture collection, on what passed for the ground floor or *pianterreno* contains some of the most famous pieces in the world. Before you lose yourself in those delights, be sure to notice the late Roman floor mosaics depicting gladiatorial combat scenes in the entrance room. These fourth-century mosaics, excavated from a family estate, are enthralling for their realism. These are portraits (the gladiators' names are written into the mosaic) and those marked with a ø, the first letter in the Greek word *thanatos* (death), got the thumbs down sign and were no more. In Room I is Canova's marble **statue of Paolina Borghese,** also known as Pauline Bonaparte, Napoleon's sister. She is reclining, seminude, on a sort of chaise longue, and legend has it that the sculpture was kept under lock and key for years by her husband, Prince Camillo, who was scandalized by her lack of modesty.

Then there are three extraordinary **sculptures by Bernini,** all done while this Roman genius was still in his mid-20s. In Room II you'll find the "David" (ca 1624) in which the young hero is preparing

Galleria Borghese

- Map pp. 106–107
- Piazzale Scipione Borgese 5
- 06 32810 (for reservations)
- Closed Sun. p.m. & Mon. Advanced booking required for visits scheduled at 9 a.m., 11 a.m., 1 p.m., 3 p.m., 5 p.m. Tickets must be picked up one half hour before scheduled admission time
- $$
- Bus: 52, 53, 116, 490, 495, 910. Metro: Linea A (Barberini) plus 95, 116

to hurl a stone at his adversary. The face, with its intense and concentrated expression, is a self-portrait of the sculptor. But wait till you get to Room III. "Apollo and Daphne" (1622–25), which depicts the young nymph's vain attempts to escape the god (the same scene is painted on the ceiling), has a quasihallucinatory quality. Daphne's hands and feet are in the process of being transformed into a laurel tree. (Remember the laurel wreath? Well, Apollo invented it to keep Daphne ever near him.) The swirling and sensual movement of the two intertwined bodies shows the artist's amazing ability to capture the surface texture of skin and hair, as does his other work (in the next room) the "Rape of Proserpine" (ca 1622). Notice the way Pluto's fingers sink into Proserpine's thigh.

The last room (VIII) on this floor is exceptional more for its paintings than its sculptures. There are six incredible **Caravaggios** here, "St. Jerome" (1605), "David with the Head of Goliath" (1609–1610), and the "Madonna dei Palafrenieri," sometimes called the "Madonna del Serpente," which was removed from an important altar in St. Peter's almost immediately as sacrilegious. The "Bacchino Malato" ("Sick Bacchus") from 1593 is a self-portrait.

Upstairs (a good place to peek out at the gardens in the back) is the painting gallery, or **Pinacoteca,** where one marvelous painting succeeds another and where some of the best known painters in Western history—Bellini, Bronzino, Correggio, Cranach, Domenichino, Fra

Bernini's "Rape of Prosperine" is only one of the magnificent sculptures housed in the refurbished Galleria Borghese, where wall and ceiling decorations vie for your attention.

Bartolomeo, Lanfranco, Lorenzo Lotto, Pinturicchio, Raphael, Reni, Rubens, Titian, and Veronese— are represented.

Room IX is particularly thrilling with Botticelli richly colored "Madonna con Bambino S. Giovanino e Angeli" (ca 1488) and Raphael's "Ritratto di Giovane Donna con Unicorno" ("Young Woman with a Unicorn"), dated 1506, as well as his very well-known "Deposition" (1507) and many other treasures. In the next room (X) is Bronzino's intriguing "Young San Giovanni Battista" (1525). Note the ceiling. Its theme is Hercules but along with the mythological scenes is a sumptuous prune-colored geometric design. The gilded eagles and dragons are the two symbols of the Borghese family.

Pauline, Napoleon Bonaparte's sister, defied convention and posed as "Venus Victrix" in Canova's magnificent neoclassical sculpture.

You might want to pay special attention to Room XIV, where there are several more works by Bernini, including two self-portraits, the busts of his patron, Scipione Borghese, and the majestic terra-cotta model of a statue of the Sun King, Louis XIV, which was never made. Room XIX contains Domenichino's famous painting of the "Cumana Sibyl," in all her turbaned glory, as well as his "Diana" (1616–17). Federico Barocci's painting of "Aeneas Fleeing the Burning Troy" (1598) inspired Scipione Borghese to commission Bernini to produce the large marble group you saw on the ground floor (Room VI). The gloriously beautiful "Sacred and Profane Love" is among several Titians in Room XX. ■

Galleria Borghese access

Access to Galleria Borghese is more complicated than to other museums. In the first place, you only have two hours to see the museum. Second, if you are carrying anything (including handbags), head straight to the basement check room, otherwise you'll be sent back there from the entrance. Strangely, coats cannot be checked. After seeing the ground floor (sculptures), you may not be able to go directly upstairs without returning first to the basement level. Never mind. What's displayed more than makes up for any organizational defects. ■

This is the heart of modern Rome; a neighborhood where the massive monuments of yesterday—temples in the round, sculpted columns and Corinthian capitals, Renaissance fountains—alternate with major modern political institutions.

Pantheon to Piazza Venezia

Detail from the marble elephant in front of the Minerva church

Pantheon to Piazza Venezia

ARTISANS AND JESUITS, BANKERS AND POLITICIANS, ROMANS AND OUT-OF-towners—the downtown area stretching from the Pantheon to Piazza Venezia is an unusual setting, a melange of ancient, medieval, and Renaissance history. Along the Via del Corso and on Piazza Venezia major Italian banks and insurance companies are ensconced in magnificent stone palaces once owned by Roman princes and noblemen.

Because of its dome, the Pantheon is often called "La Rotonda." Hence the name of the square, Piazza della Rotonda.

In Piazza Colonna the Italian prime minister's office (the 16th-century Palazzo Chigi) looks out on the Marcus Aurelius column, which dates back to A.D. 193. The quality of its workmanship is inferior to that of Trajan's Column, which is 80 years older, but it is interesting for its anthropological detail. The view from the Chamber of Deputies, located in nearby Palazzo del Montecitorio (the facade is by Bernini), includes one of the city's 13 Egyptian obelisks (see p. 80); and in this neighborhood, it is an everyday occurrence to sip a cappuccino against the thrilling backdrop of the Pantheon, a pagan temple built 1900 years ago that subsequently became a church and is today a national monument where kings and painters are buried.

The rulers of Rome have always found it difficult to keep order in Piazza della Rotonda. Recently repaved and today lined with cafés, it is now closed to traffic. But keeping out the mopeds (not an easy task) is somewhat similar to the problems of the last century when authorities tried desperately to close down the fish market and other food stands that continued to spring up there. Ironically, at least in the view of many Romans, the plaque erected by Pope Pius VII who tried to rid the area of what he called "disgraceful shops" and "things of unbelievable ugliness" is on the wall of a building that houses one of the newest arrivals to the square, a McDonald's.

Only a short distance away is Santa Maria sopra Minerva, a church steeped in history that belongs to the prestigious Dominican religious order, a major protagonist of both the Inquisition and the Counter-Reformation. The charming small stone elephant in the piazza, designed (but not sculpted) by Gian Lorenzo Bernini, was intended to be a symbol of intelligence. Perhaps more telling, given the political reality of the 16th century, is the overhead bridge spanning Via di Sant'Ignazio (behind the Minerva church); the walkway gave Dominican prelates access to their Jesuit counterparts and to the Jesuit church of Sant'Ignazio.

Across the street from the Collegio Romano, today a high school but once a Jesuit college, is Palazzo Doria Pamphili. That noble Roman family, which boasts both popes and princes among its ancestors, has now turned its imposing block-wide palace with its magnificent private art collection into a very modern museum. A short distance away is the Jesuit mother church, Il Gesu, where baroque opulence has been unstintingly employed to the glory of God.

The Via del Corso terminates at Piazza Venezia which, since several major streets converge there, today seems less a city square than a traffic hub. The helmeted *vigile*, traffic policeman, on his podium in the center of the intersection, is a fixture of the piazza and has appeared in countless films and advertisements. From an architectural point of view Piazza Venezia marks the beginning of the modern city, and clearly represents a transition from the medieval to the Renaissance. But it was the construction of the monument to Victor Emanuel II, at the end of the 19th century, that totally changed the look of the square. Then, in order to create a clear view of the monument from Via del Corso, the Palazzetto di Venezia, with its lovely

PIAZZA
SAN LORENZO
IN LUCINA

VIA MARZIO

CAMPO MARZIO

VIA DEL CORSO

VIA DI SCROFA

VIA DELLA

PIAZZA DEL
PARLAMENTO

Palazzo di
Montecitorio

V. D. UFFICI D. VICARIO

Palazzo
Chigi

PIAZZA DI
MONTECITORIO

PIAZZA
COLONNA

Colonna
di Marco
Aurelio

Obelisco

PIAZZA
DI PIETRA

Fontana e
Obelisco

PIAZZA DELLA
ROTONDA

VIA DEL SEMINARIO

PIAZZA DI
SANT'IGNAZIO

Sant'
Ignazio

VIA D. SANTIGNAZIO

Collegio
Romano

VIA DEL CORSO

Pantheon

Obelisco

PIAZZA
DELLA
MINERVA

**Santa Maria
sopra Minerva**

PIAZZA DEL
COLLEGIO
ROMANO

VIA D. TORRE ARGENTINA

PIGNA

**Palazzo
Doria
Pamphilj**

V. C. BATTISTI

| 0 | | 200 yards |
| 0 | | 200 meters |

LARGO DI
TORRE
ARGENTINA

VIA DEL PLEBISCITO

**Piazza
Venezia**

Palazzo
Venezia

San Marco
Evangelista al
Campidoglio

PIAZZA
DEL GESU

Madame Lucrezia

Palazzetto
di Venezia

**Monumento
a Vittorio
Emanuele II**

Il Gesu

VIA SAN MARCO

VIA DELLE BOTTEGHE OSCURE

PIAZZA
D'ARACOELI

**Santa Maria
in Aracoeli**

Rome

Tevere

Area of map detail

courtyard and garden, was dismantled and rebuilt around the corner in nearby Piazza San Marco. The Basilica of San Marco, instead, was founded in the fourth century to honor St. Mark, who according to legend wrote his gospel in a nearby oratory. Right outside is one of Rome's famous talking statues, the bosomy Madama Lucrezia (see p. 145). ∎

Pantheon

FIRST A PAGAN TEMPLE, DEDICATED TO THE GODS (BUT NO one is sure exactly which) and later a Christian church, the Pantheon is generally considered a perfect example of classical architectural harmony. This is largely because of its proportions (its height and diameter are equal) and because the structure, a circular building or rotunda fronted by a rectangular porch that the ancients called a *pronaos* (the latter topped by a triangular pediment), gracefully combines a variety of shapes and forms. Above all, the massive dome of the Pantheon represents an architectural and engineering feat so important that it became a prototype in much of the world.

Pantheon

- Map p. 125
- Piazza della Rotonda
- 06 6830 0230
- Closed Sun. p.m.
- Free
- Bus: 52/116, 53/116, 56, 81, 87, 95, 115/116, 119, 492

With a diameter of 142 feet (43 m) the **cupola,** which was cast by pouring concrete over a temporary wooden frame, is wider than that of St. Peter's. At the base, the dome measures almost 20 feet (6 m), but the thickness gradually diminishes with height, as do the widths of the five rows of coffers lining it. The architectonic function of these was to reduce the weight of the vault, but they also create an optical effect that draws attention towards the center. The opening or "eye" in the ceiling is 30 feet (9 m) in diameter. Apart from any allusion to an eye

looking at the cosmos, the *oculus*, as it is called in Latin, is the only source of light and air in the building, the walls of which are too thick at around 20 feet (6 m) to have made windows an option.

Built by the philosopher-emperor Hadrian between A.D. 118 and 125 to replace an earlier edifice, the Pantheon—it is important to remember—was also built as an astronomical instrument. In ancient times great significance was given to the two equinoxes (March 21 and September 22), the dates when day and night are of equal

From Paganism to Christianity

The Pantheon was the first pagan temple in Rome to be converted into a church, a development of major significance. True, as early as the sixth century other pagan structures had been turned into Christian places of worship (examples are Santi Cosma and Damiano in the Roman Forum, and Santa Maria in Cosmedin near the Forum Boarium, see pp. 200–201), but the buildings involved had been constructed for secular, not religious, purposes.

Furthermore, many of the early Christian churches, such as San Giovanni in Laterano, Santa Croce,

and indeed St. Peter's, were built on what were then the outskirts of the city. If this was partly to make things easy for incoming pilgrims, it was also to avoid offending or incurring the ire of Rome's pagan classes. After all, the spread of Christianity did not take place overnight nor without considerable conflict and resistance. The conversion of a major pagan temple located in the very center of the city was, therefore, of great consequence. It denotes the fact that Christianity had by then become the most important religion in Rome. ∎

Opposite: The Pantheon's large oculus lets in rain as well as light. There are drainage holes below in the center of the pavement.

length, and to the summer and winter solstices (June 21 and December 21 or 22), all of which had a particular significance for agriculture and for checking the accuracy of the calendar. It also had ceremonial possibilities. If every June 21 at noon the beam of light streaming through the oculus hit the floor right in front of the main door, it'd be a good time, wouldn't you think, for an appearance-conscious emperor in full regalia to make a sun-kissed entrance?

The outside **portico,** once preceded by a short staircase, consists of 16 columns of red or gray granite, each 41 feet (12 m) tall and 15 feet (4 m) in circumference and only three of which (on the left side) are replacements. The inscription running below the pediment, *"M. Agrippa F.L.Cos. Tertium Fecit"* ("Marcus Agrippa, son of Lucius, in his third consulate, built this") refers to an earlier structure erected in 27 B.C. by Agrippa to honor his friend and father-in-law, the Emperor Augustus. The bronze letters are new—19th-century fittings made for the original letter holes.

However, there have been changes throughout the centuries. The Byzantine emperor, Constans II, plundered the gilded bronze sheeting that originally covered the dome during his visit to Rome in 663. It was replaced with lead in the 8th century. In the Middle Ages a central bell tower was briefly added,

The Pantheon's remarkable state of preservation testifies to the advanced technical expertise of the later Empire's architects and engineers.

Portico

Pediment

Coffering

Panels and blind windows (18th century)

Granite columns

Corinthian capitals

Interior

only to be replaced in the 17th century by twin turrets designed by Bernini but so hated that they were nicknamed "the donkey's ears" until their removal in 1883. The enormous **bronze doors** are ancient but may have been taken from another structure and placed here. In the mid-1600s, the bronze covering of the portico beams was stripped away to make the cannon for Castel Sant'Angelo and the beautiful spiraled columns for Bernini's *baldacchino*, or canopy, over the main altar in St. Peter's. Pope Urban VIII of the Barberini family ordered this done and his act of sacrilege led the Romans to come up with the famous Latin quip, "*quod non fecerunt barberi, fecerunt Barberini*" ("what the barbarians did not do, the Barberini did").

The Pantheon is the best preserved ancient monument in Rome, largely thanks to its transformation into a Christian church after the Byzantine emperor Phocas gave the building to Pope Boniface IV in 608 or 609. The interior is awe inspiring. The cavernous **central body** or *cella* (unlike other pagan temples in the Pantheon this cella was accessible to ordinary worshippers and was not, as was usually the case, reserved for priests or notables alone) is divided into three distinct segments. The lower part has six niches (not including the apse), which originally contained statues of the principal gods. In between, there are eight *aediculae* (shrines) flanked by marble columns. The floor, restored in 1872, repeats the colored, geometric patterns of antiquity. Except for a small area, the original marble decoration of the attic, the segment that runs around the base of the dome, no longer exists.

The current decor, begun in the 15th century but added to over the following 400 years, contains few major artworks. One exception is Lorenzetto's "Madonna del Sasso" ("Madonna of the Stone"), which stands on the altar in the third aedicula to the left above the **tomb of the painter, Raphael,** who died in 1520. Two Italian kings and a queen are buried here as well as several other painters. This is not surprising since for centuries the Pantheon has been associated with the arts, and one of the most famous artists' groups in Rome, the Accademia dei Virtuosi, had its headquarters in here. The **fountain** outside, built in 1578, was designed by Giacomo della Porta. The Egyptian **obelisk** was placed on the fountain trough in 1711 by Pope Clement XI. ∎

Oculus

Relieving arches

Walls up to 20 feet thick

Exterior

Coffee & cafés

Whatever you do, don't ask for a "*latte*" (unless, of course, you want a glass of milk). What Americans have taken to calling "latte," here in its country of origin is properly known as a *caffèlatte*, the term Italians mostly use for a breakfast drink of warm milk with a small amount of coffee added. It is normally imbibed at home, especially by children, but can be drunk at the corner bar, where the custom is to take one's pleasure at the counter (although in most places tables are generally available).

The most popular form of coffee outside the home is, however, espresso. But wait! That would be too simple. Everyone crowding the counter seems to have his or her own special request. *Un caffè macchiato* is an espresso with a few drops of warm milk (for cold milk you say *"un caffè macchiato freddo"*). Some prefer a somewhat weaker, more abundant *caffè lungo*. A really strong espresso is, instead, *un caffè ristretto*. And then there are those who don't like cups and want their coffee in a small glass (*un caffè al vetro*). A decaffeinated espresso is un *caffè Hag* or *un decaffeinato*, while the worker in overalls who's been toiling since 7 a.m. wants *un caffè corretto*, an espresso spiked with something alcoholic—grappa, brandy, or anisette. Then, of course, there is the legion of cappuccino drinkers. Cappuccino, made with less milk than a caffèlatte, is also generally a morning drink (and something an Italian would never even remotely consider drinking after a meal!). But here, too, there are variations. It can be ordered *senza schiuma* (without foam), *chiaro* (light), or *scuro* (dark). A *caffè americano* comes in a larger cup and is probably Nescafé, whereas a *caffè d'orzo* is made from barley.

Coffee has been known to Italy since the 16th century, when a Venetian botanist brought some back from Egypt, and today it comes close to being a national obsession. It can also be a short cut to social interaction. *"Prendiamo un caffè"* can be a successful opening gambit. The Tazza d'Oro on the corner of the Piazza della Rotonda sells excellent fresh-ground for home use in a moka or neapolitan coffeepot, and Bar S. Eustacchio a couple of blocks away in the piazza of the same name is said to have a secret procedure to make its particularly strong and ristretto brew. But ambience counts, too. And Rome boasts a selection of cafés where the city's denizens go for chat and people-watching, another national sport. Along with the cafés at Pantheon square, there are two in this area that, unusually, offer ample indoor seating: Giolitti, on Via degli Uffici del Vicario 40, also known for its ice cream, and La Caffetteria at Piazza di Pietra.

For decades, the best-known café in Rome was the Caffè del Greco on the fashionable Via dei Condotti, almost facing the Spanish Steps. This was the place where writers and artists gathered to discuss cultural trends and to gossip, and it is still a charming place (indoors only, however) for a rendezvous. But many prefer Rosati and Canova with their outdoor tables on opposite sides of the now car-free Piazza del Popolo. Piazza Navona is lined with cafés, but the Antico Caffè della Pace on Via della Pace a block away has much more atmosphere. Ciampini on the repaved piazza in Lucina (off the Corso) is an in place. And if you happen to be on Trinità dei Monti, above the Spanish Steps, try Ciampini's outdoor café, immersed in greenery and overlooking the rooftops of Piazza di Spagna. The weatherproofed sidewalk cafés that line the Via Veneto are very pricey but can make a nice change. If you're over on the Trastevere side of the river, De Marzio on Piazza Santa Maria di Trastevere, the bar facing the facade of the basilica, isn't fancy but it's where most residents of Rome's "Greenwich Village" gather on weekend mornings. Other popular cafés in the area are Ombre Rosse at Piazza S. Egidio and Friends at Piazza Trilussa. ■

The cafés in Rome allow you to enjoy espresso, sandwiches, and ice cream while feasting your eyes on some of the city's major monuments. Here, convivial conversation takes places in the shadow of the Pantheon, the first version of which was built by Agrippa, Augustus's son-in-law.

Santa Maria sopra Minerva

THIS LOVELY CHURCH, WITH ITS THREE AISLES AND vaulted ceilings, is said to be the one true Gothic church in Rome, although the facade is early Renaissance and the interior, complete with rose windows, has been changed all too often. As an overall structure, however, the church dates back to the 13th century when its construction as the religious center of the Dominican order was begun by two monks, Brother Sisto and Brother Ristoro, who had already overseen the building of Santa Maria Novella in Florence.

Santa Maria sopra Minvera

🅰 Map p. 125

✉ Piazza della Minerva 42

☎ 06 679 3926

🖷 Bus: 52/116, 53/116, 56, 81, 87, 95, 115/116, 119, 492

This being Rome, however, the monks did not have to break new ground. An earlier church had already been erected in the eighth century amid the remains of a pagan temple probably dedicated to the Roman goddess of war, Minerva. Note the wall plaques on the right side of the facade, which show the waterline from the frequent floods that inundated the area until the 19th-century Tiber embankments were built.

Because of the power and influence of the Dominicans, the order that would later spearhead the Inquisition and (together with the Jesuits) act as standard-bearers to the popes during the Counter-Reformation, this became a very prestigious church. Four popes are buried here, as are the Tuscan painter Fra Angelico, and St. Catherine of Siena, one of Italy's two patron saints (the other is St. Francis). Most of the major Roman families had chapels here, hiring the most famous artists and architects to decorate them. For example, the Carafa family chapel at the end of the right transept has an important cycle of glorious **frescoes** by Filippino Lippi illustrating the life of the Dominican saint, Thomas Aquinas, as well as a splendid "Assumption" and an "Annunciation." In the "Triumph of St. Thomas" on the right wall, the two small boys are said to be the future Medici popes, Clemente VII and Leo X, who are buried in the church. On the left wall is the tomb of Pope Paul IV, also a Carafa and the man who in the 16th century put the Jews of Rome into the Ghetto.

To the left of the chapel, note the cosmatesque funeral monument (see p. 206), a mosaic "Virgin and Child Enthroned," flanked by two saints on a gold background. The statue to the left of the main altar, **"Christ Bearing the Cross,"** was begun by Michelangelo. In the fifth chapel on the right see the interesting detail in Antoniazzo Romano's "Annunciation," with the Madonna handing money bags (for dowries) to three girls. The seventh, has the marvelous Renaissance tomb by Andrea Bregno. The sarcophagus under the main altar holds the remains of St. Catherine, who convinced the popes to return from exile in Avignon. Behind the altar are the wall tombs of Clement VII and Leo X, created by Antonio Sangallo the Younger. On the left, in a poorly lit passageway near the rear door, is **Fra Angelico's** strikingly simple floor **tomb.**

Right: Jesus was originally naked in Michelangelo's statue, but later prelates decided greater modesty called for an added bronze "loincloth."

Ask to see the *sacrestia* (sacristy) where two papal conclaves were held in the 15th century and the room where Catherine died, which is now a chapel. In the 1566 *chiostro* (cloister), the vaulted ceiling of the fourth arch on the right side of the portico bears the headless images of four Inquisitors who were themselves tried and executed. After all, it was in the adjoining monastery that Galileo was forced to repudiate his teachings that the earth moved around the sun. Legend has it that as he was getting off his knees, he whispered under his breath "*E pur si muove*" ("But it does move"). In the piazza outside is the delightful **stone elephant** designed by Bernini in 1667. Pope Alexander VII composed the inscription, which speaks of the elephant's wisdom and intelligence. ∎

A walk through the heart of Rome

As it has through the centuries, this area includes some of Rome's major political institutions and is really the heart of contemporary Rome. The walk will take you from Piazza di Montecitorio to Piazza San Marco, enabling you to bear witness to the city's intricate mix of old and even older.

Piazza Colonna gets its name from the column of Marcus Aurelius. Behind it is the Palazzo Wedekind.

Start at Piazza di Montecitorio, where one of the Egyptian obelisks (see pp. 80–81) that Augustus brought back to Rome stands in front of the massive Palazzo dei Montecitorio, now the Chamber of Deputies, the lower house of Parliament. From this piazza, where protesters sometimes gather, walk right toward the newly repaved Piazza Colonna, named as you will immediately appreciate for the **Colonna de Marco Aurelio ❶** (Marcus Aurelius's triumphal column), erected in A.D. 193 to celebrate that emperor's victory over the Marcomanni, one of the barbarian tribes that were beginning to threaten Rome. The column stands in front of **Palazzo Chigi** (built in the 16th and 17th centuries), the prime minister's office and the seat of the Italian government. The column may seem out of place in the modern hustle and bustle, but as you saw from the Pantheon, this area was also very important in Roman times.

Leaving Piazza Colonna by Via dei Bergamaschi, you'll see 11 massive Corinthian columns in **Piazza di Pietra ❷,** now paved and closed to traffic. Embedded in the wall of the **Borsa,** or Rome Stock Exchange, these columns were part of the temple to honor Hadrian, built in A.D. 145 by his successor,

Antoninus Pius. Continue in the same direction along Via del Burro, and you're in for another treat. **Piazza di Sant'Ignazio ❸** is a tiny rococo jewel, constructed by an 18th-century architect to resemble a theatrical stage, wings and all. View it from the central door of **Sant'Ignazio** (see p. 140), a major Jesuit church. Now walk along the side of the church (on Via di Sant'Ignazio), noting the overhead arch that connected the Jesuits to their Counter-Reformation allies, the Dominicans, masters of the Minerva church (see pp. 132–33) around the corner. Via di Sant'Ignazio ends at **Piazza del Collegio Romano ❹,** where you will find the entrance to the **Palazzo Doria Pamphili** and Galleria Doria Pamphili (see p. 136).

Turn right on Via di Pie'di Marmo, being sure to note the huge marble foot (from which this street gets its name) at the intersection with Via Santo Stefano del Cacco. Like the obelisk on the elephant in front of the Minerva, it probably came from a nearby Temple of Isis and Serap. Facing it at No. 21 is a marvelous chocolate shop. The next cross street along, just before you get to the Minerva church, is Via del Gesu. Turn left, making sure you peek into the courtyards, most of which have fountains (observe the beautiful water clock at No. 62). At the intersection with Corso Vittorio Emanuele II, you'll see the

---

🅰 Also see area map, p. 125
▶ Piazza Montecitorio
🔄 1.5 miles (2.4 km)
🕐 2 hours
▶ Piazza San Marco

NOT TO BE MISSED
- Column of Marcus Aurelius
- Piazza de Pietra
- Sant'Ignazio
- Galleria Doria Pamphili
- Il Gesu

Jesuit mother church, **Il Gesu** ⑤ (see p. 137).

Now turn right and walk a block to **Largo di Torre Argentina** ⑥, more commonly known as Largo Argentina, to see the remains of four Republican-era Roman temples **(Templi Repubblicani).** On the other side of the Largo, cross Via delle Botteghe Oscure (Street of the Dark Shops) and walk back along it in the direction you came from. At the corner with Via dei Polacchi, turn right and

walk to lovely **Piazza Margana** ⑦. At this point turn left and take Via Margana to Via d'Aracoeli. On the right you'll see Santa Maria in Aracoeli and the Campidoglio. Turn left and return to the Botteghe Oscure, which becomes Via di San Marco. Cross and walk right along Via di San Marco and you'll find yourself at **Piazza di San Marco** ⑧, where you'll see the basilica (see p. 140) and the "talking statue," Madama Lucrezia. ■

Palazzo Doria Pamphili

You can visit
the private
apartments of the
Doria Pamphili
(still inhabited
by the family)
but only in
the mornings.

THIS ENORMOUS BLOCK-LONG BUILDING, WHICH TODAY
houses the Doria Pamphili Museum, dates back to 1435 when it
belonged to Cardinal Santorio, an obedient prelate who allowed himself to be "convinced" by Pope Julius II to cede the palazzo to the
Duke of Urbino, who just happened to be the pontiff's nephew. The
rococo facade on Via del Corso, considered notable, was added later.

**Palazzo Doria
Pamphili**

- Map p. 125
- Piazza del Collegio
  Romano 2
- 06 679 7323
- Closed Thurs.
  Apartments 10:30
  a.m., 11 a.m., 11:30
  a.m., & 12 a.m.
  only
- $$, includes audio
  guide. Apartments $
- Bus: 56, 64, 70, 81,
  87, 95,116, 119,
  492. Metro: Linea A
  (Spagna) and 116
  bus or walk

The Pamphilis moved here in the
1700s, bringing with them the
collection, begun a century earlier
by Donna (or Lady) Olimpia,
when the family still lived at Piazza
Navona. It is the largest and most
important patrician collection
still in private Roman hands and
the walls are really overcrowded.
But as we are talking about works
by the likes of Titian, Raphael,
Velázquez, and Rubens, it's a minor
annoyance. As there are no labels,
use the free audio guide included
in the entry price, or buy the
museum catalog.

The collection is spread through
the first floor, the so-called *piano
nobile* where the family lived, which
runs around a vast courtyard that
was once turned into a ballroom to
honor a Hapsburg emperor!

The star attraction is probably
the corner room (between
Corridors 1 and 2) in which
Velázquez's portrait of Pope
Innocent X (1644–1655) is dis-
played next to Bernini's bust of the
same pontiff. Corridor 2 is a tri-
umph of gold, crystal, and mirrors.
Two Caravaggios (the "Maddalena"
and the "Riposo Durante la Fuga in
Egitto") are in Sala del 600, between
corridors 2 and 3, and the third (a
"San Giovanni Battista") is in the
fourth corridor. There is fine statu-
ary, Roman and otherwise, in Sala
Aldobrandini, where corridors 3
and 4 meet. And don't miss the
wonderful bust of Lady Olimpia by
Algardi in the corner. The private
apartments, with their sumptuous
decoration and artwork, are also
open to the public. ∎

Il Gesu

THE MOTHER CHURCH OF THE JESUIT ORDER, THIS IS A pre-baroque structure that, in ecclesiastical terms, fully embodies the Counter-Reformation spirit. Begun by St. Ignatius Loyola (1491–1556) to complement the new Jesuit headquarters at Collegio Romano, it was consecrated in 1584, although the decoration of the interior continued, to be completed in the 19th century.

Il Gesu

Map p. 125

Piazza del Gesu 1

06 697 001

Closed 12:30–4 p.m. St. Ignatius's rooms open 4–6 p.m. Mon.–Sat., & 10 a.m.–noon Sun.

Bus: 56, 64, 70, 81, 87, 95, 119, 492. Metro: Linea A (Spagna) and bus 116

This church, like many, is built in the form of a Latin cross, meaning that there is a long central nave, making one of the four arms that radiate out from the center under the dome longer than all the others. The decoration is extremely opulent. These things were done deliberately. To counter the influence of Protestantism (which stressed simplicity and personal responsibility), the Jesuits sought to emphasize the importance of the Church and the clergy. The long nave made processions more dramatic, while darkness encouraged the faithful to focus on the priest who stood on a raised main altar. The ample use of marble, gilded bronze, lapis lazuli, and silver in the decoration of the chapels (especially the two at the opposite ends of the main transept) was another way to stress the magnificence of God.

The chapel on the right by Pietro da Cortona is dedicated to St. Francis Xavier (the relic case is said to contain the saint's arm), that on the left, to St. Ignatius, whose remains are buried here. The silver statue of the saint is attributed to the sculptor Canova. It replaced a more valuable effigy, melted down by Pope Pius VI to pay a tribute to Napoleon. The ceiling fresco and the cupola, decorated with prophets, Evangelists, and Doctors of the Church, are from the end of the 17th century. The ornate bronze banister in front of the chapel is decorated with cherubs and with candelabra set on elaborate marble bases. Note the cherub at the top holding up a lapis lazuli globe.

At Piazza del Gesu 45 next door are the **rooms where St. Ignatius lived.** There are paintings in a magnificent trompe l'oeil style by Padre Andrea Pozzo and some memorabilia. ■

The facade of Il Gesu

Piazza Venezia

FROM THE POINT OF VIEW OF SIZE AND VISIBILITY, THE white marble monument to King Victor Emanuel II (Monumento a Vittorio Emanuele II), the Savoy monarch, dominates the piazza. Begun in 1885 and inaugurated in 1911, it commemorates national unification, obtained in 1870. Though attractive at night when lit, the "wedding cake" or "typewriter" is considered an eyesore by many. It also serves as Italy's Tomb of the Unknown Soldier and houses a small museum commemorating the Italian Risorgimento.

Piazza Venezia

Map p. 125

Bus: 56, 64, 70, 81, 87, 95, 119, 492

Museo del Palazzo Venezia

Via del Plebiscito 118

06 679 8865

Closed p.m. & Mon. Note that for special exhibitions hours may be different.

$$

Palazzo Venezia was built in the second half of the 15th century by the Venetian Cardinal Pietro Barbo (the future Pope Paul II), and is Rome's first important Renaissance palace. Incorporating an existing medieval tower and retaining some of its battlements, it symbolizes the transition from the medieval to the Renaissance. It was constructed at a time of significant change in the city's urban development. Until the early 14th century, when the popes fled to Avignon in France, the city's center was around the papal residence in the Lateran Palace. On their return, the Lateran having fallen into disrepair, the popes moved to the Vatican, giving new importance to the area in between.

Over the centuries the palace has served as a papal residence, as the embassy of the Venetian Republic, and, from 1797 to 1916, as the residence of the Austrian ambassador to the Holy See. Under Fascism it became the residence of Mussolini, who made most of his speeches from the balcony overlooking the piazza and whose office, the Sala del Mappamondo, was spoofed in Charlie Chaplin's *The Great Dictator*. Remember the scene where Hitler and Mussolini play volleyball with a *mappamondo* or large globe? The building now houses the **Museo del Palazzo Venezia,** with a vast collection of artworks and objets d'art, which often hosts special exhibitions. ■

Santa Maria in Aracoeli

Santa Maria in
Aracoeli
🅰 Map p. 125
✉ Piazza del
    Campidoglio 4
☎ 06 679 8155
🚌 Bus: 56, 64, 70, 81,
    87, 95, 119, 492

PERHAPS NO OTHER CHURCH IN ROME BETTER EMBODIES
the stratified nature of Rome's development, and this is not just
because its 22 columns were recycled from some important Roman
structure. Santa Maria d'Aracoeli (St. Mary of the Altar of Heaven)
was built over the ruins of a Roman temple to Juno.

The early Christian church marks
the site where, in the first century
B.C., Octavius, the future emperor
Augustus, is said to have experienced a vision foretelling the birth
of Jesus. He built an altar here and
for this reason, in a break with
tradition, he is depicted in the apse
fresco on the arch of the apse—
quite a place of honor for a ruler of
ancient Rome. Rebuilt in the 13th
century by the Franciscans, the
church has retained the rather
austere Romanesque style of that
era, intensified by the fact that the
facade was never completed. The
painfully steep staircase (a reflection of the medieval view that salvation can only be obtained by
sacrifice) was built in 1348,
probably as a sign of thanksgiving
for the end of the Black Death.

Inside, despite the chandeliers
and considerable restoration, the
church retains its aura of mystery.
The cosmatesque pavement (see
p. 206) is interspersed with floor
tombs (Donatello created that of
Archdeacon Crivelli). The ceiling
decoration commemorates the
European naval victory at Lepanto
in 1571. Don't miss the **Bufalini
chapel** (the first on the right) with
Pinturicchio's magnificently colored
rendition of scenes from the "Life of
San Bernardino" (1485). Note how
the Renaissance realism of this
painting contrasts with the stylized
Byzantine "Madonna" on the main
altar. Other works are by Benozzo
Gozzoli, Arnolfo di Cambio, Andrea
Sansovino, and Pietro Cavallini.
Nearby is the chapel of the

Santissimo Bambino (the Holy
Infant). Romans were outraged
when, in February 1994, thieves
"abducted" its occupant, a gem-
studded statue of the Infant Jesus
(said to be carved out of olive wood
from the garden of Gethsemane)
reputed to have miraculous healing
powers. It was replaced by a copy. ■

**Edward Gibbon is
said to have been
in this church
when he got the
idea to write his
famous "Decline
and Fall of the
Roman Empire."**

More places to visit

PIAZZA DI SANT'IGNAZIO

This piazza (1727–28) is something really special. Designed by architect Filippo Raguzzini, it resembles a theatrical stage setting, especially when viewed from the central door of the church of **Sant'Ignazio** *(Tel 06 679 5206 or 2422, closed 12:30–4 p.m.)*. Historically the official place of worship for the nearby Jesuit Collegio Romano, the church, completed in 1650, was built to celebrate St. Ignatius Loyola, the founder of the Jesuit order. Funds ran out before the cupola could be built. But never mind. Ingenious artists painted a 56-foot (17-m) wide circular trompe l'oeil canvas that magnificently simulates the interior of a dome.

Built in the form of a Latin cross, this church is heavily and ornately decorated with an abundance of stucco, gilt, and colored marbles. The most notable artwork is Padre Andrea Pozzo's ceiling fresco depicting "St. Ignatius' Entrance into Paradise" and, along the sides, his frescoes commemorating the order's worldwide missionary activities. The best view of all is from the yellow marble disk set for this purpose in the floor of the central nave. Note the four large female figures representing the continents on which the Jesuits were active. Guess which one is meant to personify the Americas.

Map p. 125 Bus: 56, 64, 70, 81, 87, 95, 116, 119, 492 Metro: Linea A (Spagna), then bus 116 or walk

SAN MARCO EVANGELISTA AL CAMPIDOGLIO

The basilica of San Marco is one of Rome's 25 titular churches, that is, nonparish churches founded in early Christian times. Established by Pope St. Mark in A.D. 336 and dedicated to his namesake, St. Mark the Evangelist (who some believe may have written his gospel here), it has been rebuilt and restored more than once, leaving it with a decidedly baroque interior. However, the apse mosaic dates from the ninth century. It shows Jesus, flanked by saints, his arm lifted in a blessing. Note that the fingers are positioned in the Greek style,

which means the index and middle fingers are raised while the thumb is crossed over. This is said to mimic the first letter, in Greek, of Jesus' name, while the Western blessing style—the thumb plus the first two fingers—signifies the Trinity. Pope Gregory IV, on the far left, holds a model of the church.

The facade, with a two-story portico, is considered a fine example of Renaissance church architecture and may be the work of Leon Battista Alberti (historians can't decide). Right next door is an entrance to the Palazzo Venezia (see p. 138) from which you can get a good peep at the courtyard with its charming 18th-century fountain and its beautiful, if incomplete, two-story Renaissance loggia.

Map p. 125 Piazza San Marco 48 06 679 5206 Closed 1:30–4 p.m. Bus: 56, 64, 70, 81, 87, 95, 119, 492 ■

Family & papal heraldic crests

Bears, bulls, castles, bees, fleurs-de-lis, doves, and dragons. These are everywhere in Rome, gracing facades, fountains, occasionally a pavement, and often a ceiling (especially in churches). In case you've wondered about these ubiquitous symbols, they are the heraldic crests of Rome's noble families. These coats of arms may be carved in marble or wood, molded in bronze and in one case (in the Aracoeli Church) represented in stained glass. If the symbol is topped by a papal tiara (a large beehive-shaped crown) and two crisscrossed keys, then there is a pope somewhere on the family tree. (A broad brimmed hat with tassels means a cardinal.) As the city's rulers over centuries, the pontiffs left more traces then most. Some, like Urban VIII Barberini (a baroque period Donald Trump?) went on real building binges; in fact, the Barberini bees are probably more frequent than the Chigi star, the Farnese fleurs-de-lis, the Pamphili dove and the Borghese dragon and eagle. ■

This was once a vast and largely uninhabited flood plain. But the popes' decision in the 14th century to set up house across the river on the Vatican Hill made it a prime residential area for Rome's Renaissance elite.

Campo Marzio

A cupid from the fountain in Piazza Navona

Campo Marzio

THE CAMPO MARZIO OR CAMPUS MARTIUS (FIELD OF MARS) WAS THE NAME given by the ancient Romans to the broad expanse of largely uninhabited land that stretched from the Quirinal Hill to the Tiber River and which, until Trajan's engineering, was separated from the Roman Forum by a land ridge. From about the fourth century B.C. on, this vast flood plain was used, first for military encampment and exercises, and subsequently for games and athletic competitions.

Antique shops abound in some streets of the Campo Marzio area, mainly Via Giulia, Via di Monserrato, and Via dei Coronari.

Numerous porticoes, set among grass and trees, were built for the citizens' enjoyment and relaxation. At first, the Campus Martius area included most of what is today downtown Rome, but subsequently, it shrank in size and came to be identified primarily with the area tucked into the curve of the Tiber that faces Castel Sant'Angelo and St. Peter's, enclosing more or less everything from Via del Corso to the river. Only in 1377 when the popes returned from Avignon and took up residence across the river in the Vatican did it became a focus for residential construction. In fact, this is one of the oldest parts of modern Rome and, indeed, in vast areas much has remained more or less as it was when broad avenues like Corso Vittorio Emanuele II had yet to be even imagined. Then, as now, there was a warren of narrow streets, interrupted only by spacious squares such as Piazza Navona with its magnificent baroque fountains, Campo dei Fiori (a food and flower market), and Piazza Farnese, a study in Renaissance elegance.

Traces of the past are everywhere in this area. The remains of Emperor Domitian's stadium are underneath Piazza Navona, parts of which (several yards below today's ground level) you can see by exiting the square at the north, along Via Agonale, and turning left at the end of it. There are medieval arches and passageways that bring to mind the image of tradesmen in leather jerkins and soldiers in clanking armor. Buildings bear flood marks from the pre-embankment days. It is in this neighborhood that the Renaissance and baroque best meet. Renaissance palaces such as Palazzo Altemps and the Cancelleria alternate with baroque baronies and churches such as Palazzo Pamphili, Sant'Agnese in Agone, or Sant'Andrea della Valle. High-rent elegant streets such as Via Giulia, Via di Monserrato, and Via dei Coronari, with their churches, art galleries, and exquisite antique shops, give way to humbler crossways. On Via dei Giubbonari (full of cut-rate clothing and shoe shops) and the streets around Teatro di Pompeo or, in the other direction, on Via del Governo Vecchio you will find countless small *botteghe* (shops of craftsmen and artisans), the direct descendants of the guilds of an earlier era that more often than not gave their names to the streets of today. ■

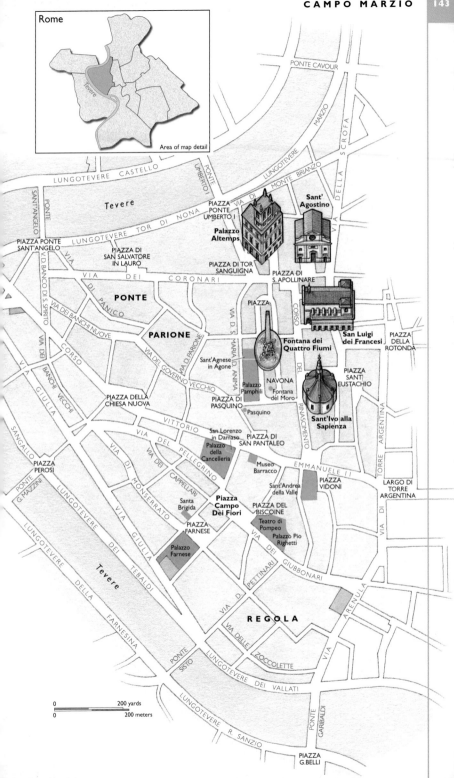

Rome

Area of map detail

LUNGOTEVERE CASTELLO

Tevere

PONTE UMBERTO I

LUNGOTEVERE TOR DI NONA

PIAZZA PONTE SANT'ANGELO

PIAZZA DI SAN SALVATORE IN LAURO

VIA DEI CORONARI

PONTE

PARIONE

V.D. BANCO DI S. SPIRITO

VIA DEI BANCHI NUOVI

CORSO

VIA DEL GOVERNO VECCHIO

VIA DEI BANCHI VECCHI

VIA GIULIA

PIAZZA DELLA CHIESA NUOVA

PIAZZA PEROSI

G. MAZZINI

PONTE

LUNGOTEVERE DELLA FARNESINA

Tevere

VIA DI MONSERRATO

VIA GIULIA

VIA DEI CAPPELLARI

VIA DEL PELLEGRINO

VITTORIO

San Lorenzo in Damaso
Palazzo della Cancelleria

PIAZZA DI SAN PANTALEO

Museo Barracco

Santa Brigida

PIAZZA FARNESE

Palazzo Farnese

Piazza Campo Dei Fiori

PIAZZA DEL BISCIONE

Teatro di Pompeo

Palazzo Pio Righetti

Sant'Andrea della Valle

PIAZZA VIDONI

EMMANUELE II

LARGO DI TORRE ARGENTINA

REGOLA

VIA DEI TEBALDI

VIA D. PETTINARI

VIA DELLE ZOCCOLETTE

VIA GIUBBONARI

VIA ARENULA

PONTE SISTO

LUNGOTEVERE DEI VALLATI

LUNGOTEVERE R. SANZIO

PONTE GARIBALDI

PIAZZA G. BELLI

PIAZZA PONTE UMBERTO I

Palazzo Altemps

Sant' Agostino

PIAZZA DI TOR SANGUIGNA

PIAZZA DI S. APOLLINARE

VIA D. S. MARIA DELL'ANIMA

VIA DELLA SCROFA

MONTE BRIANZO

CORSO DEL RINASCIMENTO

PIAZZA

Fontana dei Quattro Fiumi

Sant'Agnese in Agone

Palazzo Pamphili

NAVONA

Fontana del Moro

PIAZZA DI PASQUINO

Pasquino

San Luigi dei Francesi

PIAZZA DELLA ROTONDA

PIAZZA SANT' EUSTACHIO

Sant'Ivo alla Sapienza

TORRE ARGENTINA

0   200 yards
0   200 meters

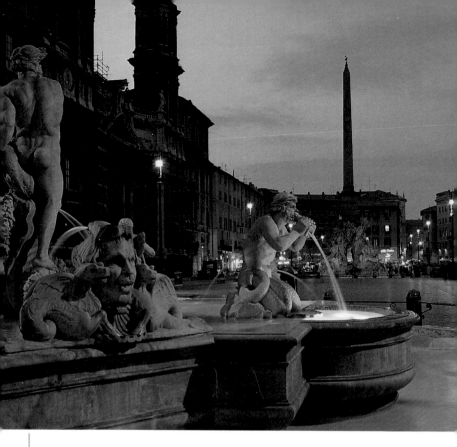

Piazza Navona

ONE OF THE WORLD'S MOST BEAUTIFUL SQUARES, PIAZZA Navona gives the visitor an opportunity to grasp the complexity of 2,000 years of Roman history. A spectacular baroque composition, the piazza lies within the contours of an ancient Roman stadium. Today it plays host to those who flock here for a moment of relaxation—a chat, an *aperitivo*, a meal—against a backdrop of magnificent man-made beauty.

Piazza Navona

Map pp. 142–43

Bus: 64, 115 & 116 (weekdays only), 70, 87, 95/81

Look closely at the buildings that form the perimeter of the piazza. They were built over the tiers of seats of the Circus Agonalis, a stadium constructed by Emperor Domitian in A.D. 86 to host Greek-style games, in which contestants competed nude. Note that as usual one end of the stadium, which could seat 30,000, was rounded.

After the popes returned from Avignon (1377) and chose the Vatican as their new residence, urban development began in earnest in this area. In 1477, for example, Pope Sixtus IV moved the central market here, where it remained for 390 years, from its historic site at the Capitol (Campidoglio)—a tradition that today survives only in the Christmas stalls set up every December to sell toys and decorations. Today's Piazza Navona, however, dates from the 1640s when Pope Innocent X, a Pamphili, chose the square as a site for a new family residence, a plan that included elaborate fountains and a church. Both the resulting Palazzo Pamphili, completed in 1650, and Sant'Agnese in Agone, completed over a decade later, are the work of Girolomo Rainaldi, his son Carlo, and of Francesco Borromini. **Palazzo Pamphili** (now an embassy) has frescoes by Pietro da Cortona depicting the story of Aeneas.

Sant'Agnese in Agone, on the other hand, was built over the spot where 13-year-old Agnes, a fourth-century Christian maiden who rejected the advances of a Roman official's son, was reportedly stripped naked in public. The story goes that, thanks to a miracle, the girl's hair grew so long and so fast as to cover her nudity. Agnes was martyred all the same, beheaded (in A.D. 304) during Emperor Diocletian's anti-Christian persecutions. The facade was designed by the temperamental Borromini, who worked on it until falling out with the family in 1657.

The magnificent baroque fountains in the piazza (see p. 96–97) conceal another tale of the legendary Bernini–Borromini rivalry. Borromini lost his commission for the central Fountain of the Four

Right: Originally designed for Greek-style athletic games in which the contestants competed in the nude, today Piazza Navona is a place for repose and relaxation.

Rivers **(Fontana dei Quattro Fiumi)** because of the savvier, more diplomatic Bernini's successful flattery of Donna Olimpia, the pope's sister-in-law. The story goes that Bernini gave one of the fountain's statues a raised arm to ward off the imminent collapse of Sant'Agnese, and that Borromini's statue of the saint on the church, her hand on her heart, replies, "I will not fall." But it just ain't so. The fountain was completed in 1651, years before Borromini's facade. The Fountain of the Moor **(Fontana del Moro)** is by Giacomo della Porta but Bernini designed the central figure. ■

Pasquino, the talking statue

D issidents and anticlerics affixed radical messages to his torso, hoping to incite the populace against the popes. The story of Pasquino, the talking statue, gives us our word "pasquinade" (a brief, anonymous satirical comment, generally on current events). Pasquino, however, was not alone. Named after an outspoken neighborhood tailor, he had several friends with whom he could converse: Marforio, the river god, now in the Capitoline Museum; the Facchino (the porter) on Via Lata off the Corso; Abbot Luigi on Piazza Vidoni near Corso Vittorio Emanuele; and buxom Madama Lucrezia, who stands outside the Palazzetto di Venezia. ■

Cardinal Marco Sittico Altemps commissioned Martino Longhi the Elder to renovate his palazzo, and the architect created this elegant central courtyard.

Palazzo Altemps

AFTER A LONG PERIOD OF DECLINE AND ABANDON, Palazzo Altemps—once the residence of 16th- and 17th-century noblemen and cardinals—has been superbly restored by the Italian government. Part of the Museo Nazionale Romano complex, it is a site not to be missed. Not only does it contain many priceless pieces of classical statuary but, as you will see, the building's structure and its decor compete for the visitor's attention with the artworks exhibited within. The *altana*, the characteristic Roman belvedere tower over one corner of the building, is believed to be the first of a genre that became a must for any patrician palace. Look up from across the street to see four obelisks, and the family's heraldic symbol, an ibex.

Like many buildings of its era, the palazzo belonged to a succession of noble Italian families. Constructed about 1477 by a Riario, in 1568 it was purchased by Cardinal Marco Sittico Altemps, who amassed a magnificent library and a rich collection of ancient sculpture. Today they are scattered among the world's major museums, although 16 pieces of the original collection have now been returned here. The building remained in the family until it was sold to the Holy See,

Museum is one of a very few that explains this. Panels near the statues use shading to indicate the parts that were added. There are also ample explanations in English.

The Painted Loggia on the first floor (one flight up) is now the setting for the Ludovisi **busts of the Caesars.** In the beautiful, tiny **church of Sant'Aniceto,** richly decorated in high baroque style, you will see some striking examples of marble and mother-of-pearl inlay work. By the way, this church (inaugurated in 1617) may well have been the only private church to house the remains of a saint: Anicetus, an early pope and martyr. The frescoes tell the story of the saint's death by decapitation. In reality, Anicetus's story was altered by the family to fit that of Roberto Altemps, who earlier had been sentenced to death by decapitation (for adultery) by Pope Sixtus V.

Like the Villa Borghese, Palazzo Altemps is as much a protagonist as the objects on display. The original **wall** and **ceiling decorations** have been restored to their former glory, that of a patrician palace whose decor embodies the gradual transition in style from Renaissance to baroque. The **courtyard,** with its statues, four of which are from the original Altemps collections, and its nymphaeum (a curved wall-fountain decorated with mosaic, paste shells, and colored gravel of the type often found in ancient Roman villas), is breathtaking. Don't miss the Fireplace Room, with Cardinal Altemps's monumental fireplace, the room of the Painted Landscapes, and the Cupboard Room. The wall fresco there, in what was the 15th-century reception room, shows wedding gifts and greeting cards received by Girolamo Riario and Caterina Sforza (the palace's first occupants). ■

which turned it into a seminary. In a dismal state, it was purchased by the Italian government in 1982.

The museum's inventory includes artworks from several major Roman art collections, in particular the Boncompagni Ludovisi collection that for years was accessible only to scholars. Now, world-famous pieces such as the magnificent **Ludovisi throne** depicting the birth of Aphrodite, the breathtaking **Grande Ludovisi Sarcophagus** with its violent battles between Roman and barbarian soldiers, the tragically moving "Gaul Committing Suicide," and the inspiring, noble "Ares," the latter restored by Bernini, are all displayed here. In the 16th and 17th centuries, restoration meant reconstructing the missing parts, and the Altemps

Palazzo Altemps

- Map pp. 142–43
- Piazza Sant'Apollinare 44
- 06 481 5576
- Closed Mon.
- $$
- Bus: 70, 115 & 116 (weekdays only), 81, 87

Caravaggio's dramatic realism and strong chiaroscuro effects are amply displayed in "The Martyrdom of St. Matthew."

San Luigi dei Francesi

COMPLETED IN 1589, THE CHURCH HAS A RENAISSANCE facade attributed to Giacomo della Porta, but the statues date from the 18th century. Dedicated to Louis IX, the French king who was later made a saint, this is the French national church and you will see that the stone dragons decorating the first story bear the fleur-de-lis.

The interior is somewhat overwhelming, a profusion of marble decoration and monuments. The star attraction, however, is the Contarelli Chapel with its three Caravaggio paintings, all scenes from the life of St. Matthew and masterpieces of dramatic composition, chiaroscuro, and realism. The dramatic content in the "Vocation of St. Matthew," in which Jesus points at Matthew, the indirect lighting from the right, and the incredulous expression on the saint's face are alone enough to rank Caravaggio among the world's great artists. Domenichino's "Scenes from the Life of St. Cecilia," are in the second chapel on the right. ■

San Luigi dei Francesi

- Map pp. 142–43
- Piazza San Luigi dei Francesi 5
- 06 688271
- Closed 12:30–3:30 p.m. & Thurs. p.m.
- Bus: 70, 115 & 116 (weekdays only)

Caravaggio

His real name was Michelangelo Merisi, and at his birth in September 1573, in the tiny northern town of Caravaggio, no one could have imagined the heights of talent and the depths of torment that his life would encompass. Trained in Milan, far from the centers of classical Renaissance art like Florence, Rome, and Venice, he was to bring to his paintings an extraordinary mix of realism and dramatic lighting. Only 17 when he arrived in Rome, his lifestyle soon took on the characteristics—dissoluteness, drunkenness, and disorderly conduct—that were to bring about his downfall: scrapes with the law, murder (albeit unintentional), impoverishment, illness,

and, at only 37, death. The artist was not loved by everyone. For example, the priests of San Luigi rejected his first version of "St. Matthew and the Angel," labelling its extreme realism "disrespectful." For his time, Caravaggio's work was truly revolutionary. He was one of the first to use to its maximum effect the "chiaroscuro" technique (the use of light and dark). His masterly use of this dramatic method, the wealth of detail, and his ability to depict humanity with all of its defects and frailty (even when painting subjects from scripture) were exceptional. His works can be found in Sant'Agostino and Santa Maria del Popolo as well as in most of the major Rome museums. ■

Sant'Agostino

A wide flight of stairs and an imposing Renaissance facade, possibly one of the earliest in Rome, are your introduction to the church of St. Augustine. Completed in 1483 (but the main altar was refashioned in the 1600s to Bernini's design), this church has several major artworks. Raphael's magnificent fresco of the "Prophet Isaiah" is on the third pilaster on the left, against which stands a lovely sculpture group ("St. Anne, the Virgin and Child," 1512) by Andrea Sansovino. The first chapel on the left houses Caravaggio's remarkable "Madonna dei Pellegrini," highly controversial at the time (1605) because its pilgrims were depicted realistically, that is as old and poor. To the right of the main portal is Jacopo Sansovino's statue, the "Madonna del Parto" (*parto* in Italian means childbirth) with unusual Junoesque proportions. ■

Sant'Agostino
- 🗺 Map pp. 142–43
- ✉ Piazza di Sant'Agostino
- ☎ 06 6880 1962
- 🕐 Closed noon–4 p.m.
- 🚌 Bus: 115 & 116 (weekdays only) 81, 87, 95/70

Although it contains several sculptures and paintings that celebrate motherhood, this church was also favored by Renaissance courtesans.

Sant'Ivo alla Sapienza

Named for the patron saint of lawyers, Sant'Ivo is located inside the Palazzo della Sapienza (*sapienza* means "knowledge" in Latin), today the National Archives. Until 1935, this was the site of Rome's La Sapienza University, founded by Boniface VIII in 1303. Many artists were commissioned to work on the structure by a variety of popes, as can be seen from the papal insignias in the courtyard (eagles and dragons for the Borghese family, bees for the Barberini). But credit for the facade and the courtyard goes to Giacomo della Porta, while the 17th-century church was designed by the temperamental Francesco Borromini and is an architectural play of fantasy and mystery with Gothic overtones. The lower portion of the facade is concave. The convex curves of the cupola culminate in a spiral pinnacle. Inside, the church is all whiteness, again an unusual composition of alternating convex and concave forms.

Outside, around the corner to the right, is a small **fountain:** Books on a shelf with a deer's antlered head and a cross, illustrate the symbol of this neighborhood called Sant'Eustacchio after Eustace, a martyred Roman soldier. He converted to Christianity after suddenly seeing a cross between the horns of a deer he was hunting and was about to kill. ■

Sant'Ivo alla Sapienza
- 🗺 Map pp. 142–43
- ✉ Corso Rinascimento 40
- ☎ 06 686 4987
- 🕐 Closed Sat. & Sun. p.m.
- 🚌 Bus: 10, 81, 87,115, 116

Medieval mystery & Renaissance riches walk

In Roman times, the vast area of the Campo Marzio was given over to army encampments, stadiums, and pleasure porticoes. It's mostly all gone or buried now, but many of the medieval and Renaissance buildings which came later remain, bearing witness to the intrigues and riches of a not-so-distant past.

This walk starts just north of Piazza Navona at **Piazza di Tor Sanguigna,** where you can still see a piece of the past: Below the railing is a chunk of the first-century foundations of **Domitian's Stadium.** Behind you is the medieval tower that gave its name to the piazza. On your left, near the lovely 17th- century wall *aedicola* (shrine) at No. 2, is the start of **Via dei Coronari,** where souvenir vendors once sold *corone* (rosary beads) to Catholic pilgrims. Today it is filled with wonderful (and expensive) antiques stores. The side streets offer intriguing views. Down the Vicolo del Volpe, on your left, is the colorful tiled spire of

A view of what was originally Hadrian's Mausoleum. The angel on the top gave the castle its name, Castel Sant'Angelo.

Santa Maria dell'Anima. On your right, the Vicolo di San Trifone, is a really tight fit. Further on is **Piazza di San Salvatore in Lauro ❶,** with the church of the same name. Here you'll want to see the church's beautiful double *chiostro* (cloister).

Now return to Via dei Coronari and walk on (away from Piazza di Tor Sanguigna) until you get to Via di Panico, where you turn right. At No. 40 note the small marble relief on the wall, a stonecutter's shingle. At the end of the street, carefully cross the Lungotevere river road (Lungotevere Tor di Nona) to the onset of Ponte Sant'Angelo ❷, from which the view of Castel Sant'Angelo and St. Peter's dome is breathtaking. The bridge is magnificently decorated with the monumental Bernini-designed statues, each holding a symbol (a crown of thorns, a whip, a nail) of the Crucifixion.

Crossing back over the Lungotevere Tor di Nona, this time take the Via del Banco di Santo Spirito, the middle street (note the columns of a medieval portico embedded in the corner building) of the three that fan out from what was formerly called Piazza del Ponte, where public executions were once held. Just after the church on your left, there is a dark, medieval passage on the other side of the street, the **Arco dei Banchi,** where an ancient inscription marks the height of the flood waters of 1277. At the Banco di Santo Spirito at No. 3, the road forks. Take the picturesque Via dei Banchi Nuovi on your left to **Piazza dell'Orologio ❸,** named for the large clock on the tower. On the left, take Vicolo degli Orsini, and at the end, sneak a peek at the lush, green inner courtyard of a baronial palace built by the Orsinis. Backtrack to the piazza and continue along the same street (now called Via del Governo Vecchio) to Via della Chiesa Nuova. Turn right here, and right again at the end, and you'll find yourself in front of the late Renaissance church that Romans call the **Chiesa Nuova** ➍ (officially, Santa Maria della Vallicella). Stand near the statue (dedicated to Metastasio) for a better view of the church and the interesting Borromini facade of the **Oratorio dei Filippini** on the left. This has a curious porticoed courtyard and, upstairs on the top floor, a charming if somewhat musty library (the Biblioteca Vallicelliana) designed by Borromini in 1581. The church, which has a ceiling fresco by Pietro da Cortona, has three Rubens paintings over the main altar. Leaving by the side door, return to Via del Governo Vecchio and proceed to **Piazza di Pasquino** ➎, with its "talking" statue (see p. 145). The statue stands against the back wall of Palazzo Braschi, seat of the Museo di Roma.

Then follow the street on the left, Via di Santa Maria dell'Anima, to **Tor Millina,** a

medieval tower. Turn left here and walk a block until you find yourself at the beginning of Via della Pace and, facing you, Pietro da Cortona's spectacularly dramatic facade of the church of **Santa Maria della Pace.** The piazza here has some interesting cafés. ∎

- 🔼 Also see area map, pp. 142–43
- ▶ Piazza di Tor Sanguigna
- ↔ I mile (1.5 km)
- 🕒 1.5–2 hours
- ▶ Piazza Santa Maria della Pace

NOT TO BE MISSED

- Domitian's Stadium
- San Salvatore in Lauro
- View from Ponte Sant'Angelo
- Chiesa Nuova
- Oratorio dei Filippini

Piazza Campo dei Fiori

THIS PIAZZA, AN OUTDOOR MARKETPLACE SINCE 1869 when the market at Piazza Navona was closed, is one of the few important squares in Rome not linked to a particular patrician family or edifice. The only building of note is the Palazzo Pio Righetti, at the southeastern end, which has an imposing facade, although it's around the corner on Piazza del Biscione.

The spread of supermarkets and fast food has changed eating habits. But although smaller, this open-air market, moved here from Piazza Navona in 1869, is still vibrant.

Piazza Campo dei Fiori

Map pp. 142–43

Bus: 64, 70, 81, 87, 95/64, 116

As is true of the rest of the Campo Marzio area, Campo dei Fiori became increasingly central following the Holy See's decision in the 14th century to set up residence in the Vatican. The square was, after all, directly on the Via Papalis (gone today) and the Via del Pellegrino, the pedestrian routes for pilgrims arriving from the south side of the city. After Pope Sixtus IV built his bridge over the Tiber (Ponte Sisto) for the 1475 Holy Year, this piazza became a transit point for anyone coming from Trastevere. Not surprisingly, until the 17th century when most such activity moved to the Spanish Steps area, it was the center of a flourishing tourist trade. Indeed, the Albergo del Sole, just around the corner on Via del Biscione, is reputedly the oldest hotel in Rome. Number 13 on the corner of the Via dei Cappellari and Vicolo del Gallo was an inn, La Vacca, run by Vanozza Cattanei, a grande dame who for a time was the mistress of Rodrigo Borgia (the future Pope Alexander VI), and mother of the lovely, but infamous Lucrezia.

The Campo dei Fiori (the name means "field of flowers") was paved in 1440 and since that time has been one of the most lively and colorful piazzas in the city. Mornings (which in Rome last until about 2 p.m.) the square is abuzz with activity, the market stalls stacked high with fresh produce and the air filled with vendors' cries. Sundays and evenings the inexpensive trattorias and pubs are a magnet for the young. Gentrification has made the apartments in the area attractive to professionals and young marrieds. In the past, this large, open space was well suited to all sorts of games and processions, not to mention public executions. The heretic, Giordano Bruno, whose statue now stands in the center of the square, was burned at the stake here on February 17, 1600. ■

Right: Campo dei Fiori straddles two of Rome's *rioni* (neighborhoods), Regola and Parione. See the wall plaques marking their borders at Nos. 14 and 30.

Street names

In medieval and Renaissance times, artisans tended to set up their shops in clusters, a practice often imposed by law as well as by convenience, and many of the streets in this central area of old Rome took (and kept) their names from the tradesmen who worked there. Thus we have Via dei Cappellari, the street of the hatmakers, which starts at the northwest corner of Campo dei Fiori; Via dei Baullari, the street of the trunkmakers, which leads toward Piazza Navona; and Via dei Giubbonari, the street of jacket- or jerkinmakers, which runs toward via Arenula and the Ghetto. Other examples are Via dei Chiavari, the street of the locksmiths; Via dei Sediari, the street of the chairmakers; and Via dei Balestrari, the street of the crossbowmakers. On Via dei Coronari, artisans specialized in the making of rosaries; the Cestari and the Canestrari made baskets; the Funari made ropes; the Staderari weighed things; and, on Vicolo del Bollo, jewelers brought gold or silver to be hallmarked. A small dictionary will help you get a better idea of the historical context. Thus, Piazza del Fico is named after its centuries-old fig tree, Via del Governo Vecchio after the large building that was once the seat of government, while Via dei Soldati, near Piazza Navona, was on a military patrol route. ■

Piazza Farnese

PALAZZO FARNESE IS WIDELY CONSIDERED TO BE THE most beautiful Renaissance building in Rome, if not in Italy, and the imposing building cannot be separated from the lovely piazza in which it stands. Begun in 1514 by Alessandro Farnese (the future Pope Paul III), the palazzo's magnificent proportions are the work of some of the major architects of the time, including Antonio Sangallo, Michelangelo, who designed the cornice and the loggia on the facade, and Giacomo della Porta.

The interior was also decorated by the best artists of the era, such as Annibale and Agostino Caracci, Domenichino, and Lanfranco—but most of the artwork is inaccessible since the building houses the French Embassy and is not open to the public. However, the fleurs-de-lis seen everywhere on the exterior and on the fountains have nothing to do with France. These are the Farnese lilies, the symbol of that noble Roman family.

During the Renaissance a piazza was always considered an integral part of any aristocratic residence and this one was adorned with granite basins from the Baths of Caracalla. It seems to be among the very few in the city not designed by Giacomo della Porta. Della Porta is instead credited with the back facade of the palace, that facing the garden and the river. A project, attributed to Michelangelo, to link the palazzo to property on the Trastevere side of the river with an overhead bridge, was never completed. The only part of the project realized is the lovely arch that romantically spans the Via Giulia. The church of **Santa Brigida** to the left of the palace is the Swedish National Church. The convent next door is where St. Bridget died in 1373. ∎

Above: The Caracci Gallery, decorated with mythological love scenes like that of "Jupiter and Juno," was to exert a tremendous influence on 17th-century painting.

Left: Along with the basins, the Farnese pope, Paul III, also removed statues from Caracalla.

Piazza Farnese

🅰 Map pp. 142–43

🚌 Bus: 64, 70, 81, 87, 95/64, 116

Casa di Santa Brigida

🅰 Map pp. 142–43

✉ Piazza Farnese 96

☎ 06 6889 2596, 06 689 2497

🕐 Closed noon–5 p.m.

Right: Bernini's genius, and his preference for indirect lighting, is fully displayed in the marble rendering of the spiritual ecstasy of the "Blessed Ludovica Albertoni."

"Ecstasies"

This relatively small marble wall relief in the **Casa di Santa Brigida** showing St. Bridget's ecstatic face after a mystical communication with God was probably inspired by Bernini. But it cannot be compared to the Maestro's work. The marble rendering of the ecstasy of the "Blessed Ludovica Albertoni" in **San Francesco a Ripa** (see p. 196) is magnificent. As for the breathtaking and dramatically baroque "The Ecstasy of St. Teresa" in **Santa Maria della Vittoria** (see p. 90), it led one 19th-century traveler to quip, "If that's celestial ecstasy, I've experienced it, too." ∎

Among popes & princes walk

This walk will let you feast your eyes on a wealth of Renaissance and baroque detail. Unlike other areas of Rome, the Campo Marzio area is remarkably homogeneous. This is because most construction here took place only after the popes returned from exile in Avignon in 1377 and decided to set up house in the Vatican, setting off a new period of urban development in the area.

An ivy-draped arch over the Via Giulia is the only trace of an unrealized project to link Farnese properties on both sides of the Tiber.

Facing the Palazzo Farnese with its newly restored splendid facade, take Via di Monserrato on the right. Though tiny, the first square you come to, Piazza Santa Caterina della Rota, has three churches. The cream-colored **San Girolamo della Carita** ❶ on your left (1650–1660) is a must. The Spada Chapel, to the left of the entrance, has opulent, polychromatic marble decor created by Francesco Borromini. Note the drapery between the two kneeling angels; it looks like cloth but it is marble.

Continue along Via di Monserrato and you'll find yourself at Piazza dei Ricci with its *palazzo istoriato* (painted building)—the L-shaped, 16th-century **Palazzo Ricci** ❷. Continuing on, at the juncture of Monserrato and Via del Pellegrino, where **Via dei**

Banchi Vecchi ❸ begins, don't miss the marble plaque, inscribed in Latin, on No. 145. This marks the perimeter of an ancient Roman neighborhood and dates from the reign of Emperor Claudius (A.D. 41–54). Via dei Banchi Vecchi has charming little shops selling antiques and bric-a-brac. Peek into the old pharmacy at No. 24 (red lanterns hang outside above the door), then cross the street to look at its facade. You'll see why the building is called the **Palazzo dei Pupazzi** (puppets). At No. 118 you'll see the imposing *portone* to the **Palazzo Sforza Cesarini,** originally built by the infamous 15th-century Borgia pope, Alessandro VI.

Continuing on, you will come to Via dei Cimatori, which leads to the most beautiful street in Rome—the Via Giulia—built by Pope Julius II in the early 16th century to provide a better link to the Vatican. To the right is the church of the Florentine residents of Rome, **San Giovanni dei Fiorentini.** Now turn left on **Via Giulia** ❹ where you'll pass some of the most beautiful Renaissance palaces in the city. At No. 85, note the inscription "*Raf Sanzio*" (for Raphael, the painter) above the second-floor balcony. In Renaissance times many famous architects lived right next door to their patrician clients. The travertine "sofas" on the building at No. 62 were part of the grandiose courthouse (Palazzo dei Tribunali) begun by Bramante for Julius II but never completed. Just past the ivy-clad overhead arch is the rear facade of **Palazzo Farnese.** After the arch, you can't miss the striking Mascherone fountain, incorporating a giant marble mask of ancient Roman origin.

Before getting to Ponte Sisto, turn left on to the Vicolo del Polverone. Number 15B is the entrance to the **Galleria Spada** ❺ (*Tel 06 686 1158, closed Sun. p.m. & Mon.*), which contains paintings by Rubens, Titian, Guido Reni, Andrea del Sarto, and others, but the palazzo is equally interesting. From the central courtyard you can look at Borromini's famous trompe l'oeil perspective; the optical illusion created by this genius of the baroque makes a tiny statue at the end of a short, 30-foot (9-m), corridor appear to be a colossus at the end of a long and imposing hallway.

After visiting the gallery, continue up the Vicolo del Polverone to the Piazza Capo di Ferro to see the main facade of **Palazzo Spada** with its magnificent stucco decorations, including statues of Caesar, Augustus, and Trajan. From here walk down the Via dei Balestrari, skirt the end of Piazza Campo dei Fiori, and bear right to the Piazza del Biscione. Venture through the iron gate at the far end and down the covered passageway (Passetto del Biscione). You are now on the **Via di Grotta Pinta** ❻. See how the street forms a curve to the right? The buildings are built over the bleachers of what was Pompey's Theater

(Teatro di Pompeo), the probable site of Julius Caesar's assassination on March 15, 44 B.C. Now heading left, cross the Largo del Pallaro and follow Via dei Chiavari to Corso Vittorio Emanuele II. The large church on your right is **Sant'Andrea della Valle** (see p. 158), setting of the first act of Puccini's *Tosca*. ■

🅰 Also see area map, pp. 142–43
▶ Piazza Farnese
🔁 1.5 miles (2.5 km)
🕐 2.5–3 hours
▶ Sant'Andrea della Valle

NOT TO BE MISSED
- San Girolamo della Carita
- Via Giulia
- Galleria Spada
- Sant'Andrea della Valle

More places to visit

MUSEO BARRACCO

This is a little-known but delightful museum, commonly called La Piccola Farnesina although there is no connection with Palazzo Farnese. The misunderstanding derives from the fact that its builders, a French noble family named Le Roys, were allowed to use the royal fleur-de-lis in their coat of arms. Built in 1523, probably by Antonio Sangallo the Younger, it has been altered several times. Currently the property of the Rome city government, it now houses the Barracco collection of ancient artwork, primarily sculptures—Egyptian, Assyrian, Greek, Etruscan, and Roman—donated to the city in 1902. It is built over Roman ruins (often accessible to the public) dating from the late empire.

Map pp. 142–43   Corso Vittorio Emanuele II 168   06 6880 6848   Closed Sun. p.m. & Mon. $. Special exhibitions $$ Bus: 64, 70, 81, 87, 95/64, 116

PALAZZO DELLA CANCELLERIA

Completed in 1517, this palazzo ranks as one of the finest Renaissance buildings in the city, and its history is intimately linked to that of Roman nobility. It was paid for with the 60,000 scudi that Raffaele Riario, a nephew of Pope Sixtus IV, received from Franceschetto Cibo, the nephew of Pope Innocent VIII as payment for a gambling debt. The stone roses on the facade and in the courtyard (walls and pavement) were the heraldic symbol of the Riario family. Today, it is owned by the Vatican, which at one time used it as a chancellery (hence the name) and enjoys extraterritorial status. Bramante did some work on the palazzo, and you should not miss its marvelous *cortile*, courtyard, with its impressive two-story double loggia.

The **Sala dei 100 Giorni,** the Hundred Days Room upstairs, where concerts are sometimes held, was frescoed by Giorgio Vasari depicting scenes from the life of Pope Paul III, a Farnese. The name comes from Vasari's claim to have painted the room in 100 days and Michelangelo's reported riposte, *"Si vede bene"* ("You can tell"). This is the Vasari who eventually gained fame with his written biographies *(Lives of the Artists)* of the most important painters of the day rather than with his own brush strokes. Incorporated into the palazzo on the right is the church of **San Lorenzo in Damaso.** Note the columns in the courtyard, some of which were taken from a preexisting fourth-century church.

Map pp. 142–43   Piazza della Cancelleria 1   Closed 2–4 p.m. daily, Sat., & Sun.   Bus: 64, 70, 81, 87, 95/64,116

SANT'ANDREA DELLA VALLE

Similar in style to the Jesuit church of the Gesu (see p. 137), Sant'Andrea della Valle was designed by Giacomo della Porta. But the facade and the dome—the largest in Rome, except of course for St. Peter's—are fundamentally the work of Carlo Maderno, although the travertine facade was added in the 1650s by Carlo Rainaldi. You might want to note the single angel that graces the top of the facade. One story goes that there were supposed to be two of them but the sculptor, irritated by criticisms, told his episcopal patron to "do it himself."

The interior decor is sumptuous. The magnificent dome fresco, the "Glory of Paradise," was done by Lanfranco while his archrival Domenichino only got to paint (brilliantly) the pendentives. Domenchino also did the scenes from the Life of St. Andrew in the upper portion of the apse. Two popes of the Piccolomini family are buried here. The lovely Strozzi chapel is in the Michelangelo style. The Barberini chapel, the first on the left, corresponds to the chapel Puccini chose as the setting for the first act of *Tosca*. It was here that Tosca accused her lover, Cavaradossi, of betrayal when she notices that the Mary Magdalen he is painting strongly resembles another woman.

Map pp. 142–43   Piazza Vidoni 6   06 686 1339   Closed 12:30–4:30 p.m. daily, Sun. p.m., & Mon. $$ Bus: 64, 70, 81, 87, 95, 115, 116 ■

The Vatican is the world's smallest independent state, but its importance is immense. The historical seat of Roman Catholicism, it is, with St. Peter's and the Vatican Museums, the repository of some of mankind's major artistic treasures.

Vaticano

Detail from Michelangelo's ceiling fresco of the "Creation" in the Sistine Chapel

Vaticano

ST. PETER'S IS THE CENTER OF ROMAN CATHOLICISM, THE CHURCH BUILT over the tomb of Peter, the Apostle to whom Jesus said, "You are Peter and on this rock I will build my church." This enormous basilica is the largest of Christianity and, with the massive dome created by Michelangelo, is known throughout the world. Built in the 16th century to replace an older church founded by Constantine, St. Peter's contains priceless monuments including Michelangelo's "Pietà" and Bernini's bronze canopy over the altar. However, it represents only the external face of the Vatican, the world's smallest independent city-state. Despite its minuscule geographical dimensions, the Vatican wields immense power and influence, although no longer that of the traditional, temporal sort. "How many battalions does the pope have?" Stalin once asked scornfully.

Behind its walls, built to keep out marauding Saracens, is a miniature urban tapestry. The Vatican has its own post office and stamps, a judicial system, a pharmacy, a gas station, a railway station, a commissary, a television station, and its own special police force, the Swiss Guards corps, which dates back to 1505. It publishes a daily newspaper, the influential *Osservatore Romano*, and beams out daily radio broadcasts in over a dozen languages. The Church once ruled much of Italy; but the Papal States were conquered by Piedmontese troops between 1860 and 1870. As a result the pope did not leave the Vatican for almost 50 years, but in 1929 peace was made with Italy through the signing of the Concordat.

The popes have lived in the Vatican since the end of the 14th

century when they returned from exile in Avignon and found the Lateran Palace (see p. 79) in ruins. Settlement of the Vatican plain (Ager Vaticanus) occurred more slowly than it did on the left bank of the Tiber and was spurred on largely by the presence of St. Peter's shrine. But the papal move to the Vatican accelerated this trend, and the 15th and 16th centuries saw a rash of construction on what was called the Mons Vaticanus. The result was a somewhat labyrinthine complex of interconnected palaces that grew up around St. Peter's in a largely disordered fashion. In the mid-1400s, Nicholas V (1447–1455) enlarged and beautified earlier structures, and his successors were to follow suit. Sixtus IV, for example, built the chapel that bears his name (the Cappella Sistina), Alexander VI (1492–1503) built a tower over that (the Torre del Borgia), and Julius II (1503–1513) arranged for Bramante, Raphael's mentor, to construct the new St. Peter's.

Outside, in the surrounding area, is the Borgo neighborhood, flanked by the remains of the ninth-century Leonine Wall, a portion of which connects the Vatican to Castel Sant' Angelo, first a mausoleum for a Roman emperor, later a fortress and, when necessary, a refuge for the popes. In the 1930s Mussolini gave Pope Pius XI (1922–1939) permission to connect the two by another means, the broad Via della Conciliazione (reconciliation). This made St. Peter's ever more visible but in the process destroyed an ancient neighborhood.

Much of the Vatican today is occupied by the Musei Vaticani or Vatican Museums, which along with the Sistine Chapel and the Rooms of Raphael include the Museo Pio-Clementino, the Pinacoteca, and the Gregorian Profane, the Egyptian, and the Etruscan museums. The

The number of cardinals may vary, but only those under 80 can be members of the conclave that elects a new pope.

entrance is well around the back of Vatican City—beyond Piazza del Risorgimento—on winding Viale Vaticano. To the right of St. Peter's, instead, is the Apostolic Palace with Bernini's Portone di Bronzo, the Papal Apartments (the pope appears in a window every Sunday when he is in residence to bless the faithful), and the offices of the Secretariat of State (the foreign ministry). It is from here that the pontiff rules his largely (but not entirely) spiritual empire. ■

Basilica di San Pietro

NOBODY KNOWS EXACTLY IN WHAT YEAR PETER CAME TO Rome, other than that it was after A.D. 50. And no one knows the exact year of his martyrdom, only that he was crucified in an Imperial Circus near the Vatican during Nero's persecutions and therefore sometime between A.D. 64 and 67. What we do know is that from early on his gravesite assumed a particular importance for the members of the then recently born Christian sect.

Basilica di San Pietro

- Map pp. 160–61
- Piazza di San Pietro
- 06 6988 4466
- Bus: 64, 62 to St. Peter's or 81, 492 to Piazza del Risorgimento

The present St. Peter's stands on the site of an earlier fourth-century church, built by the Emperor Constantine over the Apostle's grave.

Eager to help (and perhaps to be helped by) the growing religion, in the early fourth century Emperor Constantine laid the foundations for the first St. Peter's. Consecrated by Pope Sylvester I on November 18, A.D. 326, it had a spacious atrium and was elaborately decorated. However, when the popes returned from Avignon, opting for the Vatican over the aging Lateran Palace, they found that the old church had deteriorated and risked collapse. Exactly 1,300 years later to the day (November 18, 1626), a new St. Peter's would open its doors, but its birth was to be slow and painful. Shortly after his reign began, Julius II (1503–1513) commissioned Bramante to build a new church, and in 1506 the foundation stone was laid. But 120 more years were to pass before this massive construction, built over Peter's tomb and known throughout the world, would actually be completed.

Who built St. Peter's? Over the decades, just about everybody. And the fact that so many cooks did not spoil the broth can be considered a minor miracle in itself. The first problem was whether to use a Greek cross (four arms of equal length) or a Latin cross (a long vertical arm and a shorter crossbar towards one end, like the crucifix) as the basic plan. "Greek" said Bramante, who wanted a church similar to Santa Sophia in Constantinople. "Latin" said

Raphael. "Greek" said Baldassare Peruzzi. "Latin" said Antonio Sangallo the Younger. Michelangelo, who joined the fray in 1546 but only (only!) had time to conceive the giant dome that dominates much of the Roman skyline, was also in favor of the Greek cross plan. In the end, decades later, it was Pope Paul V (1605–1621) who finally made the decision, deciding in favor of the Latin cross and, in 1607, awarding the commission to architect Carlo Maderno.

At that time the Catholic Church was fully caught up in the Counter-Reformation, and Paul wanted the church to be at least as big as its predecessor and, for liturgical reasons, to have an even longer nave (615 feet/187 m) to heighten the importance of ritual, making processions and other rites more dramatic. Alas, this meant that Michelangelo's dome was not to be immediately visible to the entering faithful as originally planned. When completed, the dome designed by the 71-year-old maestro was also higher and more elaborately decorated than he had intended. Nevertheless, his mark on the church's structure, including the massive pilasters and the magnificent windows, is indelible.

In contrast, there is no doubt about who created **Piazza di San Pietro** (St. Peter's Square). With its elliptical shape and its two semicircular colonnades, Gian Lorenzo

The newly-restored travertine **facade**—white and ocher, with red and green accents on the Loggia della Benedizione—was also the work of Carlo Maderno and has become an internationally known landmark, although back then not everyone was pleased with the wide (360 foot/110 m), two-story facade: the French painter Henri Matisse once said it looked more like a train station than a church. There are five entrances into the portico (and another five doors into the church). The central loggia is used when the pope delivers his *Urbi et Orbi* ("To the city and to the world") blessing on Christmas and Easter as well as for the "*habemus Papem*" announcement after a successful papal election. Inside the **portico,** where Maderno's stuccoed ceiling has now been gloriously restored, note the two equestrian statues: "Constantine" (by Bernini) at the extreme right and "Charlemagne" (1725) on the extreme left; they represented the temporal power of

Pope Sixtus V moved the ancient Egyptian obelisk to its present place from its original position somewhat to the left of the basilica.

Bernini's design, commissioned by Pope Alexander VII Chigi (1655–1667), has been universally acclaimed as an architectural masterpiece. There are 284 gigantic Doric columns in the colonnade, 88 other pilasters, and 140 statues on top. Statues of Jesus, John the Baptist, and 11 Apostles decorate the church facade. Three sets of steps, flanked by statues of St. Peter and St. Paul, lead to the entrance. In the middle of the piazza is an Egyptian obelisk (see pp. 80–81) placed there before the colonnade was created, and two fountains, one by Maderno and a copy done in 1677 by Bernini. Halfway between the obelisk and each fountain is a plain stone disk reading "Centro del Colonnato." Go stand on one and see the four rows of columns in the corresponding hemicycle miraculously line into one.

Central loggia

Entrance

Facade by Carlo Maderno

Porta Santa

the Church. Right over the central doorway, and very difficult to see, is what is left of the famous "Navicella" mosaic, ("Jesus Walking on Water") by Giotto, which once graced the atrium of the old St. Peter's built by Constantine. The "Navicella" is best seen if you stand with your back to the central bronze doors to the church itself. Also from Constantine's time, they were decorated in the 15th century by Florentine sculptor, Filarete (Antonio Averulino).

The Holy Door, or Porta Santa, opened only during Holy Years, is that on the far right. The baroque interior of St. Peter's, for which Bernini must get much of the cred-

it, is overwhelming. Stand briefly on the large porphyry circle just inside Filarete's door, where Charlemagne (and others after him) knelt when crowned emperor. Now walk straight up the center nave to the transept. The bronze strips on the floor mark the lengths of other famous, but shorter, cathedrals. Just as Bernini intended, your eyes

Lantern and vault added in 1588–90 by Giacomo della Porta

Mosaics by Cavaliere d'Alpino

Cupola by Michelangelo

Cupola by Vignola (1507–1575), above the Cappella Clementina

Apse

Baldacchino

South transept

Nave

Pieta chapel

Statue of St. Peter

Tabernacle by Bernini (1674)

Papal altar

Entrance to Vatican Grottoes

One of two clocks by Giuseppe Valadier

go immediately to the enormous bronze canopy **(baldacchino)** over the papal altar, made with bronze stripped from the portico of the Pantheon. Don't miss the "Woman-in-childbirth" sequence on the columns' bases; marble reliefs depict her changing expressions and end with a smiling *bambino* (baby). The sunken *confessio* in front of the canopy, designed by Maderno, is surrounded by a balustrade with 95 perennially lit lamps and marks the tomb of St. Peter which is several levels below. Now head for the *gloria* or sunburst in the apse. This is part of a magnificent baroque monument, the **"Cattedra Petri,"** into which Bernini incorporated an early ninth-century papal throne (once thought to have been Peter's). An alabaster window with a dove (the symbol of the Holy Spirit) is in the center. Flanking this are the tombs of Pope Paul III (left) and Pope Urban VIII (right).

Naturally, you musn't forget to look up into the **cupola,** Michelangelo's architectural masterpiece, although completed well after his death in 1564. Warmly illuminated by the light from 16 windows and, in the upper portion, divided into 16 wedges by ribs that run up to the lantern at the top where God the Father is depicted, the dome is supported by four enormous pilasters. Note the mosaic decoration in the four pendentives (the triangular spaces where the pilasters reach the dome), each representing one of the four Evangelists. Their proportions are enormous. For example, St. Mark's pen is over 5 feet long (1.5 m). The Latin inscription around the base of the dome repeats an excerpt from St. Matthew (16:18) affirming Peter's importance and that of his successors: "You are Peter and on this rock I will build my church. I

will entrust to you the keys to the kingdom of Heaven."

Pope Urban VIII requested that the dome's four enormous **supporting piers** be decorated by Bernini with large *aedicolae* (niches) with oversize statues each more than 16 feet (4.8m) tall: St. Longinus (done by Bernini, himself), St. Andrew, St. Veronica, and St. Helen. Sometimes precious relics are exhibited on the balconies above them. The lance of St. Longinus (the Roman soldier who prodded the crucified Jesus with his spear), portions of the cross brought back from the Holy Land by St. Helen, and St. Veronica's veil, said to bear the image of Jesus' face. Standing against the Longinus pier is Arnolfo di Cambio's wonderful bronze **statue of St. Peter.** Once thought to be much older, it dates from the late 1200s. Naturally, you won't want to miss Michelangelo's marble **"Pieta"** in the first chapel of the right aisle and, ever since an attack, protected by a transparent bullet-proof panel. This is Michelangelo's only signed sculpture (see his signature on the sash across the Virgin's breast).

At present, 147 popes are buried in St. Peter's and some of the **tombs** are interesting. Check out that of Alexander VII (a Chigi) in a corridor off the left transept. Rich in colored marbles and statuary, this magnificent late Bernini work (1678) shows the pope kneeling in prayer and surrounded by statues representing the virtues. But lo! From underneath the folds of patterned marble, Winged Death— with hourglass in hand—rears his ugly head. The tomb of Innocent VIII stands against a pilaster in the left aisle. It was done by Antonio del Pollaiuolo and is the only papal tomb taken directly from the old St. Peter's, other than those in the Grottoes.

Keep in mind that with only two exceptions (a ceiling fresco over the "Pietà" and a Pietro da Cortona oil in the Cappella del Santi Sacramento) all the "paintings" you see here are mosaic copies of famous paintings in other churches or in the Vatican Museums. Only three monuments in the church are dedicated to women, a queen (Queen Christina of Sweden who abdicated to convert), a countess (Countess Matilda of Tuscany) who sided with the papacy in the 11th-century conflict with the Holy Roman Emperor, and a mother (Maria Clementina Sobieski, mother of the last Stuart pretender to the English throne, the Stuarts). Other things to see include the **Treasury Museum** (off the left transept) where for a small fee you can see magnificent church vestments and crucifixes, a Bernini angel and another Pollaiuolo tomb, and the **Grottoes.** Many popes including John XXIII are buried here (take the stairs at the base of one of the piers) and it will allow you a glimpse of St. Peter's shrine. Do not miss the **dome** or cupola. An elevator (there is a charge) from the far end of the portico is advisable to get you to the first level. A short climb from there will get you inside the dome where you can really appreciate the church's immense proportions. Another narrow, seemingly endless circular staircase will take you to the balcony atop the cupola from which the view is superb. But be sure you're up to it physically and are not claustrophobic. This closed-in staircase is one way so you can't change your mind halfway up. ∎

The inscription around the base of Michelangelo's dome repeats a verse from Matthew's Gospel (16:18), the basis for the Petrine theory, the primacy of the Roman pontiffs.

Musei Vaticani

EVEN IN THE BEST OF CIRCUMSTANCES, NAVIGATION around the Vatican's museum complex is not easy. To make matters worse, the museum authorities open and close entrances throughout the day, to better regulate the heavy flow of visitors. However, at the entrance on the Viale Vaticano you will find audio cassettes and panels describing the various itineraries. In peak periods, try scheduling your visit somewhat later in the day, perhaps at 12:30 or 1 p.m. This can help you avoid the long lines at opening time.

Once you have decided which itinerary to follow, select the sites that interest you the most and concentrate on those. Do not try to absorb or read everything along the way, and remember there is a lot of walking: about 0.3 mile (0.5 km) from the museum entrance to the Sistine Chapel!

Walk up the impressive spiral ramp, or take the elevator, to the ticket office and start making choices. For first-time visitors, you'll want to head for the Rooms of Raphael and the Sistine Chapel. To do this, proceed left to the **Vestibolo dei Quattro Cancelli** (Vestibule of the Four Gates), stopping to peek into the large **Cortile della Pigna** (courtyard) to see the enormous, bronze Roman pinecone found near Santa Maria sopra Minerva.

Now, turn left and walk up the stairs to the first landing to the **Greek Cross Room,** part of the Pio-Clementine Museum (see p. 175). Note the two stupendous porphyry sarcophagi here. The one on the left comes from Santa Costanza. The other, with battle scenes, was used to bury St. Helena, Constantine's mother.

Take the stairs to the second floor and walk down the long corridor, divided into three sections: the **Galleria dei Candelabri** (candelabras), the **Galleria degli Arazzi** (tapestries), and finally the **Galleria delle Carte Geografiche,** for the map frescoes showing Italy and the Church's possessions in the 1580s. From the window you can see the Vatican gardens with a Renaissance villa, the Casina di Pio IV, and, to the left,

Musei Vaticani

🅰 Map pp. 160–61

✉ Viale Vaticano

☎ 06 6988 3333

🕐 Closed Sat. p.m,. & Sun. except last Sun. a.m. every month.

💲 $$$. Free on Sun. Tours ($$$) run every day except Wed., Sun. and holidays at 10 a.m. Book on 06 6988 4466

🚌 Bus: 64 to St. Peter's or 81, 492, to Piazza del Risorgimento. Metro: Cipro-Musei Vaticani an unusual view of Michelangelo's dome. The Sala dell'Immacolata leads to the Stanze di Rafaello.

STANZE DI RAFFAELLO

Raphael's Rooms (of which there are four) were commissioned by Julius II in 1508, supposedly because the existing papal apartment reminded him too much of his hated predecessor, Alexander VI (a Borgia), and his family, including daughter Lucrezia. The first two, the Stanza della Segnatura and the Stanza di Eliodoro, are considered to be examples of Raphael's greatest work. The Stanza dell'Incendio was based on Raphael's designs but was painted primarily by his assistants. The last room, the **Sala di Costantino,** was finished in 1524 after Raphael's death, and he probably only did some preliminary

sketches. The underlying theme of this room, attributed largely to Giulio Romano, Francesco Penni, and Raffaellino del Colle, and told through scenes from the life of Constantine, is the triumph of Christianity over paganism.

The **Stanza della Segnatura** was Julius's library or study. The room is justly famous because among others it contains two of Raphael's best known paintings, the "Disputation of the Sacrament" and the "School of Athens," painted between 1508 and 1511 and meant to glorify respectively faith and philosophy. In the first, Jesus, the Virgin, and St. John the Baptist are flanked by figures from the Old and New Testaments—although only those from the New Testament have halos. Below is an altar with the Host and farther down you see

Above: Papal coats of arms decorate the balustrade of the monumental spiral staircase, designed in the 1930s by Giuseppe Momo.

Left: The bronze pinecone gave its name not only to this courtyard, but to the neighborhood near the Pantheon where it was found.

Doctors of the Church, saints, and scholars. You can pick out Dante on the right in the lower section. In the "School of Athens," Plato and Aristotle are shown in animated conversation inside a large classical building. Raphael clearly enjoyed painting his contemporaries into historical tableaus, and these abound here. Raphael himself is second to last in the group of hatted gentlemen on the right. Just in front is Bramante, in the guise of Euclid who is bending over, compass in hand, to explain a problem to his students. (Bramante is also in the "Disputation of the Sacrament," leaning over the bannister, on the

The statue of the Laocoön was found in 1506 minus its right arm, which was discovered 400 years later in a marble-worker's shop and eventually reattached (see p. 176).

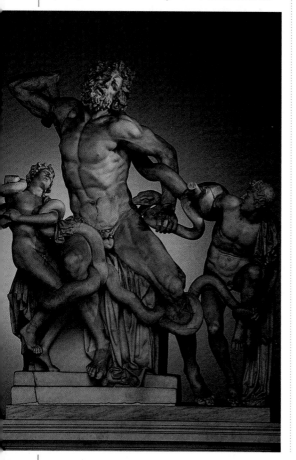

far left.) The pensive figure seated in the forefront, his head leaning on his left hand and taking notes, is Michelangelo (as Heraclitus, the pessimist).

The **Stanza di Eliodoro** (Heliodorus) is particularly noteworthy for the stunning use of color (note the Swiss Guards in the lower right corner of the "Mass of Bolsena," which depicts a 13th-century miracle) and for the dramatic use of lighting in "The Liberation of St. Peter." This room, originally a bedroom, was decorated between 1512 and 1514. The room also contains the "Expulsion of Heliodorus" (from the temple in Jerusalem), and "Pope Leo Meets Attila the Hun," recounting how St. Leo the Great (Pope Leo I, 440–461) turned Attila and his Huns away during an attack on Rome in the fifth century. Here, Raphael's penchant for painting his contemporaries' faces on historical figures created a problem. After Julius II died, Raphael repainted the face of St. Leo with the features of the new pope, Leo X (1513–1521). However, Leo X's features had already been painted onto one of the accompanying cardinals so he appears twice in the same scene.

The **Stanza dell'Incendio** (fire) was a dining room. Painted between 1514 and 1517 by Raphael's pupils, it depicts events from the lives of two of Leo X's namesakes (Leo III and Leo IV, the pope who built the ninth-century Vatican walls). The most famous painting shows how, in 847, Leo IV quenched a fire in the surrounding Borgo neighborhood by making the sign of the cross. Nearby is the small, private **Cappella di Niccolo V** (chapel of Pope Nicholas V), which was frescoed by the Florentine artist Fra Angelico. Before reaching the Sistine Chapel, you might want to visit the

Borgia Apartment, decorated with lovely frescoes by Pinturicchio and his disciples.

CAPPELLA SISTINA

Built by Giovanni di Dolce during the reign of Sixtus IV (1471–1484), this rectangular hall has seen a lot of history. It was the private chapel of the pontiffs, and for centuries it has been the room where the conclaves, or papal elections, are held. The floor is decorated in an exquisite "*opus alexandrinum*" pattern reminiscent of the cosmatesque pavements (see p. 206) from the 13th and 14th centuries, and an elegant sculpted screen—by Mino da Fiesole, Andrea Bregno, and Giovanni

Cortile della Pigna

Vestibolo dei Quattro Cancelli

Cappella di Niccolo V

Upper floor

Entrance

Stanze di Raffaello

Galleria dei Candelabri, Galleria degli Arazzi, Galleria delle Carte Geografiche

Cappella Sistina

Museo Etrusco

Pinacoteca

Borgia Apartment

Lower floor

Oriental antiquities

Classical antiquities

Etruscan/Italic antiquities

Early Christian & Medieval art

15th–19th century

Ethnology of history

20th-century art

Museo Chiaramonti

Museo Egizio

Cortile Ottagonale

Museo Pio-Clementino

Museo Pio-Christiano

Museo Gregoriano Profano

Greek Cross Room

**After 20 years of
painstaking work,
all the frescoes in
the Sistine Chapel
have been
restored to their
original glory.**

Dalmata—divides the chapel into
two sections. But the room is best
known for the recently restored wall
and ceiling frescoes, considered by
many to be the supreme example of
Renaissance, if not universal, art.

The decoration of the Sistine
Chapel can be divided into three
periods, each coinciding with an
important stage in the development
of Renaissance art. The frescoes on
the long walls were painted between
1481 and 1483; the ceiling was
painted by Michelangelo between
1508 and 1512; and his "Last
Judgment" was executed some 20
years later between 1534 and 1541.

The **long walls** were decorated
by some of the most important
15th-century Renaissance painters
(Pinturicchio, Botticelli, Perugino,
Ghirlandaio, Rosselli, Signorelli),
significantly all of Tuscan or
Umbrian origin. It was a time when,
under the impetus of a reinvigorated
and dynamic papacy, the cultural
epicenter of the Renaissance was
shifting to Rome from Florence and
its environs. On the left, starting
from the "Last Judgment," are scenes
from the Old Testament including
the "Burning Bush" and "Moses

**Opposite: The
Sistine Chapel is
the place where
the College of
Cardinals elects
the successor to
St. Peter's Throne
after a pope dies.**

slaying Egyptians" (Botticelli), the
"Punishment of Korah, Dathan, and
Abiram" (Botticelli), and the "Last
Days of Moses" by Signorelli. The
scenes on the right, from the New
Testament, include the "Baptism of
Jesus" (Pinturicchio or Perugino),
the "Temptation of Christ"
(Botticelli), the "Calling of Peter
and Andrew" (Domenico
Ghirlandaio), and "Jesus Giving the
Keys to Peter" (Perugino). On the
end wall opposite the "Last
Judgment," are the "Resurrection"
by Ghirlandaio and Salviati's "St.
Michael," both later repainted.

Michelangelo's decoration of the
ceiling (originally it was blue with
stars on it) coincided with the
mood of cultural and political self-
confidence that characterized the
early Renaissance. Michelangelo
was not particularly keen on
accepting this commission; he considered himself a sculptor, not a
painter, and wanted to keep working on Julius II's tomb, the one
which was never finished but did
spawn the magnificent "Moses" you
saw in San Pietro in Vincoli (see p.
63). When he did accept (possibly
to foil his implacable rival,

Bramante) he turned a simpler project (the "Twelve Apostles") into the more ambitious "Creation." As everyone now knows he spent four years lying on his back on scaffolding to do it.

Michelangelo's choice of subject matter was not accidental. The cosmology of the time divided world history into various epochs: The period before the Law, the period of Law (as given to Moses), and finally the period of Grace which began with the coming of Jesus. The older decoration on the side walls corresponded to the second two eras (Law and Grace), so Michelangelo decided to dedicate the ceiling to the pre-Law era, that is to the Creation, the Garden of Eden, and original sin. The decoration is sublime and has been recognized as such since the start. Hopefully,

you've brought your binoculars or at least a decent-size mirror to view the ceiling comfortably. Remember, start your gazing from the altar end of the room. There are nine central scenes on the ceiling. Alternating in larger and smaller rectangles are: "The Separation of Light and Darkness"; "The Creation of the Sun, the Moon, and Planets"; "The Separation of Land from the Sea" and "The Creation of Plants and Animals"; "The Creation of Adam"; "The Creation of Eve from Adam's Rib"; "The Expulsion from the Garden of Paradise"; "The Sacrifice of Noah"; "The Flood"; and "Noah Drunk."

Forming a border around them are portraits of prophets (going clockwise Jonah, Jeremiah, Ezekiel, Joel, Zecheriah, Isaiah, Daniel). Alternating with these are the oracles of the ancient world known as sibyls (clockwise the Persian, Erythrean, Delphic, Cumaean, and Libyan Sibyls). The triangular lunettes between the sibyls and prophets contain images of the forerunners and ancestors of Jesus Christ, while the four larger corner lunettes represent Old Testament scenes. Between the prophets and sibyls and above the triangular lunettes bearing the forerunners of Jesus, we see the figures known as the "Ignudi, athletic male nudes," painted in various poses between low, trompe l'oeil pedestals.

By the time Michelangelo got around to painting **"The Last Judgment,"** commissioned by Pope Paul III (1534–1549), the mood in Rome had changed drastically to one of pessimism. The 1527 Sack of Rome had created insecurity, and the burgeoning Protestant movement was stimulating renewed religious uncertainty and fervor. In the "Last Judgment" (which got far less favorable reviews than the "Creation," with many critics crying obscenity), you can read the drama, terror, and pathos of the era. In the center of the composition is an athletic, beardless, and severe Christ in Judgment, flanked by Mary and a collection of saints. Below, on the left, are the blessed on their way to Heaven (note the two figures suspended by a rosary, a clear anti-Lutheran statement). In contrast, on the right the damned are being pushed down to Hell while Charon, in his boat, watches. Michelangelo gave Minos, the judge of the damned (the figure in the lower right-hand corner with the donkey's ears entwined in a serpent's coils), the face of one of his sharpest critics, Biagio da Cesena, a member of the papal court. And there is a self-portrait: St. Bartholomew (below and right of the Redeemer) is holding his flayed

Right: Roman pontiffs ruled much of central Italy until the 1860s, using seals like these on important documents.

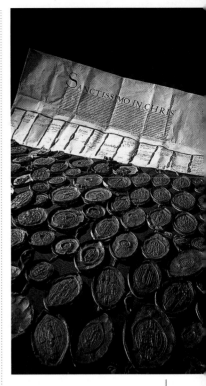

skin (recalling the method of his martyrdom) but has no beard. How so? Because the face is that of the beardless Michelangelo.

MUSEO PIO-CLEMENTINO

Access to the Pio-Clementine Museum is through the ground-floor Cortile della Pigna and up the stairs to the Palazzo del Belvedere, built during the reign of Innocent VIII. This museum has a variety of sections, but the most impressive may well be that of the vast display of classical statuary in the Cortile Ottagonale. You could say that the foundations of the entire Vatican museum complex were laid right here when, in 1503, Pope Julius II placed a statue of Apollo, ever since called the **Belvedere Apollo,** in the Belvedere's courtyard. The papal collection was significantly enlarged by Clement XIV in 1770, and the museum was opened shortly thereafter.

The list of sculptures is endless, but there are several pieces that are not to be missed, most of which are in the first several rooms. The Cabinet of Apoxyomenos, just beyond the round vestibule, houses the statue of an athlete, called the **"Apoxyomenos Athlete,"** a first-century Roman marble copy of a Lysippus bronze from about 320 B.C. An athlete in the process of scraping oil from his body, it was found in Trastevere in 1849 on the street that is named for it, the Vicolo dell'Atleta. In the Octagonal Court you'll find not only the Belvedere Apollo, but the **"Laocoön,"** possibly the most sublime classical marble group to have survived. Excavated in 1506 on the Esquiline Hill and possibly from the Domus Aurea, it is attributed to three first-century sculptors from Rhodes working from an older bronze original. It tells the story (related by Virgil in the *Aeneid*) of the Trojan priest, Laocoön, and his two sons whose warnings about the wooden horse angered Athena who sent two huge serpents to kill them. Their facial expressions convey human suffering in an unparalleled fashion. The remaining rooms include the Animal Room, the Gallery of Statues, the Gallery of Busts, the Mask Room, and the Hall of the Muses. Near the exit is a domed room with a reconstructed *biga*, or two-horse chariot.

PINACOTECA, THE OTHER MUSEUMS, & THE GARDENS

As you can imagine, over the centuries the popes have also built quite a collection of paintings, and these are kept in the **Pinacoteca**

(to get here turn right after you buy your ticket rather than left). Though not enormous, the collection is impressive. This, for example, is where you can see Raphael's "Transfiguration," his "Madonna di Foligno," and his "Coronation of the Virgin," all in the same room. There are also paintings by Giotto, Fra Angelico, Simone Martini, Perugino, Bellini, and Titian to name only a few.

For more specialized interests there are the **Museo Egizio** (Egyptian Museum), the **Museo Etrusco** (Etruscan Museum), and the **Museo Gregoriano Profano** (Gregorian Profane Museum) which displays several Greek and Roman collections, arranged either by era (Roman sculpture of the first and early second centuries) or thematically (sarcophagi, Greek originals, for example). It is in this museum that you can see the famous mosaics of athletes found in the Baths of Caracalla (see pp. 210–11). The Braccio Nuovo of the **Chiaramonti Museo,** a smaller adjunct to the Pio-Clementino that was organized by the sculptor Canova in the early 19th century, also displays Roman floor mosaics. There you will also find the famous statue of Augustus from the villa of his wife, Livia, at Prima Porta. The **Museo Pio-Christiano** (Pio-Christian Museum), displays early Christian antiquities.

It is also possible to visit the 16th-century **Giardini Vaticani** (Vatican Gardens) on guided tours that last about two hours. You get to see the medieval German cemetery attached to the Teutonic College, several major fountains, and the main buildings (mostly from outside) including the new (1971) Aula delle Udienze (Audience Hall), the Governatorato (Governor's Palace), and Casina di Pio IV, today seat of the Pontifical Science Academy. ■

Castel Sant'Angelo

THIS BUILDING HAS QUITE A HISTORY. BUILT AS A mausoleum by Emperor Hadrian (but completed after his death by his successor, Antoninus Pius), Castel Sant'Angelo has also been a fortress, a prison, a papal refuge, a barracks, a pleasure palace, and even the setting for the last act of a famous opera, *Tosca*. Like Augustus's mausoleum on the other side of the river, this circular structure with a 210-foot (64m) diameter was once topped with trees and a large statue of the emperor or, some say, a four-horse chariot.

The mausoleum served its original function for a very short time. In the third century, Aurelian incorporated it into his walls in an attempt to protect the city from barbarian encroachment. Theodoric, the city's fifth-century barbarian ruler (clearly the walls didn't work!), was the first to use it as a prison. The castle got its name only at the end of the sixth century. The city's population was being decimated by the plague when Pope Gregory the Great decided to ask for divine intercession. As he was leading a massive procession to St. Peter's he saw the Archangel Michael above the tomb in the process of sheathing his sword, as if to say that the scourge was over. Subsequently, a statue of the Archangel was placed atop the tomb, hence the new name, Castel Sant'Angelo. The bronze statue you see dates back to 1753, replacing an earlier stone one by Raffaele da Montelupo that is now in one of the courtyards.

Throughout the Middle Ages, the castle was often the scene of conflict between the papacy and one or other of the noble families vying for control of the city. During the famous Sack of Rome in 1527, Clement VII took refuge here, probably using the secret corridor (*il passetto*) that was built into the Leonine wall in 1277 and which is soon to be opened to the public.

The ancient Pons Adrianus in front of Castel Sant'Angelo was built in the second century A.D. to afford ready access to the Emperor Hadrian's Mausoleum.

Castel Sant'Angelo
- Map pp. 160–61
- Lungotevere Castello 50
- 06 681 9111
- Closed Mon.
- $$
- Bus: 87, 280, 492. Get off 62, 64 on left bank and cross over Sant'Angelo bridge

For centuries parts of the castle were used as a prison. The 16th-century Florentine goldsmith, Benvenuto Cellini, tells in his autobiography of being imprisoned here, and Puccini made it the scene for Tosca's suicide. In the 1930s it was restored and turned into a museum.

Because bits and pieces have been added on over the centuries, you'll need imagination and a discerning eye to separate the original Roman portions from the additions of later eras. In the vestibule downstairs you'll find a very useful model that shows what is left of the original structure. This, like the rooms directly above it, is in the central Roman core of the building. Walk up the long ramp, which dates back to Roman times with portions of the original mosaic flooring until, turning left, you come to the **Cordonata di Alexander VI,** a very gradual staircase that cuts diagonally across the structure and eventually ends at the **Cortile dell'Angelo.** Along the way you will walk over a drawbridge, which until 1822 could still be pulled up to protect the upper stories of the castle from unwanted intruders. The bridge spans the funeral chamber where Hadrian's remains were originally kept.

At the top is the Cortile delle Palle, named after the cannonballs stored there (the white marble plaques on the walls indicate the diameters of the balls in each pile). This is also known as the Cortile dell'Angelo because da Montelupo's gigantic angel statue was put here after its replacement. The rooms on the left are named after the various popes who inhabited them or the subject matter of their decoration. The **Sala di Apollo** has lovely "grotesque" decoration on the walls. When you come to the **Sala di Giustizia,** once a courtroom, you will be back in the Roman part of the structure. Be sure to note the fresco of the Angel of Justice, over one of the doors, by Perin del Vaga. A corridor from the Apollo Room leads to a courtyard, called either the **Cortile del Teatro,** because theatrical performances were given there during the Renaissance, or the Cortile del Pozzo dell'Olio, because of the wellhead. Just past the entrance, a short flight of stairs (through the door on the right) will take you to **Pope Clement VII's bathroom,** complete with frescoes by Giulio Romano. The other rooms off this circular courtyard were used as **prison cells** for centuries; the ones on this floor were for VIPs, the dingy ones downstairs for ordinary prisoners.

Farther upstairs is the **Loggia of Julius II,** which overlooks the Ponte Sant'Angelo, Roman in origin but lengthened in the 19th century when the walls along the Tiber were built. Up a short flight of stairs from the loggia are the **Papal Apartments** frescoed by Perin del Vaga for Paul III (1534–1549). Note another angel frescoed on the far wall and the amusing portrait of a gentleman peering out of a trompe l'oeil door. A curving corridor, decorated with more grotesques, leads to what was once the library; here, only the upper portion of the walls was frescoed because the lower part was covered by bookcases. Through a door in the center of the wall is the **Camera del Tesoro** or dell'Archivio Segreto. Until 1870 the Vatican kept its secret archives here. This room, too, is in the central Roman core. A narrow winding staircase excavated into the thick Roman walls leads up to the terrace where the bronze statue of the archangel stands and where there is a spectacular view of St. Peter's and the entire city. ∎

Trastevere: The other side of the Tiber is a warren of narrow streets and small squares. Under the Romans this was an enclave largely inhabited by foreigners and nonconformists; it still attracts those groups as well as casual visitors.

Trastevere to Gianicolo

Detail of the ceiling of the master bedroom in Villa Farnesina

Trastevere to Gianicolo

TRASTEVERE IS WHAT THE ITALIANS CALL A VERY *POPOLARE* NEIGHBOR-
hood, by which they mean one of the few still inhabited by real Romans. Until recently this was a working-class area and your typical *Trasteverino* would thus be
lower-income, extroverted, sharp-tongued—and possibly a bit
arrogant, since the residents of this area consider themselves to be the true descendants of the ancient
Romans and are also proud that this was an
insurrectionist hotbed during the short-
lived 1849 revolt against the papacy.

No one really knows why, but the Trasteverini
tend to have loud, rather hoarse voices and to
speak with a very heavy Roman intonation,
the equivalent—let's say—of a very thick
Brooklyn accent. They drink lots of coffee,
breakfast on *maritozzi* (a plain, sweet roll filled
with fresh whipped cream), and favor heavy
dishes such as *spaghetti cacio e pepe* (spaghetti
with grated *caciotta* cheese and pepper) or
coda alla vaccinara (oxtail in tomato sauce).
They are a dwindling race, since over the last
several decades many have left the area either
by choice, preferring the newer, more modern
apartments built in the postwar period, or
forced out by gentrification and spiraling
rentals. But enough remain to allow the neighborhood to keep much of its traditional color
and character.

At the same time this area—the name
means trans-Tiber (across the Tiber)—also
has a long history as a favorite residential
area for foreigners or nonconformists. This
was already the case back in ancient Roman
times when many outsiders settled here,
including tens of thousands of Jews. According
to local parish officials, in Roman times there
may have been as many as ten synagogues in
the neighborhood. The first Christians settled
here as well, explaining the presence of several
major early Christian basilicas. And the
area's international flavor was certainly
heightened following World War II, when
many foreigners chose this area because it
seemed so Roman and was (alas, this is no
longer the case) considerably cheaper than
other central neighborhoods.

Artisans abound, as do small local shops,
bars, and eateries. In fact, the trattorias of
Trastevere have always been a draw for

outsiders, espe-
cially on weekends or during the Festa de'Noiantri
("our own festival") held
every July. Nowadays, in the
evenings the restaurants
have been supplemented by
scores of small *locali* (clubs),
sometimes only a few tables,
which appeal to young people.
Many intellectuals—filmmakers,
artists, and students—also live
here. This, along with an abundance of street peddlers, art galleries, and boutiques, explains why
Trastevere is often compared to
Soho in London or New York's SoHo
or Greenwich Village.

Trastevere is divided into two
parts, one stretching upriver from

Viale Trastevere to the Vatican and nestling on the lower slopes of Monte Gianicolo (Janiculum Hill), the other extending beyond the Viale, running by Tiber Island and including lovely Piazza in Piscinula, the church of Santa Cecilia, and, at its outer limit, Porta Portese. The heart of the neighborhood, however, is Piazza Santa Maria in Trastevere, the piazza facing the magnificent basilica of the same name and which, with its cafés and restaurants, newsstand, and pharmacy, is akin to a village square for the area's residents. Many people still shop in the outdoor market at nearby Piazza San Cosimato or buy bread on Sunday mornings at the *forno* in Via del Moro. Passing through Porta Settimiana on Via della Lungara, for centuries the only road linking Trastevere to the Vatican, you come to the Botanical Gardens, once part of the beautiful,

post-baroque Palazzo Corsini, and to Villa Farnesina, on the grounds of which archaeologists found the ruins of a splendid ancient Roman villa (rooms from it have been rebuilt in the Palazzo Massimo Museum). Above looms the Janiculum Hill, where churches such as San Pietro in Montorio and Sant'Onofrio compete for attention with the breathtaking Roman panorama. ■

Rome

Area of map detail

Santa Maria in Trastevere

EVEN MOST TRASTEVERINI DON'T KNOW IT, BUT according to St. Jerome's fourth-century chronicle, at the time of Jesus's birth Trastevere was the scene of a sort of annunciation. In a veterans' hospice, oil gushed from the ground, lasting for an entire day and flowing down to the river; a clear sign, said the saint and scholar, of "the grace of Christ that would come to humanity." Since many early Christians settled in this area, it isn't surprising that in the third century a church was founded (probably by the martyred St. Calixtus) where the miracle took place. An illegible inscription on the church floor to the right of the altar marks the spot.

Widely believed to be one of the first churches in Rome, Santa Maria in Trastevere was certainly the first to be dedicated to Mary. As we see it today, with its charming *campanile* (bell tower), the basilica—completed in the 1140s—is primarily medieval in style, and somehow the 12th-century aura has lingered, despite later additions such as Domenichino's gilded, coffered ceiling (1617) and Carlo

Fontana's portico (1702) with its statues of four saints, including St. Calixtus.

The church is notable for the use of classical Roman architectural forms, which at the time were quite fashionable. The 22 columns in the nave, of various dimensions, types of stone, textures, and colors, were looted from ancient ruins. The straight trabeation (or architrave) over the columns was a throwback to classical Roman construction, a temporary rejection of the arches preferred by earlier and later architects. What truly sets Santa Maria apart are its glowingly beautiful **mosaics,** which mark a return to a tradition that had been largely discontinued. For this we can probably thank Abbot Desiderius of Monte Cassino who, toward the end of the 11th century, brought mosaic workers to Italy from Constantinople and used them, in turn, to train local artisans. In this regard, note the cosmatesque pavement (see p. 206) which, though restored in the 19th century, dates to the 1100s.

The mosaics on the facade date from the 12th or 13th centuries and show a Madonna enthroned, flanked on each side by five women, most probably the Wise and Foolish Virgins from the Gospel, although some historians believe that the work depicts a pro-

Santa Maria in Trastevere

- Map pp. 180–81
- Piazza Santa Maria in Trastevere
- 06 581 4802, 06 581 9443
- Bus: H, 23, 63, 64/8, 70/8

Left: The 12th-century facade of the church is the major landmark of the Trastevere neighborhood and dominates the piazza of the same name.

cession of eight virgins and two widows. (It's politically incorrect, but the widows, they insist, are the women whose lamps have gone out!) Note the two tiny figures at the Madonna's feet. This was a common way to represent the donors who paid for an artwork.

The mosaics inside the church are even more exceptional. Those in the half-dome of the apse date from the 12th century and show Mary, enthroned, next to Jesus, who has his arm around his mother's shoulder. They are flanked by a collection of saints including, on the left and holding a model of the church, Pope Innocent II, the donor. The prophets Isaiah and Jeremiah are on the two sides of the apse. On the next row down is Pietro Cavallini's 13th-century mosaic of the "Life of the Virgin

Mary" in six masterful scenes. Cavallini also did the mosaic showing the "Madonna and Child between St. Peter and St. Paul" on the apse's central lower segment.

The altar canopy has four porphyry columns. The sumptuous **Altemps Chapel** on the right (designed by Martino Longhi the Elder in the 1580s) has an ornate ceiling and numerous frescoes, including one that depicts the Council of Trent (1545–1563), a major event in Roman Catholicism's response to the Protestant challenge. Also interesting are the marble fragments, embedded in the walls of the facade, bearing Christian symbols, catacomb inscriptions from the third and fourth centuries. Between the gate and the facade are four magnificent medieval floor tombs. ∎

In Christian iconography, the 12 Apostles were often shown as sheep in mosaics. In the middle is the Agnus Dei, the Lamb of God or Jesus. On the ends are the holy cities of Bethlehem and Jerusalem.

A taste of Trastevere walk

This walk around Trastevere, divided into two parts, is designed above all to give you a feeling for a neighborhood that encloses a vast spectrum of sights and sounds. Local artisans, housewives, yuppies, and transplanted foreigners congregate in this area to enjoy what many people believe is one of the last remaining enclaves of "the real Rome."

Trastevere's old buildings form one of the city's most picturesque old quarters.

Start at Piazza di Santa Maria in Trastevere (see p. 182) where you can enjoy a coffee at the Café De Marzio (the one locals prefer), while taking one more look at the basilica of Santa Maria's glorious facade. Then, wearing your bags or cameras across your chest (better yet don't carry a bag, a Roman purse-snatcher can spot a tourist a mile off), exit the piazza by the newsstand and take Via della Lungaretta to Viale di Trastevere. On your right you'll see **San Crisogono ❶** (see p. 196), which has an exceptional cosmatesque pavement (see p. 206) that you don't want to miss.

Now cross (carefully) the busy avenue and proceed along the continuation of Via della Lungaretta. This will take you through a deliciously old neighborhood, to charming Piazza in Piscinula where the Mattei family once had a palace. Turn right before entering the piazza at the hilly Arco dei Tolomei, which brings you

under a fascinating medieval archway. Turn left at the next street (Via dei Salumi) and walk along it. Turn right on Via dei Vascellari, which soon becomes Via di Santa Cecilia and takes you to the piazza and church of the same name, **Santa Cecilia in Trastevere ❷** (see pp. 192–93), another absolute must.

After visiting the church, check out lovely **Piazza dei Mercanti** (between Piazza Santa Cecilia and the river), but avoid the restaurants there, which are for tourists only. Now continue along Via di Santa Cecilia to Via Madonna dell'Orto. Note the long **Complesso di San Michele a Ripa** building on your left, a 17th-century poorhouse today used for governmental offices (see p. 196). **Santa Maria dell'Orto ❸**, the facade at the end of the Via Madonna dell'Orto curiously decorated with obelisks, was once the headquarters for many guilds of the more humble occupations, such as fruit vendors and chicken keepers. Make a brief detour right on Via Anicia and ring the bell at No. 12. The custodian will let you into the magnificent, hidden 15th-century cloister of **San Giovanni dei Genovesi ❹**. Retracing your steps, continue along Via Anicia until you come to Piazza San Francesco d'Assisi and the church of **San Francesco a Ripa ❺** (see p. 196), where

---

🅼 Also see area map, pp. 180–81

▶ Santa Maria in Trastevere

🔄 1.5 miles (2.5 km)

🕐 2 hours

▶ Villa Farnesina

NOT TO BE MISSED

- Santa Maria in Trastevere
- San Crisogono
- Santa Cecilia in Trastevere
- San Francesco a Ripa
- Villa Farnesina

one of Bernini's three "Ecstasies" is displayed. Via San Francesco a Ripa, which faces the church, will take you back to Viale di Trastevere. Cross over and at the intersection with Via Luciano Manara, look left up the street at the lovely, moss-covered fountain set against the lower slope of the Janiculum Hill. Continuing along Via San Francesco a Ripa you will come to Piazza di San Callisto and then to **Santa Maria,** where you began.

The second, and shorter, part of this walk starts from the Via della Paglia (opposite the newsstand) and takes you to **Piazza Sant'Egidio** ⑥ on the right, where there is a folk art museum (Museo del Folklore) and the city's original English language movie theater. Here you have a choice. If you leave the Piazza by Via della Scala (the exiting street on the left) you will come to Piazza della Scala, where the Carmelite church

(Santa Maria della Scala) contains paintings by some of Caravaggio's pupils. The pharmacy outside is also very old. At the end of Via della Scala is the old stone **Porta Settimiana** gateway and Via della Lungara, which takes you to the **Orto Botanico** (Botanical Garden), **Palazzo Corsini,** and **Villa Farnesina** ⑦. If instead you take the right-hand exit out of Piazza Sant'Egidio, Vicolo del Cinque, the second on the right, will take you to **Piazza Trilussa** and the wonderful fountain facing the Ponte Sisto pedestrian bridge that spans the Tevere, or Tiber River. Now take Via Santa Dorotea on the other side of the fountain to Porta Settimiana. The house to the right of the arch, **Casa della Fornarina** (today a restaurant), is said to have been the home of La Fornarina, Raphael's mistress, whose painting hangs in Palazzo Barberini. ∎

Villa Farnesina

ABOUT A BLOCK FROM PORTA SETTIMIANA, THE crenelated gateway erected by the Borgia Pope Alexander VI in the 1490s, is Villa Farnesina. Built in the early 1500s as a country villa for the Sienese banker and businessman, Agostino Chigi, and later sold to the Farnese family, Villa Farnesina doesn't look like much from the outside, but don't be misled: It is considered a gem of Renaissance architecture. Sienese architect Baldassare Peruzzi believed interiors and exteriors should be integrated, and built what was then an open-air loggia as the main entrance. (Walk around to what is now the back to see the original facade.) In addition, Chigi himself was to spare no expense in furnishing his new residence, decorating it with scenes from Greek and Roman mythology.

In the trompe l'oeil loggias at both ends of the Perspectives Room, the villa's main reception room, Peruzzi tried to eliminate the distinction between interiors and exteriors.

The first room on the ground floor is the **Galatea Room** (also once an open loggia), known primarily for Raphael's "Triumph of Galatea." This wonderful fresco, dated around 1513, shows the sea nymph, wearing a red cloak, riding the ocean waves. Her seashell carriage is pulled by two straining dolphins (one of which is breakfasting on a small squid) and surrounded by cupids. A triton appears to be molesting Galatea's handmaiden. The sumptuous ceiling, done by Peruzzi himself, depicts the planets and constellations at the time of Chigi's birth. Some of the lunettes (by Sebastiano del Piombo) contain scenes from Ovid's *Metamorphoses*.

Next is the magnificent Loggia of Cupid and Psyche, which Raphael designed to look like a summertime pergola with fruit and flowers, although most of the artwork was done by his pupils. Craning at the ceiling may give you a stiff neck but never mind because the two large ceiling frescoes—the "Wedding of Cupid and Psyche" and the "Council of the Gods"—are breathtaking. Of the "Three Graces" in the fresco in the corner right of the door, the one with her back to you was probably Chigi's mistress and may have been painted by Raphael himself. The lunettes recount the various stages of Psyche's troubled relationship with the jealous Venus.

The upper floor is equally exciting. In the **Sala delle Prospettive,** the living room, Peruzzi repeated his indoors-outdoors theme, relying amply on trompe l'oeil landscapes and urban scenes with real landmarks such as

Porta Settimiana, an aqueduct, and the campanile of Santa Maria in Trastevere. Note the unfortunate graffiti, left by marauding soldiers during the Sack of Rome in 1527. Next door is the smallish **master bedroom**, a magnificent riot of color, painted mostly by Giovan Antonio Bazzi, generally referred to as Il Sodoma (the Sodomite) because of his homosexuality. The central wall, the "Wedding of Roxanne and Alexander" (the Great), is considered Bazzi's masterpiece. The right-hand wall, "Alexander's Meeting with the Family of Darius of Persia," is less accomplished (the artist reportedly felt he was being underpaid), whereas the central portion of the left-hand wall, the "Taming of Bucephalus" (Alexander's horse), was clearly painted by someone

else: When Chigi's enormous gem-encrusted bed was moved out of the house after his death, it left an empty space that had to be filled.

Chigi was a very wealthy bon vivant with a keen sense of one-upmanship. A lavish reception organized in 1518 in honor of Pope Leo X was staged in the stables (appropriately decorated for the occasion). The idea was to embarrass the Riario family across the street by demonstrating that the Chigi stables were as elegant as the Riario's dining rooms. Later the same year another reception was held at a loggia on the riverbank. Guests were surely impressed (or horrified?) when at the end of each course the servants tossed the silver dishes into the Tiber. But not to worry—Chigi had strung nets below to catch them. ∎

Legend has it that Il Sodoma's commission to paint the wedding of Alexander and Roxanne came in the nick of time. He had just been replaced by Raphael in the decoration of the Vatican Stanze 35.

Villa Farnesina

🅰 Map pp. 180–81

✉ Via della Lungara 230

☎ 06 6880 1767

🕐 Closed Sun. & all afternoons

💲 $$

🚌 Bus: H, 23, 63, 64/8, 70/8, 280

Palazzo Corsini

Palazzo Corsini

- 🅰 Map pp. 180–81
- ✉ Via della Lungara 10
- ☎ 06 6880 2323
- 🕐 Closed Mon., Sat. after 2 p.m., & Sun. after 1 p.m.
- 💲 $$
- 🚌 Bus: H, 23, 63, 64/8, 70/8, 280

ACROSS THE STREET FROM VILLA FARNESINA IS THE Palazzo Corsini, an 18th-century remake and amplification of the Renaissance palace owned by the Riario family in the 15th century, which in the 17th century became the home of Queen Christina of Sweden, a convert to Catholicism, who had abdicated and moved to Rome in 1655. The Corsini, who were Florentines, moved to Rome when Lorenzo Corsini was elected to the papacy (as Clement XII) in 1730.

Fernandino Fuga's restructuring gave this Renaissance palace a decidedly 18th-century flavor.

The 18th-century architect Ferdinando Fuga directed the restructuring, creating a new light-filled central body with an impressive and stately ceremonial double staircase leading up to the gallery and a monumental three-arched entry way. He also added another wing that was used to house the priceless Corsini library.

In 1883 the building and its art collection were bought by the Italian government, and today the building also houses the Accademia dei Lincei (1603), an academy of scholars founded to promote learning, and said to be the oldest of its kind. The **Galleria Corsini,** a suite of eight rooms that give off the atrium (one floor up), contains part of the collection of the Galleria Nazionale d'Arte Antica (see pp 100–101). The paintings, from the 14th to the 18th century, are somewhat haphazardly displayed but include one Caravaggio ("San Giovannino, The Young John the Baptist"), a lovely "Madonna and Child" by Beato Angelico, and a bust of Pope Alexander VII, a Chigi, by Bernini. There are also a Rubens, a Van Dyck, a Murillo, and a Poussin, as well as sculptures, bronzes, and furniture from the 1700s.

Despite several remodelings, the room in which Queen Christina of Sweden died on April 19, 1689, has remained as it was. Lavishly decorated, it has two yellow faux marble columns and elaborate ceilings. From the back rooms there is a lovely view of the Botanical Garden (formerly the gardens of the Palazzo) and of the lower slopes of the Janiculum Hill. ∎

San Pietro in Montorio & Bramante's Tempietto

From Trastevere a series of steps starting in Via Masi leads up to this landmark church and the adjacent Spanish cultural institute.

THIS MAGNIFICENTLY PLACED FRANCISCAN CHURCH IS generally the first stop for visitors to the Janiculum Hill. The view of the city from the entrance steps is superb and the church itself, with its fine travertine facade, is lovely. Dating from 1481, San Pietro in Montorio once enjoyed special significance in the erroneous belief that the cloister next door was the site of St. Peter's crucifixion.

Inside, there is a beautiful "Flagellation" by Sebastiano del Piombo, and works by Peruzzi, Pomarancio, and Vasari. The second chapel on the left was designed by Bernini. Somewhere underneath is the grave of the young noblewoman Beatrice Cenci, whose 1599 execution at the age of 22 for patricide excited the popular imagination. She was the subject of poems, plays, and paintings, such as Guido Reni's portrait in the Barberini Museum.

In the courtyard of the adjacent monastery is the small, circular **Il Tempietto** (little temple) designed by Bramante and paid for by King Ferdinand and Queen Isabella of Spain to mark the birth of their son. The structure—a colonnade with Doric capitals topped by a balustrade and a cupola—is thought to embody the Renaissance ideal of classical harmony and proportion. Farther up the hill in a commanding position is the **Fontana dell'Acqua Paola** (otherwise known as the Fontanone or Big Fountain). Like the Trevi Fountain, this is the *mostra terminale* of an aqueduct, the point where water first arrives from an extra-urban source. Built of material plundered from the Roman Forum, it is composed of three large central niches flanked by two smaller ones. Water gushes from all five into the pool below (see pp. 96–97). ■

San Pietro in Montorio & Bramante's Tempietto

🅰 Map pp. 180–81

✉ Piazza di San Pietro in Montorio 2

☎ 06 581 3940

🕐 Closed 12–4 p.m.

🚌 Bus: 23/44, 63/75, 75, 870

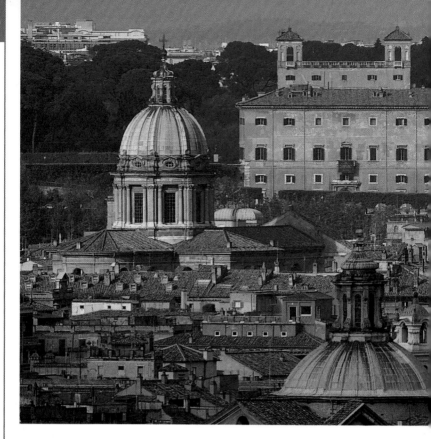

Gianicolo

THE GIANICOLO, OR JANICULUM HILL, WHICH RUNS FROM
Trastevere to the Vatican more or less parallel to the Tiber, has little sig-
nificance for ancient Roman history but was intimately associated with
the Italian Risorgimento unification movement of the 19th century.
The Porta San Pancrazio, at the top of the hill, and the surrounding
area saw major battles between the French fighting for the pope, and
Roman and Italian freedom fighters under the command of Giuseppe
Garibaldi. In the 1890s the entire area was turned into a public park.

Gianicolo
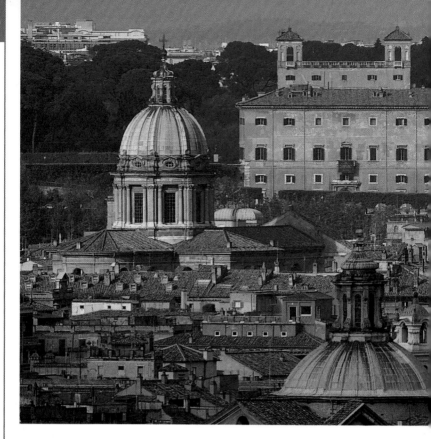 Map pp. 180–81

The Gianicolo Promenade or
Passeggiata del Gianicolo
(the main entrance is just past the
Fontana dell'Acqua Paola or
Fontanone) has a lovely tree-lined
avenue, an equestrian statue of
Garibaldi, another of his Brazilian
wife, Anita, and busts of the most
important Italian patriots. A
favorite place for the *passeggiata*

domenicale (Sunday walk) of many
families, there are souvenir sellers,
pony rides, puppet shows, and, in
the evenings, ample space for cou-
ples to park. The incomparable
view of Rome, however, is the
major attraction. From this vantage
point there is an untrammeled vista
of all of the city's major landmarks
and its magnificent domes. On

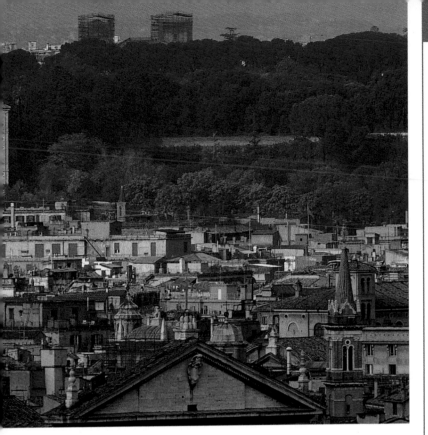

clear days, you can see all the way to the Alban Hills. Ever since 1904, a cannon shot has been fired at noon to mark the time. The view is also superb from the *faro* (lighthouse), beyond **Villa Lante,** which was donated to the city by Italians in Argentina in 1911.

Little is left of **Tasso's Oak,** the tree under which the 16th-century poet Tasso liked to sit. Tasso died, in 1595, in the convent of nearby **Sant'Onofrio,** a small single nave church founded in 1419 to honor the Egyptian acetic, Onophrius. It boasts a lovely two-part "Annunciation" by Antoniazzo Romano and a delightful 15th-century cloister, with frescoes from the life of Sant'Onofrio. ■

The seven hills of Rome

Many people think that the Janiculum was one of the original seven. Wrong. The seven hills of Rome are all on the other side of the Tiber. The Palatine, close to the river, was the site of the earliest settlements and later of the emperors' opulent residences. On the Capitoline were Rome's most important temples, and in between the two hills rose the magnificent Roman Forum. The remaining hills, which to our modern eyes do not seem terribly high, are the Caelian, the Esquiline, the Aventine, the Viminal, and the Quirinal, site of what is now the Italian president's residence (see pp. 92, 98). ■

Santa Cecilia in Trastevere

AN OASIS OF PEACE AND QUIET IN A NOISY NEIGHBOR-
hood, this church was built to honor St. Cecilia, a very important
early Christian saint, martyred by the Romans together with her husband Valerianus. It is said that on her wedding night, the well-born
Cecilia converted her husband and the two then lived together
platonically. The remains of their house, containing some sarcophagi, mosaic floors, and remnants of other classical structures, are
under the church and can be visited during church hours.

**Following a
renovation in
1725, Cavallini's
"Last Judgment"
—his only major
painting to
survive—was
covered up and
lost to sight for
almost 200 years.**

**Santa Cecilia
in Trastevere**

Map pp. 180–81
Piazza Santa Cecilia
XX
06 589 9289
Cavallini fresco in
the convent open
Tues. & Thurs.
10–11:30 a.m. only
Bus: 23, 44, 75.
Tram: H, 8

Don't expect much enlightenment
as there isn't a caption or signpost
in sight. But you should know that
Cecilia is the patron saint of music.
Some say she invented the organ,
others that she sang hymns for
three days running while confined
to the *calidarium* (steam bath) of
her house in a first, botched
attempt by third-century Roman
authorities to murder her (she was
eventually stabbed in the neck
although decapitation proved,
miraculously, impossible). Most
traces of the original Christian
shrine have been lost, but the first,
real basilica was built by Pope
Paschal I (817–824) who moved
Cecilia's body here after seeing the
location of her grave in a vision.
The church today is a hodgepodge
of styles and colors. Ferdinando
Fuga's monumental doorway open-

ing onto a garden with a fountain is
early 18th century, as is the facade.
The bell tower, however, and the
portico with its lovely mosaic decoration, are 12th century.

Inside, too, the church has a
bland, 18th-century look, probably
because of the rash decision to
encase the Roman columns in
concrete pilasters, but there are
some marvelous remnants of the
more distant past. The ninth-
century **mosaic in the apse**
showing Jesus flanked by St. Paul,
St. Agatha, and St. Valerian on the
right side and by St. Peter and
St. Cecilia on the left is a more
Byzantine version of the one you
saw in Santi Cosma e Damiano (see
p. 46). The figure farthest on the
left, holding a model of the church,
is Paschal, who cleverly had himself
placed on equal footing with the

PAVLVS·TT·S·CAECILIAE

saints and introduced to Christ by an affectionate St. Cecilia. The cosmatesque pavement (see p. 206) is, of course, medieval. The beautiful Gothic **altar canopy** by Arnolfo di Cambio dates from the late 13th century and is considered that artist's masterpiece. Below is the heart-wrenching statue of the saint sculpted by Stefano Maderno, who was allowed to view the supposedly intact body when the tomb was temporarily opened in 1599. In the chapel at the end of the right aisle there is a damaged, 12th-century fresco depicting the discovery of the saint's body.

Unfortunately, there's a lot in this church that you can't see. Church authorities have closed off the corridor where the *calidarium* is located and which also has a Guido Reni canvas. And you can't get into the Ponziani Chapel where there is a Perugino *tondo*. But don't despair: Two mornings a week, the Benedictine nuns of the adjacent convent allow you to see the enthrallingly warm colors of **Pietro Cavallini's fresco of the "Last Judgment."** Rediscovered in 1900, but dating from 1293, it is the only major Cavallini painting to survive. Christ is shown enthroned and surrounded by Apostles, saints, and angels whose multicolored wings run from cream to rose. Keep in mind that the nuns of Santa Cecilia have an extra behind-the-scenes job. Every year they are entrusted with two lambs blessed by the pope. They keep them until Easter when their wool—used to make the *pallia* (stoles) given to new patriarchs and archbishops— is shorn. ■

The sculptor Stefano Maderno is said to have carved this statue of the dead St. Cecilia after being allowed to view her body when the coffin was temporarily opened in 1599.

Isola Tiberina & San Bartolomeo

A TINY GEMSTONE OF TRAVERTINE AND PINE TREES, located in the midst of the river, Isola Tiberina (Tiber Island) has long been associated with both medicine and religion. Connected to both shores of the Tevere (Tiber), it is the site of a major hospital, Fatebenefratelli ("Do good, brothers") and a small synagogue.

San Bartolomeo

- Map pp. 180–81
- Isola Tiberina 22
- 06 687 7973
- Closed Mon.–Fri. 12–4 p.m. & weekends
- Bus: H, 23, 63, 64/8, 70/8, 280

Legend has it that in the third century B.C. a delegation of Romans returned from a visit to the sibyl in Epidaurus (Greece) with instructions to build a temple to Aesculapius, the god of healing, if they wanted an outbreak of the plague to be quelled. As they sailed up the Tiber in 219 B.C., they saw a snake like the one wound around Aesculapius' staff (traditionally the doctor's symbol). It supposedly slithered off the ship and swam to the island, indicating its choice of a temple site. Over the centuries, the island became so closely associated with this story that travertine blocks were used to give the island the appearance of a prow and a stern, and vestiges of this construction in the form of a trireme's keel (including a relief depiction of the sacred snake) can still be seen on the side facing the synagogue.

Centuries later the young Holy Roman Emperor Otto III chose the ruins of Aesculapius's temple as a site for a new church dedicated to his friend Adalbert, the first bishop of Prague, who had been martyred a year earlier in A.D. 997. Otto is said to have personally directed the building, using Roman columns and other ancient remnants for the nave and the portico. Somehow, however, poor Adalbert was to get lost in the shuffle. Otto, who would perish shortly thereafter in a skirmish with the rebellious local population, had returned from a trip to Benevento in the Italian south with the remains of the Apostle Bartholomew and

deposited them (temporarily, he thought) in his church. But then he died, St. Adalbert was quickly forgotten, and the church was subsequently rededicated to St. Bartholomew. Rebuilt in 1113 and again in 1624, San Bartolomeo has a 12th-century campanile and a baroque facade. Indoors, a marble well-head located on the steps leading up to the tribune bears four carved figures: Jesus, St. Bartholomew (holding the knife he was martyred with), St. Adalbert with his bishop's staff (although some art historians believe it to be St. Paulinus of Nola), and Otto III with crown and scepter. ∎

Tevere

It runs right through the city, but nowadays the Tevere, or Tiber does not play much of a role in the lives of everyday Romans. It's there, it's picturesque, and it is spanned by a variety of bridges, including charming Ponte Sisto from which there is a glorious view that includes St. Peter's. But ever since the end of the 19th century, when high embankments were built to put an end to frequent flooding, the *"Biondo Tevere"* ("the Blonde Tiber," named for its yellowish, muddy bottom) has taken a back seat to other major city rivers. This, however, was

not always the case. Romulus and Remus, supposedly the founders of Rome, were discovered on the banks of the Tiber by the she-wolf who adopted them. In ancient times, the Tiber was a major point of access for ships sailing the Tyrrhenian Sea. The Ripa Grande, the large commercial river port in Trastevere, and the smaller Porto di Ripetta (which until the 19th century boasted a monumental, tiered riverside staircase believed to be the inspiration for the Spanish Steps), were of vital importance to the city. ∎

"Tiber in Rome" (1685) by Gaspar van Wittel shows how accessible the Tiber was to Romans before the 19th-century embankments closed it in. Both bridges to the island, still in use today, date back to Roman times.

More places to visit

COMPLESSO DI SAN MICHELE A RIPA

Today the massive 1,099-foot-long (335 m) San Michele complex houses government offices, a branch of the Central Restoration Institute, and is open to the public when temporary exhibits are hosted. Located on the bank of the Tiber once occupied by the ancient river port called Ripa Grande, it was founded in the late 17th century to give refuge, and in some cases to teach a trade to society's rejects: orphans, delinquents, and vagabonds. For this reason its history is linked to that of Roman artisanship. For example, in the 18th century it housed a well-known tapestry workshop. San Michele was also a home for old folks and spinsters (one of the courtyards is named the "Cortile delle Zitelle" (or spinsters). Its upper end faces the Porta Portese gate, one of the entrances to the Sunday flea market.

🅰 Map pp. 180–81 ✉ Via de San Michele 25 ☎ 06 58431 🕐 Closed Mon. 💲 $$ 🚍 Bus: 75

SAN CRISOGONO

Situated on busy Viale di Trastevere, this large church is often passed over by tourists, but missing it would be an error. Built in the style of a classical Roman basilica, its cosmatesque pavement (see box p. 206) may be one of the most beautiful in Rome. Again, the baroque facade and interior decoration give little clue of its medieval beginnings. Only the Romanesque campanile (one of the few in Rome with a triangular top) and the right flank are a giveaway to the church's 12th-century origins. The two porphyry columns supporting the triumphal arch are the largest in Rome. The gilded and blue coffered ceiling is a masterpiece of the genre, but the 17th-century painting on the ceiling (the "Triumph of St. Crisogono" by Guercino) is a copy. The original is in Stafford House in London. The medieval altar has a cosmatesque finish and the framed late 13th-century mosaic in the apse ("The Virgin Between Two Saints") has been attributed to Pietro Cavallini. The

underground ruins of the original fifth-century paleo-Christian church are open to the public, although large groups should reserve. During the July Festival of Noiantri the church becomes a Marian sanctuary. "The Virgin of Mount Carmel," an icon, is carried in procession through the streets and put on view in the church for eight days.

🅰 Map pp. 180–81 ✉ Piazza Sonnino 44 (Viale Trastevere) ☎ 06 581 8225 🕐 Underground church closed 11:30 a.m.–4 p.m. daily & Sun. p.m. 💲 $ 🚍 Bus: H, 23, 63, or 64, 70, 170, then change to 44

SAN FRANCESCO A RIPA

St. Francis took a vow of poverty, but at St. Francis on the Riverbank (named for the ancient riverport that once existed near here) someone may not have been paying attention. When the 13th-century church (erected on the site of a hospice where the saint had once stayed) was rebuilt in the 17th century, it was done in no-holds-barred baroque—the decor is deliciously opulent with dramatic paintings, gold leaf, and stucco everywhere. The Pallavicini Chapel at the end of the right aisle nearest the altar is a triumph of multicolored marble; wall tombs sport garishly wicked winged skeletons. The Altieri Chapel across the aisle holds one of Bernini's majestic "Ecstasies," the magnificently dramatic statue of the "Blessed Ludovica Albertoni" (1674). Pay no attention to the putto heads gazing down on the blessed Ludovica as she reclines in mystical ecstasy; they are made of stucco and were added later. Bernini preferred natural and concealed lighting, but if the light from the side window is not enough for you, by all means ask the sacristan to turn on the electric light for a moment. He'll also take you to visit St. Francis's cell with its stone pillow.

🅰 Map pp. 180–81 ✉ Piazza di San Francesco a Ripa 88 ☎ 06 581 9020 🕐 Church closed noon–4 p.m. & Sun. 1–4:30 p.m.; St. Francis's cell closed 12–4 p.m. & Sun. a.m. 🚍 Bus: 8, 23/8, 56/8, 63/8, 70/8 ∎

Once a busy commercial center for cattle traders and farmers, this area is littered with the remains of ancient temples and monuments. On its borders are Piazza Venezia, the 16th-century Jewish Ghetto, and the quieter Aventine Hill.

Forum Boarium to Aventino

**Floor mosaic at Caracalla
depicting a gladiator**

Forum Boarium to Aventino

MILLING CATTLE, DUSTY HERDSMEN, AND TRADERS SEEKING TO SELL THEIR bovine charges for the best price possible; farmers from outside the city, their carts heaped high with pumpkins, cabbages, asparagus, lettuce, olives, lemons, figs, apples, and even truffles, loudly touting the quality of their produce; barges laden with amphorae filled with olive oil and barrels of grain. Some 2,000 years ago, the area between the Campidoglio and the Tiber was the location for the Forum Boarium and the Forum Holitorium, two bustling outdoor markets for, respectively, cattle and vegetables. Straddling a road that led straight to the city center (the Roman Forum), the Velabrium as it was called, was a marshy expanse, which according to legend was the place where the herdsman, Faustulus, found Romulus and Remus after they had washed up on the shore and been suckled by a friendly she-wolf.

The adjacent area also abounds in vestiges of Roman rule. The remains of the Teatro di Marcellus, designed by Julius Caesar's architects (but completed by Augustus), were incorporated into an elegant 16th-century palazzo. Three columns from the temple of Apollo Sosianus are dramatically outlined against a medieval urban background, and the remnants of the Portico d'Ottavia, which Octavius dedicated to his sister, lie within the area known as the Ghetto, to which the Jews of Rome were confined for centuries.

Today's hustle and bustle, however, differs drastically from that of yore. A large modern thoroughfare, opened in 1933 and now called Via Luigi Petroselli, takes car and bus traffic past the large central Registry Office (the Anagrafe) to Piazza Venezia. But some remarkable remnants of those earlier times remain, and all you need to enjoy them is a vivid imagination. Picture the cattle traders as they crowded under the Arch of Janus to avoid the winter rain or the scorching summer sun. Imagine how they and their business partners decided to build a second arch (the Arch of the Moneylenders) to honor (let's say, flatter) Emperor Septimius Severus. Surely you can appreciate why an anonymous wealthy cattle-owner would be willing to spend many, many *sesterces* to build a circular temple in honor of Hercules Victor, considered the god of merchants and traders. A second rectangular temple was built to provide offerings to Portunus, the god of ports. The church of San Nicola in Carcere (note the columns embedded in its walls) incorporates the ruins of three other temples. Several of the other churches in the

area, in particular San Giorgio in Velabro, San Teodoro, and the hauntingly beautiful Santa Maria in Cosmedin, were once *diaconates*, food distribution centers for the poor run by the early Christian Church. Centuries later, the powerful Crescenzi family built its medieval fortress (again incorporating many classical bits and pieces) to serve as a toll house for the Pons Aemilius (Emilian bridge). Only a

small section of this remains, and later Romans appropriately named it the Ponte Rotto (broken bridge).

To the south, in contrast then as now, lies the Aventine, a tree-lined residential area that today, as in the past, is an oasis of tranquility. Despite its proximity to the center, the Aventine has always been somewhat removed from the scramble of everyday life. The

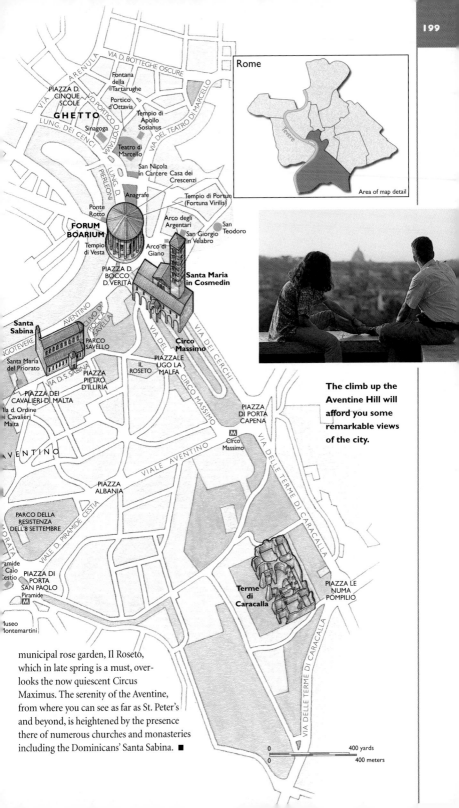

Rome

Area of map detail

The climb up the Aventine Hill will afford you some remarkable views of the city.

municipal rose garden, Il Roseto, which in late spring is a must, over-looks the now quiescent Circus Maximus. The serenity of the Aventine, from where you can see as far as St. Peter's and beyond, is heightened by the presence there of numerous churches and monasteries including the Dominicans' Santa Sabina. ■

0   400 yards
0   400 meters

You can't see it but the fourth-century Arch of Janus stands over the Cloaca Massima, the Roman Forum's main sewage drain which empties into the Tiber.

Forum Boarium

- ⓜ Map pp. 198–99
- 🚌 Bus: 81, 95, 170, 628

Forum Boarium's temples, arches, & *diaconates*

THE MASSIVE ARCO DI GIANO, OR ARCH OF JANUS, HASN'T much in common with the triumphal arches built by emperors such as Titus and Septimius Severus, but that's because its purpose was primarily practical. Despite its decorations (the niches on the facades held statues, and various deities are depicted above the archways), this was primarily a covered crossway, erected to protect the cattle traders of the Forum Boarium from the inclement weather.

The same goes for the tiny **Arco degli Argentari** (Arch of the Moneychangers), attached to the church of San Giorgio al Velabro. Erected in A.D. 204 by the cattle merchants and their financial backers, and dedicated to the Severans, it was basically the gateway to the cattle market. If it seems dwarfish, remember that centuries of silt and debris accumulation have raised the ground level, hiding a good part of the bottom section, made of plain travertine to avoid wear and tear from passing bovines. The upper portion, of white marble, is decorated with reliefs showing members of the imperial family performing religious rituals. Septimius Severus and his wife are on the right and Caracalla (who erased his brother Geta's image after murdering him) is on the left.

Facing the arch, at Via del Velabro 3, is an iron gate and a lovely arched passageway, unfortunately now inaccessible, which leads to an entrance to the Cloaca Massima, the enormous sixth-century B.C. drain system that ran from the Roman Forum to the Tiber.

As for **San Giorgio in Velabro,** this former *diaconate* (food distribution center) is dedicated to St. George (of dragon-slaying fame) who, contrary to popular belief, was not British but rather an early Christian martyr from Palestine. Here you will find a late 13th-century Madonna and Saints fresco attributed to Pietro Cavallini and a lovely 12th-century portico and bell tower. By the way, the saint's relics (including, they say, his head) were brought to this church in the middle of the eighth century when Pope Zaccaria reportedly came across them languishing somewhere in the Lateran Palace.

Across Via Petroselli, only a stone's throw from the river, is the **Tempio di Portunus,** a first-century B.C. temple dedicated to Portunus, the god of harbors, which was long known as Fortuna Virilis (Men's Fortunes). Rectangular, with a colonnaded porch and some remnants of the stucco used to create a white, marblelike effect, it is an excellent example of basic temple architecture, and it is almost intact. Guess why? Starting in the ninth century, this building (like the Pantheon and many others) was turned into a church. The medieval house of the Crescenzi family across the narrow Via del Ponte Rotto has Roman columns embedded in its walls and a classical architrave made from ancient fragments. Right behind Portunus's temple is the lovely round shrine which for cen-

turies was mistakenly called the **Tempio di Vesta** because of its resemblance to the temple of that name in the Roman Forum. Instead, experts now say, it was almost certainly dedicated to Hercules Victor. This should not surprise us since back then every cattle owner knew that Hercules, who slew the giant Cacus for stealing his cattle, was a god well worth propagating. Indeed, the god's image is on the upper left of the Moneylender's Arch. This temple, too, was turned into a church but the original parts, in white marble, are easy to spot. Many of the 20 Corinthian columns are originals. ∎

Right: These three Corinthian columns are all that is left of the temple to Apollo, a Greek god adopted by the Romans. Rebuilt several times, these ruins are from the first century.

Romans, Jews, & Christians walk

This part of Rome encompasses the Jewish Ghetto and the few remains of an area that the ancient Romans dedicated to knowledge and entertainment as well as to commerce. Today it is home to many artisans and merchants, Jewish and not. It is also a desirable address for up-and-coming professionals.

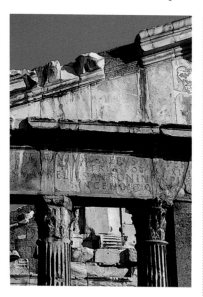

The gateway to the Porticus of Octavia, once about the size of a city block. Greek paintings and statues were displayed here.

Start this walk in front of the Tempio di Portunus and proceed up to the Lungotevere where, traffic permitting, you can cross the street to the other side. If you make it across, you will be rewarded with a magnificent view of **Isola Tiberina** (Tiber Island) with San Bartolomeo and its bell tower. Farther to the right, the restored Torre dei Caetani, or Pierleoni tower (soon to be opened to the public), stands like a sentinel over the oldest bridge in the city, the Ponte Fabricio or Ponte Quattrocapi (62 B.C.). At the stoplight by the bridge, cross back (in greater safety) and you will find yourself at the beginning of the **Via del Portico d'Ottavia ❶,** the main street of the Ghetto (see p. 204). The building on your left with the square dome is Rome's modern central **sinagoga,** or synagogue, built a century ago in an odd, but not unpleas-

ing, mock Assyro-Babylonian style. The synagogue's temple and museum *(Closed Fri. p.m. & all Sat.)* are interesting.

The small church on your right is **San Gregorio della Divina Pieta,** one of the churches where the Jews were forced to attend Christian sermons. They could avoid this torment only by paying a bribe or, as many did, using earplugs. Over the door there are inscriptions in both Hebrew and Latin. Now walk down the Via del Portico d'Ottavia to the large marble pediment supported by columns, all that's left of the **Portico d'Ottavia ❷,** the huge colonnade built by Augustus in 23 B.C. for his sister, Octavia. In the Middle Ages, the church of **Sant'Angelo in Pescheria** (*pescheria* means "fish market") was built into its ruins. See the marble plaque on the far right pilaster? It says that any fish head (considered quite a delicacy) longer than the plaque itself was to be handed over to city officials.

Where the street makes a 90-degree turn to the left, note that the buildings on the left are newer than those on the right. Why? Because of poor sanitary conditions in the over-crowded Ghetto, a century ago everything from here to the river was razed and rebuilt. At Nos. 1 and 2 is the **Casa di Lorenzo Manilio ❸,** built in 1497 by uniting several structures. Classical inscription and beautiful Roman reliefs are embedded in the walls. The pastry shop on

---

Ⓜ Also see area map, pp. 198–99
▶ Temple of Portunus
⟷ 1 mile (1.5 km)
🕐 1.5 hours
▶ Santa Maria in Cosmedin

NOT TO BE MISSED
- View of Tiber Island
- Portico d'Ottavia
- Casa di Lorenzo Manilio
- Fontana delle Tartatughe
- Teatro di Marcello

the corner (at No. 1), Boccione, makes delicious Jewish cakes and pastries, but remember that Jewish food in the Mediterranean has little to do with the Eastern European specialties known back home. Backtrack a few paces to the Via della Reginella, which leads to Piazza Mattei with its delightful Turtle Fountain. The **Fontana delle Tartarughe ❹** (see p. 96) was built in the 1580s by Taddeo Landini to a design of Giacomo della Porta. Take Via dei Funari (the Street of the Ropemakers) and peep into the courtyard of Palazzo Caetani at No. 31 to observe the fragments of classical sculpture covering the walls. **Santa Maria in Campitelli ❺** (1662–1667), in nearby

Piazza di Campitelli, is architect Carlo Rainaldi's masterpiece.

Exiting the square from its farther end, on your right you'll see the remains of the **Teatro di Marcello** and the three surviving columns of the **Tempio Apollo Sosianus**. The theater was erected between 13 and 11 B.C. and dedicated to Marcellus, Augustus's nephew and, until his premature death in 23 B.C. his probable heir. A short distance on is **San Nicola in Carcere ❻**, the medieval church built into the remains of the Forum Holitorium's three temples. Then proceed along Via Petroselli to **Santa Maria in Cosmedin ❼** with its seven-story campanile (see pp. 205–206). ■

The Ghetto

The Ghetto
 Map pp. 198–99

THE PAPAL BULL ISSUED BY POPE PAUL IV ON JULY 12, 1555, confined the Jews of Rome to a walled-off area of less than 3 acres (1.3 ha) where they were forced to live for almost 300 years. One motive was simple anti-Semitism. But the Counter-Reformation zeal inspired by the Protestant schism probably also played a key role in the creation of the Ghetto, formally abolished only in 1883.

Jews have lived in Rome since the second century B.C., settling first in areas favored by foreigners, such as the Aventine and Trastevere. However, by the time the Ghetto was decreed, many Roman Jews, especially merchants, had already moved to this commercially thriving riverport neighborhood. Tiber Island was often referred to as the Pons Judaeorum and the **Piazza delle Cinque Scole** (off today's Via Arenula) had five temples and was called Piazza Giudea by everyone, Jews included. The papal edict made it illegal for Jews to live elsewhere, barred them from certain professions and forced them to attend church services. Although enforcement was patchy, severe overcrowding was inevitable. In the 1600s, some 6,000 people crammed into this tiny area when the gates closed at sunset.

More than half of Italy's 35,000 Jews live in Rome.

Roman Jews are neither Ashkenazi nor Sephardic and pride themselves on being part of a community that pre-exists the destruction of the Jerusalem synagogue in A.D. 70. This entitles them to enjoy certain privileges such as eating lamb at Passover. But if the kosher restaurants you see start you dreaming of a pastrami sandwich or a bagel, forget it. Jewish people have been in Rome so long that often (pork dishes excluded) the Jewish and Roman cuisines are almost indistinguishable. Some favorites of Jewish origin are *carciofi alla Giudea* (fried, whole artichokes), *filetti di baccalà fritti* (fried codfish fillets), and marinated zucchini. The Jewish bakery on **Via di Portico d'Ottavia** is known for its *ricotta* cheesecakes (chocolate or berries). The area is dominated by the imposing synagogue. History was made here in 1986 with Pope John Paul II's unprecedented visit. ∎

Santa Maria in Cosmedin

UNFORTUNATELY, THIS CHURCH IS KNOWN PRIMARILY FOR the Bocca della Verità (Mouth of Truth), a stone disk inside the 12th-century portico with the carved image of a sea god that inexplicably tempts hordes of tourists to see whether, as medieval legend had it, the mouth will bite off a liar's hand. Please don't waste time on an old cistern cover that has no artistic merit. Set in the heart of an area rich in ancient monuments and memories, Santa Maria in Cosmedin has enough real, albeit understated, treasures to further illustrate this city's perennial transformations.

The two columns flanking the door inside, the three others embedded in the left wall, and the freestanding, shorter column in the sacristy are remnants of an earlier structure. In the fourth century, this was the seat of the *statio annonae*, the city office for food distribution and market inspection. By the sixth century, it had been turned into a *diaconate*, a center set up by the Church to provide food and other services to the poor. An oratory was added then, but it was only in the eighth century that Pope Hadrian (772–795) turned it into a bona fide church, donating it to Greek Christian refugees from the religious turmoil in Byzantium. It thus became Santa Maria in Cosmedin, or, as it was sometimes called Santa Maria de Schola Graeca.

Whichever name you prefer, both testify to the eastern origin of the new church's parishioners. Cosmedin is no doubt derived from Constantinople's famous Kosmidion Monastery and neighborhood whereas Schola Graeca (which means Greek School) speaks for itself.

Damaged during the Norman invasion in the late 11th century, it was restored early in the next century and the redbrick columned porch, the portico, and the lovely seven-story Romanesque bell tower date from this period. The former shelters treasures that are far more

interesting than those of the Bocca della Verita, placed on the left-hand wall only 370 years ago. The marble decoration around the portal dates from the 11th century. The tomb to

The church's Romanesque bell tower stands across from a baroque fountain, just one example of the city's artistic stratification.

to spiritual contemplation. This church abounds in Eastern or Byzantine influences, primarily the *schola cantorum*, the walled-off area reserved for worshippers, *matronei* (the balconies reserved for women), and the *iconostasis*, the marble divider delimiting the priests' domain.

The magnificently patterned floor is pre-cosmatesque (12th century), whereas the decorated Gothic canopy over the main altar is dated 1294 and is signed by Deodato, a son of one of the Cosmas (see below). There is cosmatesque decoration on the paschal candlestick (note the stylized lion at its base) just behind the right pulpit. And don't miss the framed eighth-century mosaic in the sacristy with its fine gold background, which comes from the original St. Peter's. The outstretched hand in the bottom left corner (perhaps one of the Magi) has led many experts to conclude that it was a scene from the Adoration of the Three Kings. ■

In medieval times women suspected of infidelity were questioned with their hand inside the sea god's mouth and warned they'd better tell the truth or be bitten.

its right is that of Alfano, the papal chamberlain who supervised the church's 12th-century restoration. The inscriptions on the wall record ninth-century donations. In the hush of the church's penumbra it is easy to feel yourself transported back in time and possibly moved

Santa Maria in Cosmedin

🗺 Map pp. 198–99

✉ Piazza Bocca della Verità 18

☎ 06 678 1419

🕐 Closed 1–2 p.m. in summer & 1–3 p.m. in winter

🚌 Bus: 81, 95, 170, 628

The Cosmati marble workers

Cosma must have been a common name in the 12th century; or maybe it was given to the sons of many Roman stonecutters for some other reason. These "Cosmati" can be said to have reinvented mosaic art in Rome. The cosmati technique or cosmatesque are the terms now used to describe their type of inlay decoration which relied on the use of tiny pieces of colored marble—red, green, black, white—to create intricate patterns at times resembling Islamic geometrical motifs. Often, in a break from ancient Roman techniques, the Cosmas combined them with larger stone rounds and strips to make multicolored pavements such as those in Santa Maria in Cosmedin,

San Crisogono, and Santa Maria in Trastevere. Cosmati work was also applied to church accessories such as paschal candlesticks (notable in San Lorenzo), tombs, episcopal chairs and pulpits, and the small columns often used in church cloisters and which glitter like jewels in the sun. The most impressive examples of the latter in Rome are the cloisters of San Giovanni in Laterano and of San Paulo fuori le Mura, both of which are signed by Pietro Vassalletto and his son, masters of this kind of workmanship. The production of cosmati work was interrupted in the 14th century when the popes fled temporarily to Avignon and never again reached its former levels. ■

Circo Massimo

IF YOU LOOK DOWN AT THE CIRCO MASSIMO (CIRCUS Maximus) from the imperial residences on the Palatine Hill, you can almost hear the crowds cheering on the city's most popular charioteers as their two-wheeled chariots—probably a *quadriga,* drawn by four horses—rounded the course for the seventh and last time.

Charioteers once raced here, their colors—white, red, green, or blue—signifying membership in one of the *factiones* or parties that paid for the outfitting of the equestrian teams. Today, however, there is little to see here. Archaeologists say that the starting gates and the *spina,* or raised spine, that ran down the middle of this race course, still exist. But they have yet to be excavated and here, too, you will have to rely on your imagination to picture what may have been one of the largest stadiums that humankind has known. A long rectangle about the size of a football field, it had a triple tier of stone and wood bleachers that is believed to have held over 250,000 people.

Tucked into the valley between the Palatine and the Aventine (two of Rome's famed seven hills), the Circus Maximus dates back to the fourth century B.C. and is the oldest of the known Roman circuses. During the frequent *ludi* (games), the circus was primarily for horseracing and chariot races, although gladiatorial exhibitions were sometimes held there, as were public executions. Its last use as a Roman circus dates back to A.D. 549, during the reign of the Ostrogoth (barbarian) king, Totila, who had temporarily won control of Rome from the city's then Byzantine rulers. It then gradually fell into disuse (at one point cabbages were grown here). The small medieval tower at the eastern end, has absolutely nothing to do with the original circus. It belonged to the Frangipane family, which during the Middle Ages controlled much of this area. ■

More people in ancient Rome watched chariot racing than any other sport, and charioteers vied with gladiators as the era's most popular sports heroes.

Circo Massimo
- Map pp. 198–99
- Bus: 75, 81, 95, 170, 628. Metro: Linea B (Circo Massimo)

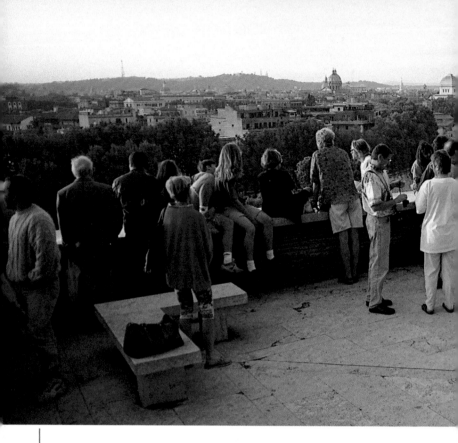

Aventino

THE MOST PICTURESQUE WAY TO GET UP TO THE AVENTINO (or Aventine Hill) and to Santa Sabina is to walk up the lovely cobblestone street called Clivo di Rocca Savella, which starts about 110 yards (100 m) from Santa Maria in Cosmedin (along Via Santa Maria in Cosmedin, the continuation of Via Petroselli).

Aventino

Map pp. 198–99

Santa Sabina

Map pp. 198–99

Piazza Pietro d'Illiria 1

06 574 3573

Closed 12:15–4 p.m.

Bus: 75, 81, 95, 170, 628

A gate in a medieval wall which was once part of the powerful Savelli family's fortress leads to the **Parco Savello,** called the Parco degli Aranci because of the orange trees brought from Spain in the 13th century by St. Dominic, founder of the Dominican order. An oasis of peace and quiet, this is one of the loveliest sites in Rome with an unbelievable panoramic view of the city.

The imposing rear view of the Dominican basilica of **Santa Sabina** makes it easy for you to grasp the essentials of fifth-century church architecture. The apse is clearly outlined, and you can see how the center part of the church, over the nave, is higher than the sides, permitting greater illumination through the clerestory windows. When you leave the park (this time through its main entrance), note the wonderful *mascherone* (mask) on the wall to your right, used in the 16th-century fountain by Giacomo della Porta.

By the time this church was built, Christianity had come out of the closet to become a mainstream religion and, as you can see from the 24 fluted Corinthian columns, the remaining mosaic decorations above the entrance door, and the beautiful Roman marble inlay ornamentation above and between the arches, this church was built to be seen. The mosaic over the entrance is particularly interesting: Two female figures, ever so much like two classical Roman matrons, represent the major components of early Christianity, the pagans or gentiles ("*Ecclesia Ex Gentibus*"), and the Jews ("*Ecclesia ex circumscisione*"). The gold lettering on a deep blue background is striking. And don't miss the cypress door on the far left of the portico. Its 18 fifth-century paleo-Christian panels depict scenes from the Old and New Testaments, including one of the earliest surviving representations of Jesus's Crucifixion.

Some 219 yards (200 m) farther along Via di Santa Sabina you'll come to a quaint piazza with obelisks set atop the surrounding walls, **Piazza del Cavalieri di Malta,** designed by the 18th-century graphic artist, Giovanni Battista Piranesi. The monumental entrance, also by Piranesi, leads to the residence of the Grand Master of the Knights of Malta, **Villa del' Ordine dei Cavalieri di Malta.** Piranesi (who is buried there) also designed the church inside, **Santa Maria del Priorato.** You can't get in there, but peep through the keyhole to see the justifiably famous picture postcard view of the dome of St. Peter's. ∎

About a thousand years ago, the Holy Roman Emperor Otto III is said to have watched from here as workmen built St. Bartholomew on Tiber Island.

Terme di Caracalla

WHEN SEPTIMIUS SEVERUS TOOK POWER IN A.D. 193, HE WAS concerned—as any new emperor would be—with consolidating the power of his dynasty. Public works were already known to generate popular support so Septimius and his son Caracalla decided to imitate Vespasian (the Colosseum) and Trajan (the Basilica Ulpia) and built the mammoth imperial baths complex which, historians say, covered 119,600 square yards (100,000 sq m) and could accommodate up to 10,000 people. Begun in A.D. 206 and inaugurated in A.D. 217 by Caracalla, the Severans' Baths sought to follow Trajan's lead in going beyond simple hygiene and pleasure to satisfy the needs of a leisured class. You came here not just for a swim and a sauna but, as in any elitist club, to while away a lazy afternoon, to catch up on you reading, or even to do some networking and make a business deal or two.

Terme di Caracalla

🅰 Map pp. 198–99

✉ Via delle Terme di Caracalla 52 (at the intersection with Via Antonina)

☎ 06 574 5748

💲 $$

🕐 Closed Sun. p.m. & Mon.

🚌 Buses: 75, 81, 95, 628. Metro: Linea B (Circo Massimo)

To build the Baths of Caracalla, an average of 9,000 workers were employed daily for five years.

The Baths of Caracalla have been "out-of-order" ever since the sixth century when the invading Goths destroyed the aqueducts and cut off its water supply. The majestic ruins which loom in the shadow of the second crest of the Aventine Hill will give you only a partial idea of the Baths' extravagant scale. Along with the bathing rooms, there were libraries (Greek and Latin), art galleries, meeting halls, and a stadium. The buildings were surrounded by a shaded esplanade with fountains, playing fields, and a covered portico. The materials used in the decorations were lavish, as can be seen from the mosaics now in the Vatican Museums, such as the "athletes in training." The sculptures were often monumental; examples are the enormous granite basins incorporated into the fountains of the Piazza Farnese of the so-called Farnese Bull and the Farnese Hercules, both in the Naples' archaeological museum.

Plundered repeatedly over the centuries, little is left of the Baths' original grandeur and as in other ancient Roman sites you will have to use your imagination. The main bathing rooms (which could reportedly seat 1,600 people at one time) formed an axis of the central quadrilateral. Secondary rooms were arranged around the *apodyterium* (dressing room), the *palaestrae* (open-air exercise rooms), the *calidarium* (hot room), *tepidarium* (warm room), and the *frigidarium* (cold room). Other structures, like the libraries, were outside the perimeter.

Your visit begins in one of the two workout rooms *(palaestrae)*. This, like its twin on the far side of the complex, contains segments of black-and-white mosaic decoration and patches of multicolor mosaic flooring. A door leading out of the workout room leads to a dressing room with a black-and-white pavement, a vestibule, and then, a few steps down, to the *natatio* (swimming pool). Another brings you to an *atrium* and then into the *frigidarium*. If you walk straight through here and the transition room on the other side, you'll come to the other *palaestra* with its many mosaic panels. Next to nothing remains of the enormous and circular *calidarium* with its seven plunge baths except two brick pilasters. The dome, now long gone, was said to have been as big as the Pantheon's. ∎

More places to visit

CIMITERO ACATTOLICO

The cemetery for non-Catholics was founded in 1738 to provide a final resting place for the foreigners who not only visited Rome but died in it as well. These include the famous—such as Keats and Shelley—and the ordinary, such as 16-year-old Rose Bathurst who in 1824 fell off her horse and drowned in the Tiber, and Devereau Plantagenet Cockburn, who died in 1850 (aged 21) after vainly traveling through Europe in search of a suitable climate.

Banked up against a piece of the Aurelian Wall, their final resting place, now almost filled to capacity, is verdantly tranquil, a place of blossom and bird song and a refuge for some of the city's most beautiful felines. Pull the bellcord and tell the gatekeeper which tomb you wish to visit. Genuine mourners pay nothing, tourists are asked to make a small donation (a few thousand lire would be suffi- cient), and if you're short of time, remember

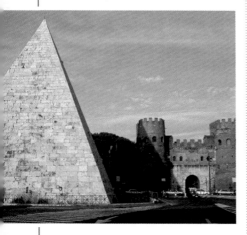

In the fifth century, Emperor Honorius doubled the height of Rome's towers, including those of the Ostiense Gate.

you can see Keats's grave from outside, through a small window in the cemetery wall at the start of Via Caio Cestio. Interestingly enough, that street is named after the first well-known non-Catholic to be buried in the area: Caius Cestius, a senior Roman magistrate who died in 12 B.C., having built himself a pyramid (on the next corner) for a tomb **(Piramide di Caio Cestio).** In the third century A.D., like other preexisting monu- ments, it was incorporated into the walls built to protect the city from the growing threat of barbarian attack. This probably accounts for its survival over the centuries.

🅜 Map pp. 198–99 ✉ Via Caio Cestio 6
☎ 06 574 1900 🕐 Closed Mon. 🚍 Bus: 23, 75, 280 🚇 Metro: Linea B (Piramide)

MUSEO MONTEMARTINI

This former power station on the Via Ostiense (the road that in ancient times led from Rome to the Basilica of San Paolo and then on to the seaport of Ostia) has been restructured, restored, and transformed into a small, decen- tralized branch of the Capitoline Museums. Originally conceived as a holding space while the Capitol's museums were undergoing restoration for the Jubilee, it has now wisely been decided to make the collection perma- nent and no more than a handful of pieces are likely to be returned to their original home.

Surprisingly, this modern-day industrial structure has proven to be a dramatic and provocative setting for the classical beauty of these 400-odd Capitoline marbles. The innova- tive juxtapositioning of ancient statuary with the dark metal machinery of this early 20th- century behemoth is entrancing. The Machine Room displays pediment sculptures and friezes from temples in the area once known as the Circus Flaminia (around the Teatro di Marcello), from Pompey's theater and from the Capitoline Hill. In the Furnace Room you can see a series of statues from the *horti*, the exten- sive monumental gardens of aristocratic resi- dences of the late Republican and Imperial eras. The Column Room, which is organized along chronological lines contains, among other things, artifacts and other remains from the ancient sanctuary dedicated to Fortune and Mater Matuta (the sacred area of S. Omobono) statuary and mosaics from the Esquiline necropolis and bronze and marble portraits (busts) etc. from the late Republican era.

🅜 Map pp. 198–99 ✉ Via Ostiense 106
☎ 0657 48030 🕐 Closed Mon. 💲 $$
🚇 Metro: Linea B (Piramide) then walk ■

Life didn't stop at the gates of Rome and neither did death. Often built over martyrs' tombs, several early Christian churches lie outside the ancient walls, while Roman tombs dot the lovely Appian Way.

Fuori le Mura (Outside the Walls)

Classical motif detail from Santa Costanza mosaic

Fuori le Mura

FUORI LE MURA, OR OUTSIDE THE WALLS. THESE ARE WORDS THAT HAVE A particular significance for a Roman even if the Aurelian Walls that once totally surrounded the city no longer have the function or the import of the past. Until fairly recently, in fact, almost all of inhabited Rome was inside the 5-mile (12 km) perimeter begun during the reign of Emperor Aurelian (A.D. 270–275), continued by Maxentius, and eventually doubled in height by subsequent emperors, such as Honorius. In a sense Rome (like most ancient settlements) has always been a walled city. A sixth-century B.C. king, Servius Tullius, built fortifications to protect the nascent city, the so-called Servian Walls, of which only a few small sections remain. But the Aurelian Wall was something else. It enclosed all seven hills, the Campus Martius, and Trastevere, which means that almost all of Rome's major monuments are within this area. What remained outside—catacombs, monasteries, vineyards, and farmland—was far more vulnerable. This included San Paolo, San Lorenzo, and Sant'Agnese, all of which have Fuori le Mura attached to their names to distinguish them from other downtown (or later) churches.

As a defensive strategy, the distance between two rampart towers could not exceed the range of arrows.

The mammoth ring of brick wall had an obvious function and a corresponding significance. Aurelian, who had already repelled the Alemanni, built the wall to protect the city in the event of another barbarian onslaught. This was not to happen for another 140 years, precisely until A.D. 410 when the Goths sacked the city, a prelude to the conquest of Spain. The feeling that the walls were necessary was the first step in the decline of an empire which had been deemed invincible. So *fuori le mura* meant vulnerability, difficulties, and distance.

As built by Aurelian, the wall was interspersed by a series of 18 *porte* (gates), many of which are still in use today, in the sense that city traffic passes through them. The *porte* often became the gateways or portals for the consular roads (in the Republican era the leaders who took the place of the kings were known as consuls) which, together with the aqueducts, made the Romans famous throughout the world. The first of these, leading out from the massive Porta San Sebastiano, was the Appia Antica, or Appian Way, inaugurated in 312 B.C. and named for the city's then ruler, Appius Claudius Caecus, who also built the first aqueduct (the Appia). The fact is that in the fourth century B.C., Rome was becoming a force to be reckoned with. The Roman Republic, founded in 509 B.C., had quickly conquered the rest of Italy and soon after had begun its expansion into much of the then known world. Military campaigns meant troop movements, and troop movements meant that roads were a major necessity. In its first stage, the Via Appia ran only to Capua in the Italian

Rome

G.R.A.

A24

Al dir

G.R.A.

Tevere

Area of map detail

south. Later its importance was assured (the historian, Statius, dubbed it the Regina Viarum, the Queen of Roads) when it was extended to Brindisi and Taranto in Apulia, in the heel of the Italian "boot," effectively becoming a pathway to the Middle East.

The Via Appia, once the site of grandiose funeral processions such as that of Emperor Augustus in A.D. 14 and of triumphal marches into the city by returning army legions, quickly became a cemetery for the rich and powerful as well. The first section of the road was apparently crowded with commemorative tombs, only a small number of which have survived

intact. With its statues, friezes, and once legible Latin inscriptions it was no doubt a site to behold. Starting in the first century A.D., when Christianity took root and began to spread, and lasting until about the fifth century, catacombs were carved out of the soft tufa rock to build deep, underground cemeteries for the multiple burials of the Christian dead (the Romans considered it unsanitary to bury the dead within the city walls). The damp, underground galleries, which sometimes ran for many miles, have interesting Greek and Latin inscriptions, faded frescoes, imperial seals, and sarcophagi. ■

Via Appia Antica

CYPRESSES AND UMBRELLA PINES; THE RUINS OF AN aqueduct silhouetted against the cobalt-blue Roman summer sky, its dried out redbrick arches now only a haven for—who knows?—an owl's nest, some crabgrass, a cluster of wild fennel or caper, a few red poppy blossoms; a long narrow road that stretches unwaveringly ahead, leading southwest, lined with the remnants of marble tombs; and—believe it or not—those large, irregular flagstones that still pave some sections of the road, often rutted by the wheels of carts and chariots that passed here so very long ago, are the originals, hewn by hand from the basaltic lava cliffs of the nearby Alban hills.

Via Appia Antica
🅜 Map p. 215
🚍 Bus: 218, 628, 714

Museo delle Mura-Porta San Sebastiano
✉ Via di Porta San Sebastiano 18
☎ 06 7047 5284
🕐 Closed Mon. (Currently closed for restoration, but due to reopen late Spring 2000.)
💲 $

Casa del Cardinale Bessarione
✉ Via di Porta San Sebastiano 9
☎ 06 5728 5738 (to arrange tours in English)
🕐 Sat. & Sun. guided visits at 10 a.m., 11 a.m. & noon

The most graphic evidence of Roman expansion, imperial roads are still visible throughout the Mediterranean, from Morocco to Turkey.

In many ways, given the impact of nature, the scene here has not changed all that much over the centuries. What you are seeing is more or less what St. Peter would have seen when he left Rome, fleeing Nero's persecution, had Jesus not appeared to him at what is now the tiny church of Domine Quo Vadis and convinced him to return to Rome and certain martyrdom. It is also approximately what the Apostle Paul saw when he entered Rome in A.D. 56 as a prisoner.

Today the Via Appia Antica, or Appian Way, is many things to many people: a mecca for pilgrims headed for the Church of San Sebastiano; a destination for the catacombs, where early Christians were buried during the last centuries of the Roman Empire; and a draw for modern-day Romans, eager for a dose of haunting beauty (or a good meal) only a few miles from downtown. The road formally begins at **Porta San Sebastiano,** the gate in the Aurelian Wall (once called Porta Appia) where, by the way, there is a small, interesting **museum** that allows you access to the tower (a great view) and a walk along the parapets. But on lovely Via di Porta San Sebastiano itself, you will find some interesting sites: the Renaissance house of Cardinal Bessarione; **Casa del Cardinale**

Bessarione (on the right at No. 9); and then, farther up on the left, the verdant **Parco degli Scipioni** with the Scipio family tomb. Out the other side of the park, across Via di Porta Latina, is the picturesque church of **San Giovanni a Porta Latina.** Right before you reach the porta is the **Arco di Druso** (Arch of Drusus), part of the Antoniana Aqueduct which supplied the **Terme** (baths) **of Caracalla.**

About 100 feet (30 m) along the Appian Way, is the road's only extant original Roman milestone, and a bit less than half a mile (1 km) farther on, on the left, is the **Domine Quo Vadis** church. Facing it is the entrance to the **Catacombe di San Callisto** (see p. 219). A little farther along is the church of **San Sebastiano fuori le Mura** with its catacombs (also see p. 219). San Sebastiano is one of the seven churches a medieval pilgrim had to visit to earn a plenary indulgence. Built in the early fourth century (the bodies of Peter and Paul were allegedly hidden here during one of the more violent periods of anti-Christian persecution), it was later dedicated to the martyr, Sebastiano. The church was rebuilt in the 17th century.

If you've enjoyed yourself so far, from now on you are really in for a treat. For those with good legs, a car,

The Appia Antica is a popular outings spot for Italians who like to picnic among the ruins.

Circo di Massenzio e Mausoleo di Romulo

- 🅰 Map p. 215
- ✉ Via Appia Antica 135
- ☎ 06 780 1324
- 🕐 Closed Mon.
- 💲 $. Guided tours Sat. a.m. ($$)
- 🚌 Bus: 218 from S. Giovanni, 714 from Termini to S. Giovani

Tomba di Cecilia Metella

- 🅰 Map p. 215
- ✉ Via Appia Antica 161
- 🚌 Bus: 218 from S. Giovanni, 714 from Termini to S. Giovani

or a bicycle, the next mile or so of the Appian Way becomes increasingly beautiful and evocative. First, on the left, are the fascinating remains of the fortified villa built by Emperor Maxentius (A.D. 306–312), whose siege mentality led him to prefer this location to the Palatine. The site includes the **Mausoleuo di Romulo,** the emperor's young son who died in A.D. 309, and a Roman circus, **Circo di Massenzio,** that, though smaller, is much better preserved than the Circus Maximus and will give you a better idea of what these racecourses were like. The stones on the ground between the remnants of two towers show where the 12 *carceres* (starting gates) were located. You can clearly see the *spina*, once decorated with obelisks and other monuments, which ran down the middle and around which the *bighe e quadrigae* (chariots drawn by two or four horses) would have raced. Built by Maxentius shortly before he was killed by his brother-in-law, Constantine, the circus was never really used. At 1,700 feet (518 m) long it is believed to have had a capacity of about 10,000 people.

Next comes the massive, circular **Tomba di Cecilia Metella.** In the 13th century, as you can see from the crenellation around the top, the powerful Caetani family transformed this monument into a sort of medieval fortress for their estate across the road. Originally this was the tomb of the wife and daughter of two of Emperor Augustus's most noble worthies, the consul Quintus Metellus Creticus and M. Licinius Crassus, scion of an extremely wealthy family. The marble frieze has reliefs of flowers, ox skulls, and weapons. Inside there are interesting inscriptions and decorations, probably taken from other tombs. Traveling on you will find yourself increasingly in the open countryside where umbrella pines alternate with funerary remains. Off to the left are the ruins of the impressive Acqua Marcia aqueduct. The last big monument, about 5 miles (8 km) from the Porta, is the **Casal Rotondo,** the largest tomb on the road. A round tomb, this time on a square base (with a house and garden on the top), it is believed to be a memorial to the poet Messala Corvinus erected by his son. ∎

Early Christian symbolism included fish, Greek letters, and animals, but never portraits of Jesus nor scenes of the Crucifixion.

Catacombe di San Sebastiano

Map p. 215

Via Appia Antica 136

06 780 8847 (church); 06 785 0350 (catacombs)

Closed 12–2:30 p.m. & all day Sun.

$$

Bus: 218 from San Giovanni. 628 to Porta San Sebastiano from the Corso or Piazza Venezia. On Sun. and holidays 760 from Circus Maximus or the Baths of Caracalla. Stop and Go bus with hourly departures stops at the Catacombs of San Sebastiano

Catacombe di San Sebastiano

Inside the Catacombs of San Sebastiano, four levels have been excavated. The tour of this catacomb, which has second-century **pagan tombs** along with Christian chapels, will take you down a staircase studded with pieces of sarcophagi with imperial seals. Underneath the church, you'll see an area with three decorated pagan tombs with some very attractive frescoes and a floor mosaic. It is believed that both Christian and pagan funerals were held in the elaborate central chapel, the vault of which has acanthus and lotus-leaf stucco decorations. The **Chapel of Symbols** has early Christian symbols carved in it. Up another staircase is a **dining room** for funeral banquets. The graffiti date back to the second century. ■

Catacombe di San Callisto

The Catacombs of San Callisto are the best known of the Roman catacombs and the first official underground burial site for early Christians, including many second- and third-century martyrs. Excavations have revealed five different levels of *loculi*, niches where the bodies, wrapped in sheets, were placed in tiers. The openings to the *loculi* were closed with slabs of marble, but these have long since disappeared, as have any artifacts of value. A major attraction of the 40-minute guided tour (available in different languages) is the **papal crypt** with the remains of several martyred early popes. Nearby, with its Byzantine frescoes, is the **Cubiculum of St. Cecilia,** whose body was discovered here by Pope Paschal I and moved to Santa Cecilia in Trastevere (see pp. 192–93). Other cubicles have frescoes and Christian symbols carved on the walls. In the crypt of St. Eusebius is a sarcophagus containing two mummified bodies. ■

Catacombe di San Callisto

Map p. 215

Via Appia Antica 110

06 513 01580

Closed 12–2 p.m. & all day Wed.

$$ (children $)

Bus: 218 from S. Giovanni, 714 from Termini to S. Giovanni

San Paolo fuori le Mura

San Paolo fuori le Mura

- 🗺 Map p. 215
- ✉ Via Ostiense 186
- ☎ 06 541 0341
- 🕐 Closed 1–3:30 p.m.
- 🚌 Bus: 23, 170. Metro: Linea B (Basilica San Paolo)

THE CHURCH OF SAN PAOLO FUORI LE MURA (ST. PAUL Outside the Walls) seems a bit isolated, but remember that until the eighth century it was physically linked to the city by a long, covered portico that led to Porta San Paolo, the city's southernmost gate. The church, originally a simple shrine, was built over the spot where St. Paul was buried after being beheaded (as a Roman citizen he could not be crucified) at the nearby Abbey of the Three Fountains (the head supposedly bounced three times before coming to rest).

San Paolo's cloister is considered by many to be the most beautiful in Rome.

A small basilica built here by Constantine was replaced later in the same century and enlarged by subsequent emperors. By the ninth century (and until the new St. Peter's was built), it was the largest church in Rome and reputedly the most beautiful. Unfortunately, it was almost totally destroyed by an 1823 fire. However grandiose its 19th-century replacement may be, it is lacking in warmth and unlikely to move you, but a visit will give you an excellent idea of what a classical Roman basilica looked like. San Paolo's construction supposedly mirrors that of Trajan's magnificent Basilica Ulpia (see p. 54), the grandest of the imperial basilicas.

San Paolo's is immense. The large central nave is flanked by two sets of side aisles that are separated by 80 enormous columns. The **bronze doors,** which survived the fire, were made in Constantinople in 1070 and decorated with Old and New Testament scenes. Other pre-fire survivors include the fifth-century mosaics in the **Triumphal Arch,** a 13th-century mosaic in the apse, and, on the inner side of the arch, more mosaic decoration, mostly attributed to Pietro Cavallini. The Gothic canopy over Paul's tomb, dated 1285, is the work of Arnolfo di Cambio. Don't miss the 18-foot (5.5 m) 13th-century cosmatesque **paschal candlestick,** decorated with figures of animals, plants, and scenes from the Passion of Christ. The Cosmati maestri who fashioned it also worked on the **cloister** which, though small, is astonishingly lovely with its fluted and spiraling colonnettes. ∎

San Lorenzo fuori le Mura

ANOTHER OF THE SEVEN PILGRIM CHURCHES, SAN LORENZO
fuori le Mura (St. Lawrence Outside the Walls), is the only church in
Rome to have suffered serious bombing damage during World War
II. Mostly, however, it is unusual in that it was formed from the fusion
of two early churches, the Minor and Major Basilicas.

St. Lawrence, one of many early
Christian martyrs, died a particularly gruesome death, roasted alive
in the year A.D. 258 on a smoldering
grid. Like many early Christians,
he was buried in a catacomb outside the city on the ancient Via
Tiburtina. St. Lawrence's gravesite
quickly became a popular destination for pilgrims, and in A.D. 330
Emperor Constantine, by now a
true friend of Christianity, built a
church in his honor. In the sixth
century the Minor Basilica was
rebuilt (by Pope Pelagius) right
next door to a fifth-century place of
worship honoring the Virgin Mary.
Centuries later, in 1216, another
pontiff (Honorius III) joined the
buildings after knocking down their
apses. The **chancel** (the area
where the priest officiates) and the
ten columns with superb
Corinthian capitals surrounding it,
are from Pelagius's church. In fact,
on the inner face of the chancel
arch there is a sixth-century mosaic
in which Pope Pelagius is seen
holding a model of the building.

The **nave** and **aisles,** slightly
lower in level, belonged to the
second church. Its splendid 12th-
century cosmatesque pavement was
reconstructed after the war. Admire
the richly decorated cosmatesque
paschal candlestick and a magnificent *ambone* (pulpit) in the same
style. In the portico, lovely frescoes
dramatize the lives of St. Lawrence
and of St. Stephen. The remains of
both these saints, together with
those of St. Justin, are in the crypt.
From the sacristy, in the right aisle,
you come out into a charming 12th-
century cloister. The campanile is
from the same period. ■

The ciborium
over the main
altar dates from
the mid-12th
century and
stands over St.
Lawrence's tomb
in a crypt below.

**San Lorenzo fuori
le Mura**

🔼 Map p. 215
✉️ Piazzale del Verano
3
☎️ 06 491 511
🕐 Closed 12:30–3:30
p.m.
🚌 Bus: 71, 492, 204.
Tram: 30B (from
Aventine, Colosseo,
San Giovanni)

Sant'Agnese fuori le Mura

SANT'AGNESE, WHO WAS ONLY 13 AT THE TIME, WAS martyred in A.D. 304, and her cult became so popular that by the end of the century a basilica had been built over her tomb. Most impressively, the church was founded by a member of Emperor Constantine's family, although experts are still undecided whether it was Constantine's daughter (Costantina or Costantia) or perhaps a granddaughter of the same name.

Sant'Agnese fuori le Mura

- Map p. 215
- Via Nomentana 349
- 06 8620 5456
- Church: Closed 12–4 p.m. Mon.–Sat. & all p.m. Mon. & Sat. Catacomb: Closed 12–4 p.m., Mon. p.m., & Sun. a.m.
- $
- Bus: 36, 60, 62, 317. Metro: Linea B (Piazza Bologna), then walk or take bus 168, 310, 445, 542 along Via 21 Aprile

Don't let such uncertainty interfere with your appreciation of this site, and of the mausoleum around the back that Costantia/Costantina later constructed for herself, today called Santa Costanza. The mosaics in the two buildings represent different moments in the development of Western art.

Sant'Agnese outside the Walls was built by Pope Honorius I (625–638) over Agnes's catacomb (open to the public) and into the side of a hill. You enter the complex on ground level from Via Nomentana and then descend a broad staircase (early Christian tombstones and inscriptions are embedded in the walls) to reach the front entrance. The seventh-century **apse mosaic** has a gold background against which Sant'Agnese (clothed like a Byzantine princess and with the sword of martyrdom at her feet) stands between two popes. The figures are totally Byzantine, with no trace of substance or mass beneath their garments.

In contrast, the mosaic decoration in the ambulatory, or arcade, of **Santa Costanza,** the mausoleum originals of which are evident, is an eloquent example of classical mosaic art. Note the absence of any explicit Christian symbolism or iconography which had probably not yet developed. The ceiling is covered with a variety of motifs—geometric, classical leafy scrolls, amphorae, trees, and animals—all in the best pagan tradition. ∎

Rome lends itself beautifully to the Roman's passion for the *gita fuori porta* (day outing). The city's surroundings include, amid bewitching scenery, seaside resorts, lakes, charming hilltowns, and important historical monuments.

Excursions

Detail of the Fontana della Natura in the Villa d'Este in Tivoli

Excursions

THE REACH OF THE ROMAN EMPIRE WAS EXTENSIVE. AT ITS HEYDAY ITS influence was felt far and wide, as far north as Britain, as far south as North Africa, and by the end of the first century A.D. all of Asia Minor and much of the Middle East had come under its sway. But the first focus of Roman expansion was, as is natural, close to home. Rome was founded in the eighth century B.C., and when the seven early legendary kings started looking around for their first conquests and colonies they looked at their immediate surroundings. The story goes that Ancus Marcius, the fourth king of the nascent city-state, was prescient enough to have founded Ostia, the seaport at the mouth of the Tiber River. However, this is almost certainly just a legend; the earliest remains found at Ostia date from the fourth century B.C. and the colony, in the form of a *castrum* (fortified city), was probably founded at that time.

Legend or not, it was clear from the start that an outlet to the Mediterranean was essential for growth and expansion, and indeed Ostia was to have immense strategic and commercial importance for Rome. It was, for example, the terminus for the massive grain imports from North Africa that allowed Rome to implement its policy of *panem et circensis* (bread and circuses), which proved successful in assuring the affections of the populace. Ostia Antica was the headquarters for the Annona, which was responsible for supplying Rome with grain and distributing it (generally at no cost) to the people. The Annona's presence in Ostia gave impetus to the proliferation of guilds and corporations involved in other kinds of trade. The mosaic remains of their storefronts in the Piazzale delle Corporazioni testify to their importance. So does the advanced level of decorative embellishment in the city in general, the proliferation of baths and temples, and of the *insulae* (multistory apartment houses) that will give you a good idea of what life was like in Rome as well.

Early expansion also looked eastward, and it wasn't long before the Romans set their sights on Tibur in the Sabine Hills. Originally inhabited by tribes such as the Sabines and the Volsci, it was conquered first by Tiburnus or Tiburtus, the son or grandson of a Greek hero named Amphiaraos, and quickly became the object of Roman attentions because of its strategic location on the banks of the Aniene river. Not surprisingly, when conflict between the two finally broke out Rome emerged as the victor and Tibur's fate was sealed. By the first century B.C. its relatively cool climate and lush vegetation had made it a well-touted holiday resort for well-born, well-off Romans. It was here, in fact, that Augustus came to consult the Albunea Sibyl, who saw in one of the young emperor's dreams the onset of Christianity (thereby winning him an unusual special mention in the iconography of the Aracoeli church on Capitoline Hill in Rome). Brutus and Cassius, Julius Caesar's assassins, had villas here, as did the poets Horace and Catullus. And it was to Tivoli that emperors such as Trajan and his successor, Hadrian, repaired to wait out the hot and sultry summer months far from the heat of Rome. Even Totila, the Ostragoth chieftain who briefly conquered Rome in the sixth century, made Tivoli the capital of his short-lived reign.

It was, however, Hadrian, (A.D. 117–138) who really put Tibur on the map. His magnificent imperial villa (Villa Adriana) may well be the major architectural achievement of the philosopher-emperor from Spain to whom one must already feel grateful for the Pantheon and Castel Sant'Angelo. The town's traditional appeal to the Roman elite may have reached its apex during the Renaissance, most notably after 1550 when Cardinal Ippolito II, a scion of the wealthy d'Este family, became governor and settled here. The d'Estes' architects turned an old monastery into a sumptuous palace, embellishing it with magnificently elaborate terraced gardens and a Mannerist complex of secluded grottoes, classical statuary, waterfalls, and cascading fountains. ∎

Ancient Tibur was both the home of the Sibyl and the source of travertine—Roman marble.

Ostia Antica

The Baths of Neptune in Ostia got its name from a black-and-white mosaic of the sea god in his chariot.

YOU'VE SEEN THE TIBER AS IT WINDS ITS WAY THROUGH Rome. You know the location of the old river ports where barges and boats laden with everything from fresh produce to squealing livestock ended their upriver course. Now let's follow the river back down to its mouth on the Mediterranean and see what remains of the settlement, Ostia, that grew up there, becoming first a military installation and then a major port. In its heyday, the inhabitants exceeded 100,000 and the city extended over 148 acres (60 ha).

Rome (14 miles/23 km away), it can be reached easily by car or subway.

Ostia (the name comes from *ostium*, the Latin word for "river mouth") was probably Rome's first colony, and the oldest remains found date from the fourth century B.C. By late Republican times (the second century B.C.), it had become Rome's major port, as well as an important naval outpost. Throughout the first two centuries of the Imperial period, Ostia was to thrive, gradually acquiring the trappings—fora, basilicas, porticoes— of an important urban center. It

Ostia Antica

🗺 Map p. 225

✉ Viale dei Romagnoli 717, Ostia

☎ 06 5635 8036

🕐 Closed Mon.

💲 $$

�æ Metro or train: From Termini, Linea B to Magliana or San Paolo, change to the Ostia train. From the Piramide, take the Ostia train at old Stazione Ostiense, get off at the Ostia Antica stop.

A visit here will give you an excellent idea of what life was like in a normal Roman city. Unlike Pompeii, Ostia was not a resort for the rich or a pleasure dome for the powerful. Although its location on the terminus of an international trade route inevitably gave it a cosmopolitan character, it was above all a living, breathing urban complex made up for the most part of ordinary people. Much of its decorative embellishment (for example, its omnipresent mosaics) and its structures—the baths, temples, civic center, and particularly its *insulae* (multistory apartment houses)—can be assumed to be similar to those in Rome and will help you imagine lifestyles in the nearby capital. The site, easily negotiable because of its limited size, is hauntingly lovely. Not far from then had to face the competition of Portus, the newer port begun by Emperor Claudius in A.D. 42, completed by Nero, and enlarged by Trajan. It maintained its primacy until Constantine's reign in the early fourth century when a newer port was built nearby. It gradually became more residential, but was to remain an important passenger port for decades to come. For example, when St. Monica died here at the end of the fourth century, she and her bishop son, the future St. Augustine, were awaiting passage to Africa.

In later times Ostia was to be abandoned, ravaged by Saracen invasions and endemic malaria. But at its apex, it had all the amenities, cultural and otherwise: a lovely Roman theater (still used in summer), scores of bathhouses, shops, temples, and taverns, as well as commercial offices, which were concentrated in the Piazzale delle Corporazioni, a sort of ancient mall or port authority.

Who lived (and worked) in the Ostia of yore? Shippers and ship-builders, merchants and traders, grain weighers, tanners, rope-makers, carters, tavern keepers, prostitutes, and priests. Only about half of the city has been excavated, but digs have brought to light invaluable information about lifestyles and residential patterns. Unlike Pompeii, domestic architecture here mostly eschewed the one-story *domus*, a dwelling built around a central atrium and preferred by the wealthy. The lower- or middle-class dwellings of Ostia were rooms or apartments in buildings that by law were allowed to climb as high as four stories (about 46 foot/14 m high). Windows were probably made of mica or selenite (when not simply covered by fabric). Balconies were frequent and the ground floor was often, though not always, reserved for shops.

To get the best possible sense of this ancient coastal town you'll need several hours. Start at the beginning

In summer you can still see productions of classical drama in Ostia's theater, built 2,000 years ago by Augustus's son-in-law. Three surviving ancient masks are on the right side of the stage.

of the **Decumano Massimo,** the main drag as it were, lined with shops, baths, theaters, and warehouses. This street was the in-city continuation of the Via Ostiensis (which connected Ostia to Rome), and, as in most Roman colonies, was crossed at mid-point by the Cardo Massimo, which formed the north–south axis. Just inside the Porta Romana, the main gateway to the city, to the left, is a large **Statua di Minerva Vittoria** (statue of Victory), dating from the first century A.D., which may have once stood atop the gateway. To the right, a path leads to the **Terme dei Cisiari,** carter guild's bathhouse, with a black-and-white mosaic of a cart and driver that you really shouldn't miss. Farther along the Decumanus, at the **Osteria di Fortunato,** or Tavern of

Fortunatus, the mosaic inscription on the floor appears to be a form of early advertising. It reads "Fortunatus says: drink from this bowl to quench your thirst." Continuing on you will come to the **teatro** or theater, built by Agrippa, which held between 2,000 and 3,000 people. Originally, there were three tiers of seats (the top »one has not survived) and, like today, there were snack stands in the alcoves between the external arches on the ground floor.

The pulse of second-century ancient Ostia may have beat hardest, however, in the **Piazzale delle Corporazioni,** a huge portico right behind the theater where some 70 local guilds and foreign corporations had their offices and whose trademarks, which have supplied historians with invaluable depict the day's fare. You can make out eggs, fruits, and vegetables.

If at the next crossroad you turn right, you'll come to the **Museo Ostiense** that displays artworks found during the excavations. A snack bar and bookshop are behind it. Otherwise, continue on to the Cardo Massimo. Turn left and you'll find yourself in the **Foro** or Forum, which is where the Cardo and the Decumano intersect. At one end of the square was the **Capitolium.** Ostia's major temple, dedicated to Jupiter, Juno, and Minerva, still has the broad staircase that leads up to the *cella,* with niches, now empty, for statues of the gods. A second temple, **Tempio di Roma e Augusto,** dedicated to Rome and Augustus, faced it at the opposite end of the forum. The terme, or baths, and the basilica, or law courts, flanked the area on the right and left. And you won't want to miss the *forica* (public latrine) near the baths, with its 20 seats, all in a row.

Farther down the Decumano, you will eventually leave the section corresponding to the *castrum* (the earlier, fortified city) and enter the newer Ostia Antica. Take Via della Foce, to the right, from which a long pathway (to your left) leads to the **Mitreo delle Pareti Dipinte** where the sun god Mithra was worshiped. Continue along the Via delle Foce to the **Insula degli Aurighi,** where frescoed walls depict two charioteers, the sports heroes of yesteryear. Leaving the *insula* from the other side, find your way back to the Decumano, where there are more baths, a traders' guild (the **Schola di Traiano),** and a market (the Macello). Back behind the Temple of Rome and Augustus, on the Cardo, are a number of elegant one-story houses. The **Domus di Giove Fulminatore** has an interesting welcome mat, a mosaic depicting a phallus. ■

information, have been immortalized in the arcade's mosaic floors. Next turn right from the Decumanus onto the Via dei Molini, then take the first street on the left, Via di Diana. The **Casa di Diana,** a large *insula,* or apartment block, gives you a good idea of the architectural layout of the times: shops on the ground floor, apartments with windows on the first floor, and balconies higher up. Next is the **Thermopolium,** a latter-day restaurant or snack bar that is fascinating for the degree to which it shows how little things have changed. The Thermopolium has stone seats near the door (for waiting customers, perhaps?), an L-shaped counter, and near a door leading out to a patio are holes in the wall probably for coat hooks. Above a display shelf, faded frescoes

Tivoli

Tivoli

⬛ Map p. 225

Visitor information

✉ Largo Garibaldi

☎ 0774 31 1249

🕐 Closed Mon. & Sun. a.m.

🚇 Metro: Linea B to Ponte Mammolo, then bus to Tivoli (leaves every 15 minutes). Train: Departures hourly from Stazione Tiburtina in Rome

Villa d'Este

⬛ Map p. 225

✉ Piazza Trento 1

☎ 07 7431 2070 (Call ahead to make sure fountains are in working order)

🕐 Closed Mon.

💲 $$

GREEN HILLS, RIVERS, AND CASCADING WATERFALLS—FOR centuries, ancient Tibur (later Tivoli) was a well-known summer resort. The well-born of Rome were attracted by the gentler summer climate of the Sabine Hills and came here to build their villas or, as in the case of Augustus, to consult the Albunea Sibyl. Poets and princes, emperors and barbarian chieftains frequently chose it as the location of their vacation houses. If contemporary Tivoli has unfortuntely lost much of its charm in the onslaught of runaway postwar building construction, the historic center still retains much of the atmosphere of a medieval hill town.

The **Rocca Pia,** or fortress, built over the ruins of a Roman amphitheater, dates back to the 15th century. There are some lovely churches. **Santa Maria Maggiore,** a fifth-century church next door to Villa d'Este *(Closed p.m.),* was rebuilt in the 13th century and has a Gothic portal set in a Romanesque facade. The church of **San Silvestro,** charmingly Romanesque except for a hideous, recently built glass front door and a couple of garish shrines, contains some extremely attractive 13th-century frescoes. Next door is an interesting fountainhead and nearby is the attractive Casa Gotica (Gothic House). **San Lorenzo,** the Duomo, unfortunately was rebuilt in the 17th century, but the "Triptych of the Saviour" in wood (12th century) with a gold-and-silver cover (15th century) is definitely worth a look. The same goes for the disturbingly modern 13th-century "Deposition" group.

Walk down Via Valerio and along Via della Sibilla to the Sibilla restaurant to see the remains of both the circular **Tempio di Vesta** and the rectangular **Tempio della Sibilla.** Not far from here on Largo Sant'Angelo is the entrance to the gardens of **Villa Gregoriana,** with its lovely waterfall.

Throughout its history, then, Tivoli has been a favored resort destination, but its fame as a getaway location was heightened by Emperor Hadrian's decision to make it the site of his magnificent imperial villa. The inventiveness of his design enabled him to create a sprawling residence where intellectuals and friends could enjoy the pleasures of a contemplative life. More than a thousand years later a noble (but weren't they all?) Renaissance churchman decided to make life in Tivoli bearable by turning a dilapidated Benedictine monastery into a lovely villa. This was embellished by one of the most fascinating garden and fountain complexes in the world, recently listed by UNESCO as one of Italy's 31 major historical/artistic sites.

VILLA D'ESTE

Cardinal Ippolito II, a son of Lucrezia Borgia, wanted to be pope. But things didn't work out, so in around 1550 this scion of the wealthy d'Este family of Ferrara settled for the governorship of Tivoli and decided to make the best of it. Money was not a problem, and the cardinal wasted no time in engaging the services of major architects to turn an old monastery into a sumptuous palace, the Villa d'Este. After dispossessing many small landowners, they embellished

Opposite: Papal ambitions thwarted, Cardinal Ippolito spared no expense in creating his terraced gardens where hundreds of jets of water spring from sculpted fountains.

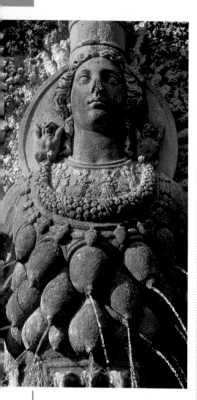

it with magnificently extensive terraced gardens and an elaborate Mannerist complex of secluded grottoes, classical statuary, and fountains. After the cardinal died, the villa fell into neglect. In the 1920s, it was restored and opened to the public.

Among the most bewitching of the mossy fountains are: the Fontana del Bicchierone (water pours out from a large shell-shaped basin), attributed by many art historians to Bernini; the Rometta fountain is a miniature Rome complete with Tiber, Tiber Island, and a wolf-suckling Romulus and Remus; in the Avenue of the Hundred Fountains, animal heads, lilies, a small boat, basins, and so on all spurt water; the sibyl in the Fontana dell'Ovato watches over naiads and river gods; the Water

Organ fountain once played music while the Owl and Bird fountain made hooting and chirping sounds. You can also visit the rooms of the *appartamento nobile,* but make sure you don't miss the Loggia dello Scalone, that is the terrace, from which there is a lovely view.

VILLA ADRIANA

Just a few miles outside of Tivoli are the ruins of Emperor Hadrian's villa, or summer estate, undoubtedly the largest and most elaborate Roman imperial palace ever to have existed. As you can see from the model in the kiosk near the entrance, it extends over a broad area and includes the remains of an enormous villa, with baths, theaters, libraries, and extensive gardens. Choose a nice day and plan on spending several hours here.

Hadrian (see p. 21) ruled between A.D. 117 and 138. He began building this pleasure palace shortly after he ascended the throne and completed it in A.D. 133, although by that time he was ill and grief-stricken by the deaths of his wife and of Antinous, his young lover. Hadrian is known for other architectural achievements such as the Pantheon and Castel Sant'Angelo in Rome, but the villa is his masterpiece. Much traveled and highly educated, when he built the villa (which took about 15 years to Úcomplete), Hadrian sought to re-create, or re-evoke, some of the world's architectural wonders. The vast sprawling site (almost 300 acres/ 121 ha) was designed both as a monument to man's achievements and as a place for study and reflection. Below is a network of tunnels, some large enough for a horse and carriage.

Your best move here is to buy a brochure in the bookstore adjacent to the café, and to follow the suggested itinerary. From the

Above: The Canopus illustrated how the philosopher-Emperor Hadrian sought to create in his Villa an atmosphere conducive to study and reflection.

Above left: Often depicted as a huntress, the goddess Diana was worshiped as a fertility symbol at her temple in Ephesus (Turkey).

Villa Adriana

🗺 Map p. 225

✉ Via di Villa Adriana 204

☎ 0774 53 0203

💲 $$

🚇 Metro: Linea B to Ponte Mammolo, then bus to Tivoli (leaves every 15 minutes). Train: Departures hourly from the Stazione Tiburtina in Rome

parking lot you enter through the high perimeter wall to find yourself at midpoint in the **Pecile,** a large square with an enormous reflecting pool, said to have been modeled on the Stoa Pokile of Athens. It was originally covered over and surrounded by a portico. As you will see, it is also the upper story of a vast construction with hundreds of rooms, probably for slaves and other palace staff. Continuing on you come to the Small Baths and the Large Baths, much of which are still standing. Next is one of the complex's most mystical monuments, the **Canopus.**

This is a reflecting pool, 750 feet (228 m) long, surrounded by columns and statuary (don't miss either the river god or the stone crocodile) and ending in a large nymphaeum (the Serapis) that once held fountains and statues. It is believed to have been inspired by the canal that linked Alexandria in Egypt to ancient Canopus. Along the west side are six caryatids like those on the Erechtheum on the Acropolis in Athens. Returning via the Stadium, and the Room with Three Exhedrae or apses (probably a large outdoor dining room), are the remains of the **palace proper,** an enormous structure composed of pavilions built around peristyles or courtyards. Don't miss the Fishpool Quadriportico, the Hall of the Doric Columns, the Heliocaminus Baths which may have been heated by solar power, the circular Maritime Theater, and the Republican Villa where you can see the remains of mosaic floors and vault decorations. ∎

More excursions from Rome

Nothing is dearer to an Italian than his Sunday outing and fortunately the regional bus company, Cotral, goes most places *(Call 800-431784 for information)*. If you have a car, so much the better, as all roads leading out of Rome go someplace interesting. Here are some suggestions.

CASTELLI ROMANI
The Castelli Romani (Roman Castles) are small hilltop towns in the Alban Hills southeast of Rome. Best known for their white wine, porchetta (roast pork), and restaurants and situated among the chestnut trees, olive groves, and vineyards that cover the slopes of these extinct volcanoes, there are also some interesting monuments.

Frascati, home of the best-known Roman white wine, was founded in the Middle Ages and because of its cooler clime became a resort for the wealthy who built luxurious villas (many of which sadly were damaged by Allied bombing during World War II). The best preserved is Villa Aldobrandini while the park attached to Villa Torlonia has wonderful fountains designed by Carlo Maderno. Nearby is **Tusculum,** an Etruscan settlement said to have been founded by Telegonus, a son of Ulysses, and the siren Circe; the view from the ruins (a forum, a small theater and an amphitheater) is wonderful.

Grottaferrata's beautiful fortified Greek-rite abbey was founded by St. Nilus in the 10th century and later incorporated into a castle. Don't miss the chapel of St. Nilus in the Church of Santa Maria, with Domenichino's wonderful frescoes. **Marino,** on Lake Castelgandolfo (or Albano), is known for its October wine festival, when the town fountains spew forth wine rather than water. There's a Guido Reni painting in the Trinità church and a Mithraeum with interesting frescos. Medieval **Rocca di Papa** is the highest of the Castelli, whereas the most charming is **Nemi,** a tiny hilltown (known for its annual strawberry festival) with a Renaissance castle that overlooks a miniscule lake in a crater. The remains of two of the Emperor Caligula's pleasure boats (unfortunately burned by the Germans in 1944) are housed in a small museum. **Genzano,** across Lake Nemi, with its lovely lakeside restaurants and a 13th-century castle, is known for the June "infiorata" when the streets are "paved" with pictures made out of flower petals. Near Albano, once the Castra Albana, headquarters of Rome's Second Legion, is the Etruscan-style Roman tomb of the Horatii and Curiatii. And **Castel Gandolfo's** castle, the Pope's summer residence, was built by Carlo Maderno over an earlier fortress. The fountain in the piazza is by Bernini.

🅼 Map p. 225 **Visitor information** ✉ Piazza Marconi 1, Frascati ☎ 06 942 0331 (for Frascati and Grottaferrata) 🕐 Closed p.m. ☎ 06 932 4081 (for Albano and the lake towns) 🕐 Closed p.m.

PALESTRINA
Some say ancient Praeneste was also founded by Telegonus. In any event this medieval-looking town outside Rome is built over the remains of the Sanctuary of Fortuna Primigenia, a Roman shrine which dates back to the second century B.C. This may have been the largest Hellenistic construction in Italy, a series of climbing terraces culminating in a (now) partially reconstructed temple. Its foundations are incorporated into the Palazzo Colonna-Barberini, currently the site of the Museo Nazionale Archeologico Prenestino *(Tel 06 953 8000)* which hosts numerous statues, artifacts, and reliefs. But its prize possession is the remarkable Nile Mosaic, discovered in the city's ancient Forum. The Cathedral of St. Agapitus has a 12th-century campanile but was built over the remains of a pagan temple. A grill opens on to a small section of Roman Road. The Renaissance musician Giovanni Pierluigi da Palestrina, the creator of contrapuntal composition, was born here.

🅼 Map p. 225 **Visitor information** ✉ Via Barberini ☎ 06 957 3176 ∎

Travelwise

Traffic policeman

TRAVELWISE INFORMATION

Rome is a very rewarding city to visit and, on the whole, it's also very welcoming. However, some aspects of life here are difficult to understand for those used to a more streamlined (and less idiosyncratic) way of doing things. Although some people feel tales of Italian inefficiency are exaggerated, there is no doubt that the pace of life (and of change) is slower here and some of the procedures you're likely to have to make may take far longer, or be much more complicated, than you would have expected.

PLANNING YOUR TRIP

WHEN TO GO

The peak tourist seasons in Rome are May–June and September–October, when temperatures are perfect for sightseeing. Easter is also busy, with pilgrims flocking to the city for Holy Week. Christmas, on the other hand, attracts fewer international visitors, but the historic center is full of celebrating Romans and people from the rest of Italy. January and February are definitely the quietest months for tourists.

From May onward most of Rome's social life takes place outdoors. Restaurants and bars move their tables on to streets and piazzas, and there is a plethora of open-air cinemas and arts festivals. Several of these now continue until September, but much of the city still grinds to a halt in August, which is an almost uncannily quiet month. People take to the beaches or mountains on holiday and most restaurants, bars, shops, and businesses close for at least a week or two. The momentum and traffic build up again gradually throughout September and, by October, when the schools reopen, the summer is truly over and the first rains arrive—October and November aren't usually particularly cold but, like April and early May, they're nearly always wet.

Not all hotels give off-season reductions, but those that do

are more likely to do so in the periods December to March and, especially if a significant proportion of their clients are business people, in July and August. Annual increases in price are usually made at Easter or the beginning of May.

CLIMATE

Rome has mild, damp winters; the temperature seldom drops below freezing and it rarely snows. Springs and falls tend to be rainy and warmish. Summers are hot—sometimes oppressively so in July and August—and, apart from the occasional dramatic thunderstorm, dry. It can be noticeably humid at any time of year but, to make up for it, you're unlikely to have more than two or three days without seeing the sun, whatever the season.

WHAT TO TAKE

Italians dress smartly for the city. As a visitor, however, you can wear pretty much what you like, although if you're planning to visit any churches make sure you're not wearing shorts or a very short skirt, and cover your arms to at least the elbow or you may not be allowed in. You'll also probably want to have one fairly elegant outfit for the evening. Natural fabrics are more comfortable at any time of year and essential in summer when the heat and humidity make synthetics sticky and sweaty. In winter, bring plenty of warm clothes because, although the outdoor temperature may not be that low, marble floors and sometimes less than efficient

central heating make for coolish, drafty interiors. In spring and fall, when daytimes are often warm and balmy, the temperature drops significantly in the evening.

Try to bring at least two pairs of comfortable shoes—even if you limit your walking to getting around museums and galleries you'll be on your feet a lot and, if you're going to be walking around the historic center, the cobbled streets can be hard-going.

Although you're unlikely to see much rain during the summer, an umbrella is a good idea at any time of year and essential in the spring and fall wet seasons (when a rain coat is also a good idea—it's not the kind of rain you can ignore). Sunglasses are also advisable because even the winter sun can be dazzling. A pair of binoculars will help you make the most of views and interiors, especially of lavishly decorated churches.

Other essentials are: your passport, driver's license, credit cards, insurance documentation, and, if you're using them, travelers' checks. In Italy you're meant to carry proof of your identity at all times—although you're unlikely to need to produce it—but you can usually get by with a photocopy of the personal information pages of your passport for this.

INSURANCE

Take out enough travel insurance to cover emergency medical treatment, repatriation, and loss or theft of money and possessions.

HOW TO GET TO ROME

PASSPORTS

U.S. and Canadian citizens do not need a visa for stays in Italy of up to three months. By law, however, all visitors are supposed to announce their presence to the local police. Hotels do this for you—leave your passport at reception when you check in and you'll get it back the following morning. You have to do this every time you check into a hotel, even if it's just for one night. Independent travelers and anybody staying for more than three months should contact the central police station (*La Questura*), tel 06 46 86, to find out what to do.

AIRLINES

Alitalia
Rome. Tel 06 65 631.

AIRPORTS

Fiumicino—Leonardo da Vinci (southwest of Rome). Tel 06 65 951.
Ciampino (southeast of Rome). Tel 06 794 941.

Although direct flights to Rome are available from many cities, they aren't particularly frequent and you may find it more convenient to fly to Milan (or another major European airport such as Frankfurt or London) and transfer from there. Rome has two international airports but nearly all scheduled flights (both national and international) arrive in and leave from Fiumicino—Leonardo da Vinci.

From here regular train services (every 30 or 60 minutes from about 7:30 a.m. to 10 p.m.) take you to the central train station at Termini or (every 15 minutes from about 6:30 a.m. to 10:30 p.m.) Tiburtina, with stops along the way including Trastevere and Ostiense. A taxi costs about L.70,000.

Many charter flights and a few cut-price scheduled services from the rest of Europe use the much smaller Ciampino airport which has, as yet, no direct transport link to the city center—you need to catch an infrequent bus to the nearest station to get an

equally infrequent train to Termini. A taxi from Ciampino should cost about L.50,000 but you may be charged a fairly hefty supplement on top of this.

GETTING AROUND

BY CAR

Car rentals
In Italy:
Avis. Tel 06 3549 8886.
Europcar. Tel 06 488 2854.
Hertz. Tel199 112 211.
Maggiore—Budget. Tel 06 488 3715.
Unless you're planning on making a lot of trips out of the city, a car in central Rome is more of a hindrance than a help. Parking is nearly impossible to find, and the local driving style is daunting to those used to more rigidly disciplined traffic. If you do want to rent a car, inquire with a travel agent before leaving home as prices are likely to be lower if the car is booked in the U.S.—car hire in Italy is about the most expensive in Europe as, incidentally, is petrol.

**Driving regulations
& conventions**
An international driver's license is not required for short-term visitors. When driving, keep all relevant documents (including at least a photocopy of your passport) in the car. Driving regulations in Italy are not always strictly adhered to so, while it's advisable to stick to them yourself, don't count on everybody else doing so. Remember also that, although it may not look like it when you're on foot yourself, pedestrians always have right of way. This becomes particularly noticeable in the narrow streets of the historic center and at the many traffic lights where cars turning right or left have to share the green light with pedestrians crossing the road—they expect to cross first. At night, many traffic lights are switched to a

constantly flashing amber light, this means they're out of use and it's up to you to decide when it's safe to go.

In spite of appearances, the law requires that seat belts be worn in the front and (when fitted) back seats. A car flashing its lights means that the driver is asserting right of way, not, as in some places, ceding it to you.

The speed limit in built-up areas is 30 mph (50 kph); other normal roads, 70 mph (110 kph); and motorways, 80 mph (130 kph). The legal limit for drinking and driving works out at about two glasses of wine, but you probably won't much want to drive unless you've got all your wits about you.

If your parked car is blocking somebody else's access, the police may tow it away. If you think this has happened, call the *Polizia Municipale* (the town police), tel 06 67 691, to find out where it is and when to collect it (you'll have to pay a charge to do so).

Car breakdown
Automobile Club d'Italia (ACI). Tel 116 (emergencies) or 06 44 77.
Rental cars will have an emergency number for breakdowns, check the information package that comes with the car. Otherwise, ACI is your best bet. It has English-speaking staff and reasonably priced services, although it costs more if your car needs to be towed away. There are emergency phones along the motorways.

PUBLIC TRANSPORTATION

Metrebus
Buses, trams, the metro, and local rail services in Rome are all integrated into one transport system. Tickets for the whole system can be bought at most tobacconists (*tabacchi*), stations, and machines near major bus

stops. An ordinary ticket (BIT—
biglietto integrato a tempo) costs
L.1,500 and entitles you to 75
minutes of unlimited bus and/or
tram travel plus one journey by
train or metro. (There is talk of
introducing tickets that can be
bought from the bus driver—
these will cost L.2,000.) A day
pass (BIG—*biglietto integrato
giornaliero*) costs L.6,000 and is
valid until midnight while weekly
passes (CIS—*carta integrata
settimanale*) cost L.24,000. You
should validate the ticket by
stamping it at the beginning of
your journey and then again if
you switch from bus to metro
or train or vice versa. Machines
for doing this are on buses or at
the entrance to metro and train
stations. Keep the validated
ticket until the end of your
journey in case of an inspector.

Metropolitana
Operates: 5:30 a.m.–11:30 p.m.
Rome has only two metro lines
(A and B) which cross at
Termini. It is not particularly
useful for getting around central
Rome unless you plan your
sight-seeing route around it.

Buses
ATAC (daytime bus service)
Operates: 5:30 a.m.–midnight
(some services stop earlier).
ATAC (night bus service)
Operates: midnight–5:30 a.m.
Central Rome is well-served
with ATAC's buses and trams,
although they tend to be
crowded and are at the mercy of
traffic, sometimes leading to
delays and long journey times.
Take particular care of your
valuables on buses (especially the
No. 64 which serves the touristy
Termini to the Vatican route)
which are a popular haunt for
pickpockets. The winding streets
of the historic center are
navigated by little, electric buses
(Nos. 116 and 117) which are
particularly useful for sightseers.

For information about ATAC and
Cotral bus, tram and metro
transport in the city and
throughout the Lazio region, tel

800 431 784 (Mon.–Fri. 9 a.m.–1
p.m. and 2 p.m.–5 p.m.)

Buses out of Rome throughout
the Lazio region are operated by
Cotral. Tickets and information
from Via Volturno 65, 00185
(near Piazza dei Cinquecento;
Metro Repubblica).

Taxis
Taxis can be hailed in the street
or picked up at one of several
ranks in the historic center;
these are clearly marked with a
blue-and-white or yellow-and-
black sign saying "Taxi." Roman
taxis are yellow or white and the
red taxi sign on the top is
illuminated when they are free.
Inside the taxi, a meter indicates
the fare which starts at L.4,800,
the minimum charge. Extras are
charged between 10:30 p.m. and
7:30 a.m., on Sundays and public
holidays, for carrying baggage, or
for airport trips. A list of all
charges is displayed in several
languages inside the taxi. Tipping
is optional but drivers often
automatically round the fare up
to the nearest L.1,000.

Calling for a taxi can be nerve-
racking as few operators speak
English but hotels or restaurants
will call for you. The meter
starts running when the driver
receives the call and may have
clocked up several thousand lire
by the time it reaches you.
When you call, you may be
asked for the number you're
phoning from. If you can't give
this say "*Non c'è numero*"
("There's no number") and give
your location. You'll then be
given the number of the taxi
that's coming for you. This is
made up of a geographic name
followed by a one- or two-digit
number (Assisi 23, for example)
and the waiting time. Some
companies have automated their
booking service and the taxi
number and wait-time are given,
in Italian, by a voice machine. If
you understand and agree with
what is said just hang up the
phone, otherwise wait until you
get a human being on the line.

Radio-dispatched taxis
Cooperativa Samarcanda, tel 06
5551. Accept payment by credit
card.
La Capitale. Tel 06 4994.
Pronto Taxi. Tel 06 6645.
Radio Taxi. Tel 06 3570.

Limousine services
Capitol 2000. Tel 06 322 5866.
Airport Shuttle. Tel 06 338 3221.

Traffic
For those new to Rome, the
city's undisciplined and fast-
moving cars and motorbikes
can be intimidating. Many
intersections have no traffic
lights but only white, painted
stripes on the ground which are
supposed to give the pedestrian
precedence, but don't count on
it. Be careful, but not overly
hesitant either as you may
confuse drivers. And don't
hesitate to hold up your arm in
a "stop" gesture. You may look
silly but it helps. Also remember
that where there are both traffic
lights and stripes, you must
observe the former.

Trains
The national Italian railroad, FS
(Ferrovia dello Stato), links
Rome and all major cities, as well
as smaller centers within the
surrounding area. Most rail
services leave from and arrive at
the recently renovated Termini,
Rome's main railroad station.
Reservations and ticket
purchases have to be made in
person at stations or through a
travel agent. Information on all FS
services (from 7 a.m. to 9 p.m.),
tel 147 888 088 or (for a
summary of the immediate
situation—strikes, delays, etc.)
tel 06 488 4466. Tickets and
information about regular
services are also available from
machines at main rail stations.
Before boarding the train, make
sure you validate your ticket with
the date and time by punching it
in the yellow machines on or
near each platform.

There's an interesting range of
services on offer. *Locale* services

stop at every station on their routes; *Diretto* stop at most; and *Express* stop at the most important (although your interpretation of what an important station is may differ from that of the FS). Intercity services are much quicker while Eurostar, which serves main towns and cities only, is the best and quickest. There are supplements to be paid on both of these services and seats often have to be reserved in advance.

Internal flights
For flights within Italy and the rest of Europe
Alitalia. Tel 06 656 41.
Air One. Tel 1478 488 800.
Meridiana. Tel 06 478 041.

TOURS & SIGHTSEEING

Independent sightseeing
Rome's a wonderful place to discover on your own, unless you're short of time or are particularly concerned not to miss certain sights. A flexible attitude is the key to enjoyment. Official opening hours in Italy are in a state of constant flux—laws are being passed to extend them but staff shortages often make this impracticable, at least in the short term. You should also be prepared to find even the most important sights closed at short notice because of a strike, major restoration, or some other apparently unforeseen circumstance. Phone before you make a special journey and try to have a contingency plan. The use of conscientious objectors (who opt to do cultural, instead of military service) as custodians is improving the situation greatly, however, and many museums and churches are now open for longer than their advertised hours, particularly during the main tourist seasons.

Much of Rome's art is displayed in more or less the settings for which it was created—aristo-cratic palazzi and churches. This means that paintings in galleries are often hung three or four deep on ornately frescoed walls, while Renaissance and baroque gems are tucked away in the little chapels of churches where the lighting and position can make them difficult to see (many churches have slot machines which illuminate their greatest treasures for a few minutes when a L.500 coin is inserted). Although display information is sometimes scarce, many monuments publish their own detailed guides which give floor-plans and details of virtually everything you can see, in English.

When you go into a church make sure you're dressed properly, which means no shorts or sleeveless tops, and try to avoid entering when there's a service in progress.

Bus tours
There's a special ATAC-run service, the No. 110, which leaves Termini about five times a day and passes several of the main tourist sites for L.15,000 (for information, tel 06 4695 2252). Other tours of the city and its monuments:
Stop-'n'-go (also organizes full- and half-day trips to surrounding area), 60 Piazza dei Cinquecento, 00185. Tel 06 321 7054. Metro: Repubblica.

Walking tours in English
Michael Brouse and Dennis Cigler are part of *In Italy's Companions.* For information and advance reservations call in the U.S. 1-323-655-1268. Fax 1-323-655-3350. E-mail:
In.Italy@inItaly.com
Website: www.initaly.com
Tours of the historic center, Vatican and archaeological area:
Scala Reale. Tel 06 4470 0898.

Bicycle & scooter hire
A good way of getting around and seeing Rome:
Happy Rent, Via Farini 3, 00185, tel 06 481 8185. Metro: Termini.
Rent Scooter Borgo, Via delle Grazie 2, 00193. Tel 06 687

7239. Metro: Ottaviano. Bus: 19, 23, 49, 51, 64, 81, 492, 982.
Trevi Tourist Center, Via dei Lucchesi 32, 00187. Tel 06 6920 0799. Bus: 52, 53, 56, 58, 60, 61, 62, 71, 81, 85, 95, 115, 116, 117, 160, 175, 204, 492, 590, 628, 850.

PRACTICAL ADVICE

COMMUNICATIONS

POST OFFICES
Main branch: Piazza San Silvestro, 00187. Tel 06 679 3064. Bus: 52, 53, 58, 61, 71, 85, 160, 850.
Open: Mon.–Fri. 9 a.m.–6 p.m., Sat. 9 a.m.–2 p.m.
Local branches: Open 8:25 a.m.–2 p.m., Sat. 8:25 a.m.–noon.

Le poste has branches in every neighborhood, however, unless you're sending unusually sized mail, your best bet is to buy stamps from a tobacconist as post offices are usually full of long lines of people waiting to pay bills, collect pensions, or do one of a host of other tasks. You can have your mail sent to the main post office by having it addressed "Fermo Posta" followed by your name and the address of the post office.

Most mailboxes are red and have two slots, one *Per la città* (for the city) and one for *Tutte le altre destinazioni* (other destinations). They are outside post offices and at other sites, including outside some tobacconists. New, blue boxes decorated with the stars of Europe are for international mail only.
Roman addresses usually put the number *after* the name of the street or piazza, so Via della Scala 15 is 15 Via della Scala.

Vatican post
Piazza San Pietro, 00193. Bus: 19, 23, 49, 51, 64, 81, 492, 982; Metro: Ottaviano. Open: Mon.–Fri. 8:30 a.m.–7 p.m., Sat. 8:30 a.m.– 6 p.m.
The Vatican has its own postal system with two post offices in

Piazza San Pietro (one on either side of the basilica). Stamps (or *Francobolli*) cost marginally more than they do for the Italian system but international mail is usually delivered far more quickly. There are mailboxes at the post offices and at the Vatican offices on Piazza San Calisto in Trastevere (behind Piazza S. Maria in Trastevere).

TELEPHONES

To call Italy from the United States, dial 011-39 (international and Italian country code) followed by the full area code (which starts with 06 for Rome) and the number.

Most public phones are now operated by phone cards which can be bought in denominations of L.5,000, L.10,000 and L.15,000 from tobacconists, bars and post offices. Most also have clearly displayed instructions in English. To make a call, lift the receiver, then insert your card (first break off the perforated corner) in the slot. The amount of money still available on your card will be shown on an LCD. Dial the number and wait for an answer. You can watch how quickly you're using up the card on the LCD—just before it's about to expire, you'll hear a shrill sound. Insert another card to continue the conversation. There are still a few coin-operated phones around (not recommended for international calls). These take coins of L.50, L.100, L.200 and L.500, and work according to the same principles.

Italian numbers can have anything from four to eight digits in addition to the area prefix. You must always use the area prefix, even when calling from within that area; the prefix for Rome is 06. Other useful prefixes are: 02 for Milan; 055 for Florence; 041 for Venice and 081 for Naples. Numbers beginning with 167 or 800 are toll free.

To make an international call, dial 00, followed by the country code (1 for the United States and Canada), the area code (omitting the initial zero if there is one) and the number. American long-distance operators include AT&T: 167 877 472; DirectLine International: 06 854 3241. For Italian directory assistance, dial 12. For international assistance, dial 176.

MEDIA

NEWSPAPERS

Many newsstands (*edicole*) have a selection of English-language papers and magazines; the *International Herald Tribune* is particularly widely available. The major Italian daily papers (published every day including Sunday) are the Milan-based *Corriere della Sera*, and the Rome-based *La Repubblica*. *Il Sole 24 Ore* is the country's leading business daily.

TELEVISION

The main national stations available without cable are the state-owned RAI-1, -2 and -3, Mediaset's Italia Uno, Rete Quattro, and Canale Cinque. TeleMonteCarlo is another privately owned station. Programs are all in Italian, including English-language imports which are dubbed. Cable and satellite stations include CNN International, Euronews, CNBC, the Cartoon Network, BBC Prime, MTV, and MCN.

RADIO

Vatican Radio (93.3 FM) broadcasts news and other programs in a wide range of languages including English. For 24-hour classical music without breaks try La Filodiffusione (100.1 FM). Radio Centro Suono plays a range of dance, reggae, ragga, Afro-Caribbean, and other music. The state-owned stations (RAI-1 on 89.7 FM, RAI-2 on 91.7 FM, and RAI-3 on 93.7 FM) broadcast a mixture of news and

chat shows combined with (usually fairly middle-of-the-road) classical and light music.

BOOKS & MOVIES SET IN ROME

Ever since ancient times, Rome has featured in literature. More recently, as Hollywood on the Tiber with its own active film industry working out of Cinecittà, it's also become a popular setting for films, many of them historic and/or romantic.

Books

If you're interested in ancient Rome, you can read all about it from the horse's mouth in Suetonius' *The Twelve Caesars,* Livy's *History of Rome,* and Tacitus' *The Histories.* Also try Robert Graves' *I Claudius* and *Claudius the God,* Marguerite Yourcenar's *Memoirs of Hadrian,* or the works of Allan Massie— *Augustus, Caesar* and *Tiberius*— which, although they're fiction give a good idea of what life was like. Literary works set in more recent times include: *Roman Fever* by Edith Wharton; *A Time in Rome* by Elizabeth Bowen; *History* by Elsa Morante; *The Marble Faun* by Nathaniel Hawthorne; *Vendetta* and others by Michael Dibdin; and, last but not least, most of the works of Roman author Alberto Moravia.

Movies

See "Hollywood on the Tiber & After" on page 32.

ELECTRICITY

Nearly all Italian circuits use 220 volts; American appliances need adaptor plugs and those that operate on 110 volts will also need a transformer. These can be bought at *casalinghe* (hardware stores) in Italy or before you leave home.

LOCAL CUSTOMS

Say *"buon giorno" ("buona sera"* after lunch) and *"arrivederci"* when entering and leaving shops, restaurants and bars. Although nobody expects you to speak Italian, an attempt to utter a few words, no matter how basic, is often greatly admired. In general Italians use "please" and "thank you" *(per favore and grazie)* less frequently than English-speakers do so don't be offended if people seem brusque. If you're presenting anybody with flowers, don't give them chrysanthemums which are usually only put on graves.

MONEY MATTERS

Banca Commerciale Italiana, Via del Corso 226, 00186. Tel 06 671 21. Bus: 56, 60, 62, 81, 85, 95, 117, 160, 175, 492, 628, 850.
American Express, Piazza di Spagna 38, 00187. Tel 06 676 41. Metro: Spagna.
Thomas Cook, Piazza Barberini 21, 00187. Tel 06 482 8082. Metro: Barberini.

In November 1999, one U.S. dollar equaled approximately 1,800 Italian lire, which come in coins of 50, 100, 200, 500 and (recently) 1,000 and bills of 1,000, 2,000, 5,000, 10,000, 50,000, 100,000 and 500,000. (Try to keep a ready supply of low-denomination notes as shops are often short of them for change.)

Since January 1999, the Euro has been the official currency of Italy—one Euro is worth just under L.2,000. Italian notes and coins continue to be legal tender during the transitional period until January 2002 and prices are often quoted in both currencies. If you can, it's best to opt for the lire price as the Euro one is often slightly inflated.

There are commercial currency exchanges all over the city, but you're nearly always better off using any of the banks displaying a sign saying *Cambio*. They charge a commission but their conversion rates tend to be considerably more advantageous than those offered by currency exchanges that

advertise "No commission." Cash withdrawals with a credit card are possible at banks and currency exchanges although you'll often need a PIN number and always need a passport or similar document for identification. The American Express office exchanges currency or gives advances on AmEx cards.

The best sources of currency with a credit card are the ATMs, called *Bancomat*, outside many banks. You'll need an international PIN and should check with your bank or credit card supplier before leaving home. ATMs have instructions in a range of different languages, including English. A fee is usually charged for credit card advances, whether done in banks or via ATMs.

NATIONAL HOLIDAYS

Jan. 1, Jan. 6, Easter Sun., Easter Mon., April 25, May 1, Aug. 15, Nov. 1, Dec. 8, Dec. 25, Dec. 26.

OPENING TIMES

Most banks are open Mon.–Fri. 8:30 a.m.–1:30 p.m. and 3–4 p.m. A few are also open on Sat. a.m. Shop opening hours are currently being extended. In general food shops are open Mon.–Sat. 9 a.m.–2 p.m. and 5–8 p.m. with one afternoon off (Thurs. in winter, Sat. in summer). Other shops are open from 9 or 10 a.m.–1 p.m. and 4 or 5–8 p.m. (shut Mon. a.m. in winter and Sat. p.m. in summer) but many are now open all day and some even on Sun.

Bars open in the early morning; some close at 8 p.m. but many in the center stay open until midnight or 2 a.m. Restaurants are open from noon–3 p.m. and from 8–11 p.m. but some open earlier or stay open later. Many shops, restaurants, bars, and other businesses close for at least a week or two in August. and several also in January.

TIME DIFFERENCES

From the last Saturday of October until the last Saturday of March, Rome is one hour ahead of Greenwich Mean Time; for the rest of the year (summer time) it is two hours ahead. If it's midnight in Rome, it is 6 p.m. in New York (summer time it's 5 p.m.) and 3 p.m. in California (summer time it's 2 p.m.).

TIPPING

If service is not included on the bill (it appears as a separate charge under *"servizio"*) add about ten per cent, which should be left in cash if you're paying with a credit card, depending on how satisfied you've been. Even when it is included, it's normal to leave an additional few thousand lire if the service has been good. In museums, tipping is never necessary but cloakroom attendants in restaurants usually get L.1,000 or so. Hotel maids and porters can be tipped at the end of your stay.

TOILETS

Rome is famous for its lack of public toilets, but most bars will let you use theirs if you ask first (especially if you order something before you do so). One toilet often serves both men and women so don't be surprised if a member of the opposite sex is using it when you arrive.

Standards of hygiene vary dramatically but tend towards the lower end of the scale and it's a good idea to carry paper hankies as toilet paper isn't guaranteed.

CRIME

Rome is much safer than most American cities, but tourists are an enticing prey for thieves and it pays to take a few simple precautions to avoid the risk of falling prey to pickpockets or bag-snatchers. Carry cameras and bags (securely fastened shut) across your body and keep a hand on them in crowded areas; be particularly aware of the whereabouts of all your valuables if somebody seems to be jostling you unnecessarily or approaches you a little too closely for comfort to ask for directions or some other help; and be especially wary of groups of scruffy children waving cardboard or newspaper in your face while their colleagues delve into your pockets and bags. Don't leave anything on tables, chairs or anywhere from which it could be grabbed by a passerby. Leave valuables, money, documents, and credit cards that you don't need immediately in a hotel safe and try not to bring out tempting wads of cash in public when you're paying for anything.

If you are robbed, go to the nearest police station to make a *denuncio* (report). You're unlikely to see your valuables again but at least you can use the denuncio for insurance.

TOURIST OFFICES

Azienda di Promozione Turistica (main tourist office): Via Parigi 5, 00187. Tel 06 4889 9253/5. Metro: Repubblica. Open Mon.–Fri. 8:15 a.m.–7:15 p.m. Staff here can help with hotel reservations and sightseeing tips for Rome and Lazio.

In addition the Comune of Rome also operate information kiosks (usually open from 9 a.m.– 6 p.m.) at several of the main tourist locations.

Tourist information is also available from tel 110.
In general, treat all published information with caution (even when it comes from official tourist offices) as it is often out of date and inaccurate. Staff at the above offices have access to more reliable information via the Internet, and most speak (sometimes limited) English.

TRAVELERS WITH DISABILITIES

Rome is not an easy city for anybody with a physical disability, and virtually impossible if you're unaccompanied. Efforts are being made to improve the situation and in the meantime many people will do all they can to help—restaurants will make sure you've got a table with enough room and hotel staff will carry you up short flights of stairs.

Lifts allow access to most of the metro stations on the "B" line (apart from Circo Massimo, Colosseo, and Cavour—three of the most useful ones for tourists) but the "A" line is unusable, as are most buses although the new trams on route No. 8 and buses used on route 590 (which follows that of Metro Line A) are accessible. The newer trains serving the faster (Intercity and Eurostar) services are also wheelchair-accessible.

Most taxis will carry wheelchairs although this usually means folding them up and putting them in the trunk—it's helpful if you can phone in advance.

Many museums and several restaurants and bars have ostentatiously advertised toilets for the disabled but these are sometimes located at the top or bottom of flights of stairs.

EMERGENCIES

EMBASSIES & CONSULATES

United States Embassy, Palazzo Margherita, Via V. Veneto 119, 00187. Tel 06 46 741. Metro: Barberini. Consulate, Via V. Veneto 121. Tel 06 46 741.

Canadian Embassy, Via G.B. de Rossi 27, 00161. Tel 06 445 981. Bus: 36, 37, 60, 62, 136, 137, 317. Consulate. Tel 06 4459 8981.

EMERGENCY PHONE NUMBERS & ADDRESSES

General emergencies. Tel 113.
Carabinieri. Tel 112. English-speaking carabinieri. Tel 06 6710 5228 or 06 4686 2876.
Fire. Tel 115.
Ambulance: Italian Red Cross. Tel 06 5510.
Emergency medical assistance. Tel 118 or 06 5820 1030.
Poisoning. Tel 06 497 971 (24 hours).
Dentist. Tel 06 578 3639 (Dr Charles Kennedy)
Rome American Hospital: Via Longoni 69, 00155. Tel 06 22 551 or 06 225 3333.
24-hour pharmacy: Piram, Via Nazionale 228, 00185. Tel 06 488 0754. Metro: Repubblica. (Closed pharmacies post signs in their windows indicating the nearest one open.)

The Vatican Pharmacy (at the Porta Sant'Anna entrance to the Vatican, 00193. Tel 06 686 4146. Bus: 23, 49, 51. Open: Mon.–Fri. 7:30 a.m.–1 p.m. and 3:30–6:30 p.m.) has English-speaking staff and a wide range of non-Italian pharmaceutical products not readily available elsewhere in Rome.

LOST PROPERTY

Oggetti Rinvenuti, Via Nicolo Bettoni 1, 00153 (Trastevere train station). Tel 06 581 6040. Tram: 8. Open Mon., Wed. and Thurs. 8 a.m.–5:45 p.m.; Tues. and Fri. 8 a.m.–1 p.m. (closed Sat. and Sun.).
Termini station at track 1. Metropolitana. Tel 06 487 4309. Open Mon., Wed. and Fri. 9 a.m.–12:30 p.m.

Lost credit cards
American Express. Tel 06 67 641. Diners Club. Tel 167 864 064. MasterCard. Tel 167 870 866. Visa. Tel 167 821 001.

HOTELS & RESTAURANTS

Accommodation in Rome (listed here by price then in alphabetical order) is scarce and expensive and you should book as much in advance as possible. You'll probably be asked for a faxed confirmation and a deposit or credit card number. When reserving, it's also a good idea to confirm that you can pay the final bill with a specific credit card as some hotels accept them only for confirmation purposes. Many of the hotels listed here are in old buildings which have been well restored to make them comfortable for modern visitors without losing their original historic charm. As a result, however, bedrooms and, even more so, bathrooms are often smaller than they are elsewhere.

Hotels

Central Rome (especially Trastevere and the areas around Piazza Navona and Campo de'Fiori) is noisy until 2 or 3 a.m. every night. Most of the central hotels listed here have some off-street rooms where the noise level is reduced (ask for a quiet room when you book), even so you may like to travel with earplugs and if you're particularly sensitive to noise, consider some of the out-of-center options. Relatively quiet hotels in noisy areas have been noted.

Few hotels have rooms that are specially adapted for disabled travelers but many will do all they can to accommodate special needs, especially if you let them know in advance.

Street parking is extremely difficult to find in the historic center but most hotels will help you and arrange for you to use a garage for which you will usually have to pay an additional daily charge. It's a good idea to inquire in advance about parking if you know you're going to need it.

Grading system

Italian hotels are rated from one to five stars by the Government's Tourist Office according to such facilities as the number of rooms with private bathrooms, rooms with TV, etc.; facilities rather than style or comfort. However, this is not always a reliable measure of a hotel's facilities as many opt to stay in a lower category. Unless otherwise noted, all the hotels here have private bathrooms in all rooms (usually, upper categories have bathtub and shower, lower only shower). English is spoken at all the hotels listed here; however the amount spoken varies and may only be sufficient to take a booking and deal with the most basic visitor requests. Value-added tax and service are included in the prices, so is breakfast, unless otherwise noted. Room price categories are given only for guidance and do not take account of seasonal variations, which can be considerable.

Restaurants

You can eat badly in Rome, but it's very difficult—even the humblest of fare is usually lovingly prepared and tasty. Italians take eating seriously and, when they eat out, tend to eat quite a lot. A typical meal starts with appetizing *antipasti* and goes on to the *primo* (usually pasta, soup, or risotto) before hitting the main, or *secondo*, course (meat or fish) accompanied by salad or vegetable *contorni*. Desserts or fruit round off the meal before a cup of strong black espresso coffee and, if you're up to it, sweet wine or after dinner liqueurs. Most restaurants will expect you to eat at least two courses and helpings are sized accordingly.

Dining hours

Lunch is between about 12:30 p.m. and 2:30 p.m. Dinner is seldom served before 8 p.m. and continues until about 10:30 p.m. or even later. It's always advisable to book in advance if you can. In some places booking is essential and may need to be done several days in advance.

Menus are displayed outside each establishment, and you usually order individual items *alla carte*. Fixed-price menus (especially when they're called tourist menus) are best avoided unless you're dealing with the *menu degustazione* offered by some of the best restaurants—these give you little tastes of several dishes accompanied by appropriate wines and are a good way of sampling far more than you'd usually manage at one sitting.

Smoking is still widely accepted (and practiced). Non-smoking areas are something of a rarity in Rome, so there's not much you can do about it—it's regarded as very bad form to complain about another person's smoking although you can politely ask them to direct a cigarette away from you if it's really (and literally) getting up your nose.

Trattorias

These are relatively simple restaurants that are often family-run and were originally geared toward serving local people with good, home-style cooking. Their clientele may have widened over the years (people will travel for miles to eat at a good trattoria) but their value for money has, in most cases, remained.

Tipping

Some establishments add a service charge to the bill and others don't. When it hasn't already been calculated, leave about ten percent; whether it's been added or not, a few thousand lire left on the table shows that you've enjoyed your meal and service, and is a gesture that will be much appreciated.

One of the anachronisms of Italian dining is the charge for *"pane e coperto"* (bread and cover), which appears on nearly all restaurant bills and is usually a few thousand lire per head. It may seem odd that you should effectively be charged for using

HOTELS & RESTAURANTS

the cutlery and table linen but it's standard practice and not an optional extra which depends on whether or not you've eaten any bread.

ANCIENT ROME

Although this area is packed with tourists during the day, in the evenings it becomes one of the quieter parts of central Rome. Most of the restaurants here are simple trattorias, some better than others.

HOTELS

▥ FORUM
$$$$ ✪✪✪✪
VIA TOR DE' CONTI 25, 00184
TEL. 06 679 2446
FAX 06 678 6479
The atmosphere and decor are vaguely reminiscent of an English gentlemen's club and the location is a comparatively quiet corner tucked behind the Imperial Forums. Rooms vary in size but all are well furnished and there's a wonderful roof garden restaurant. Breakfast is extra.
🛏 80 🚆 85, 87, 115, 175, 186, 810, 850 🅿 ⬆ ⓢ ◈ All major cards

▥ DUCA D'ALBA
$$ ✪✪✪
VIA LEONINA 14, 00184
TEL. 06 484 471
FAX 06 488 4840
Enthusiastic staff and its location on a quietish street in the Monti area, make this hotel excellent value for money. The bedrooms may not be the prettiest you'll find but they're sound-proofed and all have safes and hairdriers.
🛏 27 and one suite
🚆 Cavour ⬆ ⓢ ◈ All major cards

▥ PERUGIA
$ ✪✪
VIA DEL COLOSSEO 7, 00184
TEL. 06 679 7200
FAX 06 678 4635

Unfaultable for its class and price category, this budget hotel is spotlessly clean and conscientiously run. Single rooms do not have bathrooms. Breakfast is not served.
🛏 11 🚆 Colosseo ◈ All major cards

RESTAURANTS

🍴 CAVOUR 313
$$
VIA CAVOUR 313, 00184
TEL. 06 678 5496
This wood-lined wine bar has more than a thousand different wines from all over the world and serves an interesting range of cheeses, salamis, and freshly prepared salads. No outdoor dining.
🍽 60 seats 🚆 Cavour, 75, 115 🕐 Closed L Sat.–Sun.
◈ All major cards

🍴 SILVIO ALLA SUBURRA
$$
VIA URBANA 67–69, 00184
TEL. 06 48 6531
A real find. Silvio is a serious and passionate chef who offers a regular menu of traditional and personal cuisine augmented with exquisitely tasty seasonal dishes (he's been known to break his wrist gathering early spring's wild fennel crop). Home-made *fettuccine* is the house specialty, but every thing (from antipasti to desserts) ranges from good to stupendous.
🍽 45 seats 🚆 Cavour
🕐 Closed Mon. (not in summer) ◈ MC, V

COLOSSEO TO SAN CLEMENTE

Another good choice for those who want peace and quiet at night, although there are very few hotels in the grid of streets behind the Colosseum. Many of the bars and restaurants cater for tourists with elevated prices and dubious quality but there are some notable exceptions.

PRICES

HOTELS
An indication of the cost of a double room without breakfast is given by $ signs.
$$$$$ Over $350
$$$$ $250–$350
$$$ $150–$250
$$ $100–$150
$ Under $100

RESTAURANTS
An indication of the cost of a three-course dinner without drinks is given by $ signs.
$$$$$ Over $60
$$$$ $40–$60
$$$ $30–$40
$$ $20–$30
$ Under $20

HOTELS

▥ CELIO
$$ ✪✪✪
VIA DEI SANTI QUATTRO 35, 00184
TEL. 06 7049 5333
FAX 06 7049 6377
One of Rome's most aesthetically pleasing hotels. Bedroom walls are frescoed with reproduction Renaissance and baroque greats and the little bathrooms have mosaic floors, Located in a relatively quiet street near the Colosseum.
🛏 10 🚆 30, 75, 175, 204
🅿 Garage ⬆ ⓢ ◈ All major cards

RESTAURANTS

🍴 AI TRE SCALINI
$$$
VIA SS QUATTRO 30, 00184
TEL. 06 709 6309
Downstairs is a wine bar serving snacks and light dishes to accompany any of the 500 wines on the list. The restaurant upstairs serves imaginative Italian-based cuisine, full of mouth-watering flavor combinations that aren't afraid to break a few long-established rules.

HOTELS & RESTAURANTS

60 seats 30, 75, 175, 204 Closed Mon. & 2 weeks in Aug. All major cards.

SHAWERMA
$$

VIA OSTILIA 24, 00184
TEL. 06 700 8101

The best non-Italian cuisine in Rome tends to be North African and this bustling Egyptian restaurant is an excellent choice for couscous, meat kebabs and pastries. The reasonably priced *menu degustazione* gives you a small selection of different dishes. In the afternoon you can stop here for tea and cakes.

70 seats 30, 75, 81, 117, 175, 204, 673 Closed Mon. AE, MC, V

LATERANO TO TERME DI DIOCLEZIANO

Although the area adjacent to the main railway station is best avoided at night, the atmosphere changes quickly as you leave the station and you soon find yourself in smart residential and business areas. The range of both hotels and restaurants in this area goes from the simplest to the most luxurious.

HOTELS

GRAND HOTEL
$$$$$

VIA V.E. ORLANDO 3, 00185
TEL. 06 47 091
FAX 06 474 7307

A traditional luxury hotel whose public rooms are awe-inspiringly decorated with marble columns and richly patterned oriental carpets. The spacious and comfortable bedrooms are furnished with valuable antiques, and bathrooms are well-equipped. Efficient service matches the slightly hushed aristocratic atmosphere. Breakfast extra.

170 Repubblica All major cards

MARGHERA
$$$

VIA MARGHERA 29, 00185
TEL. 06 445 7184
FAX 06 446 2539

Its sparklingly clean interior contrasts with the slightly rundown surroundings of this street next to Termini station. Every detail has been thought of so rooms have fax connections, trouser presses, and hairdriers and some also have spa pools.

25 Termini All major cards

VIMINALE
$$$

VIA C. BALBO 31, 00184
TEL. 06 488 1910
FAX 06 487 2018

Recently restored, this hotel has spacious, attractive bedrooms, some with balconies overlooking the nearby ancient church of Santa Prudenziana. Public rooms are in Liberty style.

46 Repubblica, Termini, 70, 71 All major cards

ESQUILINO
$

PIAZZA DELL'ESQUILINO 29, 00185
TEL. 06 474 3454
FAX 06 474 1570

Recently restored and enthusiastically run, this spotless little hotel is located in a late 19th-century residential building just opposite S. Maria Maggiore.

12 Termini, 4, 9, 70, 71, 75, 204, 590, 714 All major cards

RESTAURANTS

AGATA E ROMEO
$$$$$

VIA CARLO ALBERTO 45, 00185
TEL. 06 446 6115

A family-run restaurant that's been among the best in Rome for years. The menu offers exquisite versions of traditional dishes (*spaghettini all' amatriciana*, pasta with

broccoli, beef fillet in balsamic vinegar) and *menu degustazione* with suitable wines to accompany each dish. No outdoor dining.

40 seats Vittorio Emanuele, 71, 590 Closed Sun. All major cards

MONTE CARUSO
$$$

VIA FARINI 12, 00185
TEL. 06 483 549

Of all the regional cuisines of Italy, that of Basilicata in the south is probably the least well-known and this friendly yet restrained restaurant makes sure that diners have an excellent first impression of spicy, herby dishes such as *ricotta ravioli* with mint, stuffed zucchini, and ham and *mozzarella* rolls. No outdoor dining.

40 seats Termini Closed Sun. & L Mon. All major cards

TRATTORIA MONTI
$$$

VIA DI SAN VITO 13, 00185
TEL. 06 446 6573

A warm welcome is guaranteed at this elegant trattoria serving traditional, seasonal dishes from the Lazio region—lamb with artichokes, mushrooms and truffles or thick winter soups made with pulses. No outdoor dining.

50 seats Vittorio Emanuele Closed Tues. & Aug. All major cards

EST! EST! EST!
$$

VIA GENOVA 32, 00184
TEL. 06 488 1107

This well-loved pizzeria has been here for nearly a hundred years (1905) and you may have to queue to get in. Serves both thin-crust (Roman) and thick-crust (Neapolitan) pizza and the usual range of fried *suppli*, cod fillets, and zucchini flowers.

120 seats 64, 70, 71, 115, 116, 170, 640 Closed L Mon. MC, V

HOTELS & RESTAURANTS

🍴 TRIMINI WINE BAR
$$
VIA CERNAIA 37B, 00185
TEL. 06 446 9661
Elegantly modern setting for this excellent value for money wine bar serving delicate symphonies of flavor such as pumpkin soup and rice *timballo*, followed by French and Italian cheeses and mousses for dessert. Wide and interesting range of wines. Booking essential.
🔲 80 seats 🚇 Castro Pretorio 🕐 Closed Sun. & Aug. 🔳 🃏 All major cards

FONTANA DI TREVI TO VIA VENETO

Although this is no longer the fashionable area it was in the 1950s and '60s, it still has a concentration of some of Rome's smartest and most flamboyant hotels. Be careful where you eat—many of the once fashionable names on and around Via Veneto are now over-priced tourist traps.

HOTELS

🏨 EDEN
$$$$$ ✪✪✪✪✪
VIA LUDOVISI 49, 00187
TEL. 06 478 121
FAX 06 482 1584
A massive restoration in the early 1990s created a luxury hotel that is now a favorite among international celebrities. Every detail has been thought of, from the antique furnishings to the imaginative "welcome" sets when you arrive. Stunning views from the famous roof terrace. Breakfast extra.
🛈 112 including some suites 🚇 52, 53, 58, 58b, 63, 95, 116 🅿 Garage 🔀 🔳 🃏 All major cards

🏨 EXCELSIOR
$$$$$ ✪✪✪✪✪
VIA VITTORIO VENETO 125, 00187
TEL. 06 47 081
FAX 06 482 6205
A dramatically grand hotel,

opulently decorated with swathes of rich fabric, and antique and reproduction furniture. All the more or less uniformly decorated bedrooms are luxurious while the suites look like stage sets. Breakfast extra.
🛈 327 including some suites 🚇 52, 53, 58, 58b, 63, 95, 116 🅿 At a price 🔀 🔳 🃏 All major cards

🏨 LORD BYRON
$$$$ ✪✪✪✪✪
VIA GIUSEPPE DE NOTARIS 5, 00197
TEL. 06 322 4541
FAX 06 322 0405
Tranquility is the over-riding feature of this well-run hotel in a chic residential area. The prettily decorated rooms are a good size and equipped with all you'd expect from a five-star hotel.
🛈 37 🚇 52, 53, 910 🅿 Garage 🔀 🔳 🃏 All major cards

🏨 FONTANA
$$$ ✪✪✪
PIAZZA DI TREVI 96, 00187
TEL. 06 678 6113
FAX 06 679 0024
The view over Trevi fountain from this quirky little hotel is breathtaking (also sleep-robbing—it goes on all night). Rooms come in all shapes and sizes in this rambling old building. Breakfast is extra.
🛈 25 🚇 52, 53, 58, 60, 61, 62, 63, 71, 95, 115, 116, 117, 160, 175, 492, 628, 850 (Via Tritone, Via del Corso) 🔀 🃏 All major cards

🏨 LA RESIDENZA
$$$ ✪✪✪✪
VIA EMILIA 22–24, 00187
TEL. 06 488 0789
FAX 06 485 721
A smart hotel that is far more restrained than its more ostentatious neighbors on Via Veneto, although it offers a comparable range of services and facilities. The atmosphere is serene and courteously welcoming.

🛈 28 including some junior suites 🚇 52, 53, 58, 58b, 63, 95, 116 🅿 Garage 🔀 🔳 🃏 AE, MC, V

RESTAURANTS

🍴 LA TERRAZZA DELL' EDEN
$$$$$
VIA LUDOVISI 49, 00187
TEL 06 4781 2552
Certainly not the best value in Rome but the view and elegant surroundings guarantee a memorable experience. The menu makes creative and interesting use of a wide range of Mediterranean ingredients (although some dishes are almost too ambitious in their quest for originality). Desserts are the highlight.
🔲 60 seats 🚇 52, 53, 58, 58b, 63, 95, 116 🅿 🕐 Always open 🔳 🃏 All major cards

🍴 PAPA BACCUS
$$$$
VIA TOSCANA 36, 00187
TEL. 06 4274 2808
There aren't many genuine, good restaurants this close to Via Veneto (notorious for its tourist traps) but this is one. The cuisine is Tuscan from the *salami antipasto* to the *cantuccini* and Vinsanto (after-dinner sweet wine). Suave, professional service. Has a non-smoking section.
🔲 60 seats 🚇 52, 53, 58, 58b, 63 🅿 🕐 Closed Sun. & L Sat. & Christmas period 🔳 🃏 All major cards

🍴 TRATTORIA TRITONE
$$$
VIA DEI MARONITI 1, 00187
TEL. 06 679 8181
Here you're guaranteed not just excellent Roman cuisine, but courteous, attentive (English-speaking) service and a welcome that is hard to match in a city whose attitude to tourists is sometimes slightly cynical—non-Italian eating habits are courteously

HOTELS & RESTAURANTS

accommodated. Underneath the newly opened elegant extension are some carefully preserved ancient remains. Il Tritone's popularity with journalists from the nearby *Il Messaggero* (for whom it stays open late) proves its appeal with discerning locals.

🛏 180 seats 🚌 52, 53, 58, 60, 61, 62, 63, 71, 95, 115, 116 (Via Tritone) 🕐 Closed Sun. 🏧 All major cards

🍴 PICCOLO ARANCIO
$$
VICOLO SCANDERBERG 112, 00187
TEL. 06 678 6139
Popular and thus packed little restaurant that extends over several rooms on a tiny, steep alleyway near the Trevi Fountain. The food offers a good, rather than exceptional, range of Roman standards slightly adapted for international tastes.

🛏 40 seats 🚌 52, 53, 58, 60, 61, 62, 63, 71, 95, 115, 116, 204, 492, 590 (Via del Corso) 🕐 Closed Mon. & Aug. 🏧 All major cards

🍴 VINERIA IL CHIANTI
$$
VIA DEL LAVATORE 81, 00187
TEL. 06 678 7550
Apart from the standard wine bar fare of cheeses and salamis, here you'll find some tasty *primi* and pizzas with original toppings all served in an informal setting. Not surprisingly, Chianti wines dominate the wine list.

🛏 60 seats 🚌 52, 53, 58, 60, 61, 62, 63, 71, 95, 115, 116, 204, 492, 590 (Via Tritone, Via del Corso) 🕐 Closed Sun. & Aug. 🏧 None

PIAZZA DI SPAGNA TO VILLA BORGHESE

This is an elegant area that includes Rome's smartest shopping streets along with some interesting and original hotels and restaurants. Proximity to the Villa Borghese park is an added advantage.

HOTELS

🏨 ALDROVANDI PALACE
$$$$$ ✪✪✪✪✪
VIA U. ALDROVANDI 15, 00197
TEL. 06 322 3993
FAX 06 322 1435
This elegantly restrained hotel housed in a former boarding school makes the most of its beautiful setting on the edge of Villa Borghese park. Unusually, some of the well-planned and attractively furnished public rooms and bedrooms are reserved for non-smokers. The gardens and other outdoor areas are as well cared for as the interior.

🛏 137 🚌 52, 53, 910 🅿

🏧 All major cards

SOMETHING SPECIAL

🏨 HASSLER VILLA MEDICI
This hotel's enviable position at the top of the Spanish Steps is matched by elaborate interior design (marble columns and well-upholstered seating) and bustling attentive service. The good-sized rooms are comfortably furnished and have traces of their more than one hundred-year history as a hotel. Breakfast is extra.

$$$$$ ✪✪✪✪✪
PIAZZA TRINITÀ DEI MONTI 6, 00187
TEL. 06 699 340
FAX 06 678 9991
🛏 100 plus suites
🚌 Spagna 🅿

🏧 All major cards

🏨 INGHILTERRA
$$$$ ✪✪✪✪
VIA BOCCA DI LEONE 14, 00187
TEL. 06 69 981
FAX 06 6992 2243
Famous for well over a century as one of the best in Rome, this hotel can list

Oscar Wilde among its VIP guests. Antique furnishings tend towards the lugubrious but make for an appropriately historic atmosphere. It's also perfectly placed for the city's most exclusive shopping streets. Breakfast is extra.

🛏 98 🚌 Spagna, 116, 117, 590 🚫 🏧 All major cards

🏨 SCALINETTA DI SPAGNA
$$$$ ✪✪✪✪
PIAZZA TRINITÀ DEI MONTI 17, 00187
TEL. 06 6994 0896
FAX 06 6994 0598
This delightfully rambling old building seems to be tumbling down the Spanish Steps to join Keats' house below. Charming individually furnished bedrooms (some slightly small) are fitted into the available space. Spectacular roof garden.

🛏 15 🚌 Spagna, 590 🅿 🚫 🏧 All major cards

🏨 CARRIAGE
$$$ ✪✪✪
VIA DELLE CARROZZE 36, 00187
TEL. 06 699 0124
FAX 06 678 8279
A refined, discreet hotel on one of the shopping streets below the Spanish Steps. You will need to book in advance if you want one of the two rooms with their own balconies, but there's also a roof terrace with bar. Small but carefully designed rooms.

🛏 24 🚌 Spagna, 116, 117, 590 🚫 🏧 All major cards

🏨 GREGORIANA
$$$ ✪✪✪
VIA GREGORIANA 18, 00187
TEL. 06 679 4269
FAX 06 678 4258
A charming hotel decorated in a variety of styles but over-ridingly art deco. Each room, some with private balcony, has its own personality.

HOTELS & RESTAURANTS

Breakfast served in bedrooms or, in summer, on the terrace.
ⓘ 20 🚇 Barberini, Spagna, 116, 117, 590 🅿 Garage 🔁 🔳 🌀 None

LOCARNO
$$$ ✪✪✪
VIA DELLA PENNA 22, 00186
TEL. 06 361 0841
FAX 06 321 5249
This friendly and romantic hotel is in a pretty vine-clad building just off Piazza del Popolo. The public rooms and bedrooms are tastefully decorated and there's a lovely roof garden. Guests can borrow the hotel's bicycles for a convenient way to get around the historic center.
ⓘ 42 🚇 81, 204, 590, 628, 926 🅿 Garage 🔁 🔳 🌀 All major cards

PENSIONE PARLAMENTO
$$ ✪✪
VIA DELLE CONVERTITE 5, 00187
TEL. 06 6992 1000
FAX 06 6992 1000
A simple, well-run and spotlessly clean *pensione* where not all rooms have air-conditioning but there is double-glazing to reduce noise. Breakfast is served on the little roof garden in summer.
ⓘ 22 🚇 52, 53, 58, 60, 61, 62, 63, 71, 95, 115, 116, 117, 160, 175, 492, 628, 850 (Via del Corso) 🅿 Garage 🔁 🌀 All major cards

MARGUTTA
$ ✪✪
VIA LAURINA 34, 00187
TEL. 06 322 3674
FAX 06 320 0395
Excellent value in an expensive part of town. The rooms are simply and traditionally furnished in wood with iron bedsteads. Bath and shower rooms are small but adequate.
ⓘ 21 🚇 116 🅿 Garage 🔁 🌀 All major cards

RESTAURANTS

🍴 AL 34
$$$
VIA MARIO DE'FIORI 34, 00187
TEL. 06 679 5091
Slightly cramped but with a pleasantly friendly atmosphere and good service. The menu is particularly accommodating to tourists with three *menu degustazione* for those who want to taste as many dishes as possible. The quality of food and ambience ensure that locals come too.
🍽 60 seats 🚇 Spagna, 116, 590 🕐 Closed Mon. & Aug. 🔳 🌀 All major cards

SOMETHING SPECIAL

🍴 CAFFE DELLE ARTI
Booking is essential for the glorious surroundings of the Gallery of Modern Art in Villa Borghese. Unlike many beautifully situated restaurants, here you don't have to make any compromises on the food which is good, especially fish dishes served with olives, aniseed, and a host of other compatible flavors.
$$$
VIA A. GRAMSCI 73, 00197
TEL. 06 3265 1236
🍽 130 seats 🅿 🚇 116 🕐 Closed D Mon. 🌀 All major cards

🍴 EDY
$$
VICOLO DEL BABUINO 4, 00187
TEL. 06 3600 1735
A simple, straightforward trattoria in this area is quite a find. Here, among the Roman and sea-based specialties is spaghetti with seafood cooked and served in a paper parcel to keep all the flavors in. No outdoor dining.
🍽 45 seats 🚇 Spagna, 117 🕐 Closed Sun. & Aug. 🌀 All major cards

PRICES

HOTELS
An indication of the cost of a double room without breakfast is given by $ signs.
$$$$$ Over $350
$$$$ $250–$350
$$$ $150–$250
$$ $100–$150
$ Under $100

RESTAURANTS
An indication of the cost of a three-course dinner without drinks is given by $ signs.
$$$$$ Over $60
$$$$ $40–$60
$$$ $30–$40
$$ $20–$30
$ Under $20

🍴 IL BRILLO PARLANTE
$$
VIA DELLA FONTANELLA 12, 00187
TEL. 06 323 5017
A massive range of wines is the highlight of the "Talking drunkard" but there's also a good range of cheeses, salami, pizzas, and grilled meat—the beefsteaks are particularly recommended. The informal staff greet and serve clients as though they were old friends.
🍽 100 seats 🚇 117 🕐 Closed L Sun. & all Aug. 🔳 🌀 All major cards

PANTHEON TO PIAZZA VENEZIA
The true heart of Rome includes the parliament and senate buildings, two major road intersections, and some of the city's oldest monuments as well as a labyrinth of narrow streets and alleys. It's home to some of Rome's most solidly established and dignified restaurants and hotels.

HOTELS

🏨 HOLIDAY INN CROWN PLAZA MINERVA
$$$$$ ✪✪✪✪✪

PIAZZA DELLA MINERVA 69,
00186
TEL. 06 695 201
FAX 06 679 415
The extravagant lobby was
designed by post-modernist
architect Paolo Portoghesi
and there's a wonderful
roof terrace with restaurant
and bar. Although the
bedrooms are fairly standard,
upper-range Holiday Inn,
many have unmatchable
views over the piazza and
its Bernini-designed
marble elephant.
🛏 134, including junior and
full suites 🚇 46, 60, 62, 64,
70, 81, 87, 115, 186, 492, 628,
640, 810 (Largo Argentina)
🅿 🔁 🅢 🔽 🅢 All
major cards

🏨 PLAZA
$$$$ ✪✪✪✪✪
VIA DEL CORSO 126, 00186
TEL. 06 6992 1111
FAX 06 6994 1575
Located right in the heart of
Rome on one of its busiest
shopping streets. The public
rooms are ornately decorated
in stagey aristocratic 18th-
century style and some
bedrooms have their own
balconies. There's also a
communal terrace. Breakfast
is extra.
🛏 229 🚇 81, 115, 117, 204,
590, 628, 913, 926 🔁 🅢
🅢 All major cards

🏨 SANTA CHIARA
$$$ ✪✪✪
VIA DI SANTA CHIARA 21,
00186
TEL. 06 687 2979
FAX 06 687 3144
A refined hotel with
excellent service and a
pleasant, calm atmosphere.
Larger than average, the
bright rooms are carefully
furnished to combine
functionality with comfort.
All the rooms have
satellite television.
🛏 90 🚇 46, 60, 62, 64, 70,
81, 87, 115, 186, 492, 628,
640, 810 (Largo Argentina)
🅢 🔁 🅢 All major cards

🏨 SOLE AL PANTHEON
This gem of a hotel dates
back to the 15th century
and has seen its share of
illustrious guests. Rooms are
bright and airy, furnished in
Mediterranean style with
antique, beamed ceilings,
terracotta floors, and the
addition of mod cons such as
satellite television and, in
some rooms, spa pools.
$$$$ ✪✪✪✪
PIAZZA DEL ROTONDA 63,
00186
TEL. 06 678 0441
FAX 06 6994 0689
🛏 25 🚇 46, 60, 62, 64,
70, 81, 87, 115, 186, 492,
628, 640, 810 (Largo
Argentina) 🔁 🅢

RESTAURANTS

🍴 FORTUNATO AL PANTHEON
$$$$
VIA DEL PANTHEON 55, 00186
TEL. 06 679 2788
Soberly elegant traditional
restaurant much-loved by
Italian politicians from the
nearby parliament and, as
photos attest, visiting dignitar-
ies. Ultra-professional staff
serve delicate versions of
traditional dishes—fillet steak
and fresh fish are excellent.
🪑 110 seats 🚇 46, 60, 62,
64, 70, 81, 87, 115, 186, 492,
628, 640, 810 (Largo
Argentina) 🕐 Closed Sun. &
Aug. 🅢 🅢 All major cards

🍴 L'EAU VIVE
$$$
VIA MONTERONE 85, 00186
TEL. 06 6880 1095
Lay sisters serve in this simple
restaurant located in an old
palazzo, and the proceeds go
to charity. The food and wines
are mainly French and the
range of well-prepared, tasty
dishes on offer suits all
pockets. No outdoor dining.

🪑 180 seats 🚇 46, 60, 62,
64, 70, 81, 87, 115, 186, 492,
628, 640, 810 (Largo
Argentina) 🕐 Closed Sun. &
Aug. 🅢 🅢 All major cards

🍴 SANT'EUSTACHIO
$$$
PIAZZA DEI CAPRETTARI 63,
00186
TEL. 06 687 5216
Restrained, polite atmosphere
with pleasant outdoor dining
in summer. The menu features
Roman and more elaborate
dishes—saltimbocca (veal with
ham), fried artichokes, salmon
carpaccio, and satisfying home-
made tarts for dessert.
Good service.
🪑 100 seats 🚇 46, 60, 62,
64, 70, 81, 87, 115, 186, 492,
628, 640, 810 (Largo
Argentina) 🕐 Closed Sun.
🅢 All major cards

🍴 DA GINO
$$
VICOLO ROSINI 4, 00186
TEL. 06 687 3434
Bustling no-frills trattoria
popular with politicians and
journalists who come from
parliament to grab a quick
lunch or dinner—be
prepared to wait for a
table. Specialties include
pasta with peas, and ham and
rabbit in white wine. No
outdoor dining.
🪑 60 seats 🚇 81, 115, 117,
204, 590, 628, 913, 926
🕐 Closed Sun. & Aug.
🅢 None

CAMPO MARZIO

Central Rome at its most
charming and typical and one of
the busiest areas both during the
day and at night. The range of
hotels and restaurants includes
something to suit all pockets and
tastes and each establishment
has its own distinct personality.

HOTELS

🏨 RAPHAEL
$$$$ ✪✪✪✪
LARGO FEBO 2, 00186

TEL. 06 682 831
FAX 06 687 8993

A soothing ivy-clad building in a surprisingly quiet corner just off Piazza Navona. Public rooms are furnished in a pleasing mix of real and reproduction antiques and bedrooms are well-designed if not particularly large. Attractive multitiered roof terrace and excellent restaurant. Breakfast extra.

🛈 63 🚊 70, 81, 87, 115, 116, 186, 204, 492, 628 (Corso Rinascimento) 🔁 🔇 🗢 All major cards

🏨 DUE TORRI
$$$ ◐◐◐

VICOLO DEL LEONETTO 23, 00186
TEL. 06 687 6983
FAX 06 686 5442

Elegant furnishings and a warm welcome combine with a romantic atmosphere to make this one of the most attractive hotels in its price category. The 19th-century building, on a quiet street not far from Piazza Navona, used to be the home of bishops and cardinals.

🛈 26 🚊 116 🅿 🔁 🔇 🗢 All major cards

🏨 PORTOGHESI
$$$ ◐◐◐

VIA DEI PORTOGHESI 1, 00186
TEL. 06 686 4231
FAX 06 687 6976

An atmospheric 17th-century building houses this simple, efficient hotel named after the adjacent Portuguese church. Some of the rooms have antique furnishings. In summer breakfast is served on the terrace.

🛈 28 and one suite 🚊 70, 81, 87, 115, 116, 186, 204, 492, 628 (Corso Rinascimento) 🅿 🔁 🔇 🗢 MC, V

🏨 TEATRO DI POMPEO
$$$ ◐◐◐

LARGO DEL PALLARO 8, 00186
TEL. 06 687 2812
FAX 06 6880 5531

A delightfully quirky interior is built over the remains of an ancient theater which are visible in the breakfast room. Friendly service and small yet comfortable bedrooms and bathrooms.

🛈 12 🚊 46, 62, 64, 116 🅿 Garage bookable in advance 🔁 🔇 🗢 All major cards

🏨 CAMPO DE' FIORI
$$ ◐◐

VIA DEL BISCIONE 6, 00186
TEL. 06 6880 6865
FAX 06 687 6003

Good value in pretty, individually furnished rooms a stone's throw from Campo dei Fiori. The hotel's two terraces offer lovely views over the roof-tops.

🛈 27 🚊 46, 62, 64, 116 🔁 🗢 MC, V

🏨 RINASCIMENTO
$$ ◐◐◐

VIA DEL PELLEGRINO 122, 00186
TEL. 06 687 4813
FAX 06 683 3518

Located on a narrow street near Campo dei Fiori, this old building has been refurbished recently and now offers excellent value for money in pretty, if slightly small, rooms. There is a terrace.

🛈 18 🚊 46, 62, 64, 116 🔁 🔇 🗢 DC

RESTAURANTS

🍴 CAMPONESCHI
$$$$$

PIAZZA FARNESE 50, 00186
TEL. 06 687 4927

Its location on this gracious piazza adjacent to the French embassy, combined with the courteous, red-carpet welcome extended to all diners, makes for a unique dining experience, even before you've tasted the exquisite Roman cuisine. Served with flourish and style.

🍴 75 seats 🚊 116 🕐 Closed L, daily and Sun. & Aug. 🔇 🗢 All major cards

🍴 IL CONVIVIO

Three brothers run one of the best and nicest restaurants in Rome which has moved to new, extended premises. Service is cordial and informative and the food is ambrosial—basically Italian with some touches of creative genius from the chef (one of the brothers). Every dish is a beautifully presented work of art but the desserts are masterpieces. No outdoor dining.

$$$$$

VIA DEI SOLDATI 44, 00186
TEL. 06 686 9432
🚊 70, 81, 87, 115, 116, 186, 204, 492, 628 (Corso Rinascimento) 🕐 Closed Sun. & L Mon. 🔇 🗢 All major cards

🍴 LA CARBONARA
$$$

PIAZZA CAMPO DE'FIORI 23, 00186
TEL. 06 686 4783

This vast restaurant extends over several floors and (in summer) on to the pavement outside. Its informal atmosphere appeals to both tourists and locals so it's always busy. Standard Roman cuisine of reliable, rather than outstanding, quality is served.

🍴 150 seats 🚊 46, 62, 64, 116 🕐 Closed Tues. & Aug. 🗢 All major cards

🍴 MONSERRATO
$$$

VIA DI MONSERRATO 96, 00186
TEL. 06 687 3386

High standards of cuisine and service and good value for money help to ensure this attractively laid-out restaurant remains popular with both visitors and locals. Fish is the strong point of the good menu—cuttlefish salad to start with, gnocchi with clams, and roast bream with potatoes.

🍴 60 seats 🚊 116

⚙ Closed Mon., Aug. & Dec.
⚙ AE, MC, V

🍽 PIERLUIGI
$$$
PIAZZA DE'RICCI 144, 00186
TEL. 06 686 1302
Although it has suffered
recently as a mecca for
visitors in the know (prices
have risen and it's always full),
this is still a very agreeable
place to sample deliciously
fresh dishes—pasta with
zucchini flowers, fish cooked in
various ways, and tasty
desserts. A good first
experience of a real Italian
restaurant that's used to
coping with non-Italians.
⚙ 80 seats ⚙ 116
⚙ Closed Mon. ⚙ ⚙ All
major cards

🍽 DITIRAMBO
$$
PIAZZA DELLA CANCELLERIA
74, 00186
TEL. 06 687 1626
Charming staff and attractive
decor make for a pleasantly
busy atmosphere which is
matched by the standard of
the constantly changing menu.
Innovative versions of Italian
regional dishes include a
delicious potato and broad-
bean soup, rabbit, egg-plant
croquettes, lamb with lentils,
and delicious desserts. Tasty
home-made bread and
pasta. Good value for
money. Booking is essential
in the evening.
⚙ 55 seats ⚙ 46, 62, 64,
116 ⚙ Closed L Mon. & all
Aug. ⚙ ⚙ All major cards

🍽 BAIRES
$$
CORSO RINASCIMENTO 1,
00186
TEL. 06 686 1293
Come to this Argentine
restaurant when you've got a
large appetite—starters
include *empanadas* (various
meats wrapped in pastry)
which are followed by gener-
ous portions of grilled meats.
The atmosphere is casual and

bustling. No outdoor dining.
⚙ 100 seats ⚙ 70, 81, 87,
115, 116, 186, 204, 492, 628
(Corso Rinascimento)
⚙ Always open ⚙ ⚙ All
major cards

🍽 OSTERIA ROMANESCA
$$
PIAZZA CAMPO DE'FIORI 40,
00186
TEL. 06 686 4024
This truly Roman trattoria
has been here for a hundred
years. Nowadays it's run by
Aldo, who keeps both staff
and customers in order. The
cuisine is good, simple Roman
dishes—ravioli in fresh
tomato sauce, chicken with
green peppers, meatballs in
sauce. At lunch time you can
watch the Campo dei Fiori
market being laboriously
dismantled, as it is every day
after early trading.
⚙ 40 seats ⚙ 46, 62, 64,
116 ⚙ Closed Mon.
⚙ None

🍽 DA BAFFETTO
$
VIA DEL GOVERNO VECCHIO
114, 00186
TEL. 06 686 1617
One of Rome's most popular
and best pizzerias, this is not
somewhere you'll be able to
linger—unless you come early
or late you'll have to wait for a
table and then share it when
you do sit down.
⚙ 100 seats ⚙ 46, 62, 64,
116 ⚙ Closed L & Aug.
⚙ None

🍽 INSALATA RICCA
$
PIAZZA PASQUINO 72, 00186
TEL. 06 6830 7881
Delicious, prepared-to-order
salads with a wide range of
different ingredients are the
highlight of this informal
restaurant, ideally situated for
a sightseer's lunch break.
There are also simple, fresh
primi and main courses for
those with larger appetites.
Other branches at Largo
de'Chiavari 85 (just off Corso

Vittoria Emanuele II), Via del
Gazometro 62 (in Testaccio),
and on Viale Aventino.
⚙ 50 seats ⚙ 46, 62, 64,
116 ⚙ Always open
⚙ AE, V

VATICANO

Slightly out of the hustle and
bustle, this is a solidly
respectable residential area,
much of which dates from the
late 19th and early 20th
centuries. There are a few
unflashy but luxurious hotels, but
the plethora of gaudy, touristy
eating places around the Vatican
is best avoided.

HOTELS

🏨 ATLANTE STAR
$$$$ ✪✪✪✪
VIA VITELLESCHI 34, 00193
TEL. 06 687 3233
FAX 06 687 2300
A comfortable, well-run hotel
with nice staff and spectacular
views of St. Peter's and Rome
from its roof garden. Rooms
are small and (unusually for
Rome) decorated in an
interesting ultra-modern style
with dark colors.
⚙ 70 some suites
⚙ Ottaviano, 19, 23, 34, 51,
64, 81, 492, 982 ⚙ ⚙ ⚙
⚙ All major cards

🏨 COLUMBUS
$$$ ✪✪✪
VIA DELLA CONCILIAZIONE
33, 00193
TEL. 06 686 5435
FAX 06 686 4874
A 15th-century building right
in front of St. Peter's is the
setting for this aristocratically
austere hotel. Bedrooms and
bathrooms are functional but
public areas make up with a
surfeit of carved stone and
frescoed walls.
⚙ 92 ⚙ 23, 34, 46, 62, 64,
98, 881, 982 ⚙ ⚙ ⚙
⚙ All major cards

🏨 FARNESE
$$$ ✪✪✪✪
VIA A. FARNESE 30, 00193

HOTELS & RESTAURANTS

TEL. 06 321 2553
FAX 06 321 5129
A charming choice (and value for money) in the residential Prati area near St. Peter's, connected to the center by metro. Tranquil atmosphere with 17th-century decor and comfortable bedrooms.
🛏 22 🚇 Lepanto 🅿 ⬍
♿ 💳 All major cards

RESTAURANTS

🍴 TAVERNA ANGELICA
$$$$
PIAZZA DELLE VASCHETTE 14, 00193
TEL. 06 687 4514
Reservations are essential for this romantic little corner serving delicate, flavorful, and innovative Italian cuisine—*tagliatelle* with nettles and curry, duck breast in balsamic vinegar, and chocolate crêpes, all accompanied by a carefully selected wine list.
🍽 20 seats 🚇 Ottaviano, 19, 23, 34, 51, 64, 81, 492, 982 🕒 Closed Sun. & L Mon. ♿ 💳 AE, MC, V

🍴 VERANDA OF THE HOTEL COLUMBUS
$$$$
BORGO DI SANTO SPIRITO 73, 00193
TEL. 06 687 2973
A tranquil haven off Via della Conciliazione whose menu of delicacies includes prawn and spinach *risotto*, stir-fried vegetables, and *farfalle* with fresh tomato, basil, and *caciocavallo* cheese as well as some elegant versions of Roman dishes. Service is excellent and summer dining in the garden is particularly pleasurable.
🍽 80 seats 🚇 23, 34, 46, 62, 64, 98, 881, 982 🕒 Always open ♿ 💳 All major cards

TRASTEVERE TO GIANICOLO

This old area across the river from the rest of the historic center is the place to come in the evening when the streets are throbbing with visitors and Romans looking for a good time. Apart from a few cheerful budget hotels, Trastevere doesn't offer much in the way of accommodation. However, it has the highest concentration of eating and drinking establishments of any area in Rome and its maze of pretty little alleyways is perfect for an after-dinner stroll.

HOTELS

🏨 LA CISTERNA
$ ⊙⊙
VIA DELLA CISTERNA 8, 00153
TEL. 06 581 7212
FAX 06 581 0091
Attractive, atmospheric little hotel in one of the winding streets behind Trastevere's main piazza. Rooms are simple and there's a pretty courtyard for the summer.
🛏 18 🚇 8, 23, 44, 75, 280 🅿 Garage ⬍ 💳 DC, MC, V

🏨 LOCANDA CARMEL
$ ⊙
VIA G. MAMELLI 11, 00153
TEL. 06 580 9921
Simple, bright rooms (all with private bathrooms) in this clean, airy kosher *pensione* near the heart of Trastevere. Two rooms open on to the communal roof terrace.
🛏 9 🚇 23, 44, 75, 280, H ⬍ 💳 MC, V

🏨 TRASTEVERE
$ ⊙⊙
VIA LUCIANO MANARA 24A, 00153
TEL. 06 581 4713
FAX 06 588 1016
Recently renovated and upgraded, the entrance is attractively decorated with wall paintings and repro-duction antique furniture. Small but cheerful rooms look out over the market. This is the heart of Trastevere so it's noisy at night. Breakfast extra.
🛏 12 🚇 8, 23, 44, 75, 280 💳 All major cards

PRICES

HOTELS
An indication of the cost of a double room without breakfast is given by $ signs.
$$$$$	Over $350
$$$$	$250–$350
$$$	$150–$250
$$	$100–$150
$	Under $100

RESTAURANTS
An indication of the cost of a three-course dinner without drinks is given by $ signs.
$$$$$	Over $60
$$$$	$40–$60
$$$	$30–$40
$$	$20–$30
$	Under $20

RESTAURANTS

🍴 PARIS
$$$$
PIAZZA SAN CALISTO 7A, 00153
TEL. 06 581 5378
Civilized surroundings and friendly service at this Jewish–Roman restaurant whose dishes include elegant versions of such favorites as skate-wing soup, pasta and chickpeas, ox-tail, and roast fish and meats with potatoes.
🍽 90 seats 🚇 8, 23, 44, 75, 280 🕒 Closed Mon., Aug., & D Sun. ♿ 💳 All major cards

🍴 SABATINI
$$$$
PIAZZA SANTA MARIA IN TRASTEVERE 13, 00153
TEL. 06 581 2026
Tourists come for the stunning setting and archetypal Italian restaurant ambience (complete with strumming serenaders) as well as for the good (and sometimes exceptional) mainly fish-based cuisine, which also draws locals. The menu may not be particularly innovative but the ingredients are all super-

fresh and of top quality.

🍴 120 seats 🚌 8, 23, 44, 75, 280 🕐 Closed Wed. 🆒 🚭 All major cards

🍴 L'ANTICO TEVERE
$$$
VIA PORTUENSE 45, 00153
TEL. 06 581 6054

Come here in the summer and the view from the terrace over the Tiber along this unbuilt-up stretch of the river is enough to make you think you're in the country. The restaurant has been professionally run by the same family for three generations. Fish is the mainstay of a menu which also offers good meat and vegetable dishes. It's open until after midnight and in summer serves pizzas as well as the restaurant menu.

🍴 120 seats 🚌 23, 44, 75, 280 🅿 🕐 Closed Sun. & Jan. 🚭 All major cards

🍴 BELLI
$$$
PIAZZA SANT'APOLLONIA 11, 00153
TEL. 06 580 3782

Fish takes pride of place at this popular, busy Sardinian restaurant, but there are other excellent dishes such as giant Sardinian ravioli in spicy tomato sauce, and good grilled meats. Booking is recommended.

🍴 80 seats 🚌 8, 23, 44, 75, 280 🕐 Closed Mon. & Jan. 🚭 All major cards

🍴 BOTTICELLA
$$$
VICOLO DEL LEOPARDO 39A, 00153
TEL. 06 581 4738

In summer you can eat outside on this characteristic Trastevere alley, complete with drying washing and noisy neighbors. Excellently prepared Roman dishes are offered but the highlights are the more original alternatives—*crostini* with homemade pâté and the dish

for which the restaurant is named, veal roasted with vegetables. Friendly, welcoming atmosphere and courteous service.

🍴 50 seats 🚌 8, 23, 44, 75, 280 🆒 🚭 None

🍴 CHECCO ER CARETTIERE
$$$
VIA BENEDETTA 10, 00153
TEL. 06 581 7018

Behind a modest entrance lurks a massive Trastevere institution whose glorious and long past is recorded on the hundreds of photos that cover its walls. The atmosphere is informal but efficient and the Roman cuisine it serves is reliably good.

🍴 150 seats 🚌 8, 23, 44, 75, 280 🕐 Closed Mon. & D Sun. 🆒 🚭 All major cards

🍴 CIAK
$$$
VICOLO DEL CINQUE 21, 00153
TEL. 06 589 4774

Reservations are essential for this carnivores' paradise where game and grilled meats from Tuscany are served in checked-tablecloth, informal surroundings. It can get a little crowded.

🍴 65 seats 🚌 8, 23, 44, 75, 280 🕐 Closed L Tues.–Sun. & Mon 🚭 All major cards

🍴 FERRARA
$$$
VIA DEL MORO 1, 00153
TEL. 06 580 3769

Two sisters run this excellent and popular wine bar which has an impressive list of wines and after-dinner drinks to accompany a constantly changing menu. The soups are particularly recommended. The decor is original and pleasing, with touches such as glass panels in the floor allowing you to look down into the extensive, all-important cellars.

🍴 45 seats 🚌 8, 23, 44, 75, 280 🕐 Closed Tues. & L

Sun. (winter), Sun. (summer); D other days 🚭 All major cards

🍴 RIPA 12
$$$
VIA SAN FRANCESCO A RIPA 12, 00153
TEL. 06 580 9093

Comfortable, informal setting in which to eat fish dishes with a Sardinian–Sicilian influence—watch for fresh tuna, marinated raw fish, and grilled anchovies when available. Offers consistently high standards and excellent value.

🍴 55 seats 🚌 8, 23, 44, 75, 280 🕐 Closed Sun. & Aug. 🆒 🚭 All major cards

🍴 DA LUCIA
$$
VICOLO DEL MATTONATO 2B, 00153
TEL. 06 580 3601

The same family has run this no-frills, typical trattoria for more than 60 years. In summer tables fill the alley outside. The interior is lined with wooden slats (an old form of insulation). The unchanging menu includes some standard *primi* followed by dishes such as rabbit *alla cacciatora*, cuttlefish with peas, and beef stew.

🍴 50 seats 🚌 8, 23, 44, 75, 280 🕐 Closed Mon., Aug., & Christmas 🚭 None

🍴 IVO
$
VIA SAN FRANCESCO A RIPA 158, 00153
TEL. 06 581 7082

Four decades of business have established this as a mainstay of the Rome pizza scene and the owners continue to come up with a few interesting and original toppings. The hectic atmosphere is complemented by swift, efficient service.

🍴 120 seats 🚌 8, 23, 44, 75, 280 🕐 Tues., other days open evenings only 🆒 🚭 All major cards

HOTELS & RESTAURANTS

🍴 PANATTONI
$

VIALE TRASTEVERE 53, 00153
TEL. 06 580 0919
Its marble tables earned it the nickname of the "mortuary", but there's precious little of the deathly about this hectic pizzeria which has the added advantage of staying open until 2:30 a.m.

�� 50 seats 🚍 8, 44, 75 🕐 Closed Wed., Aug., & L Thurs.–Tues. 🚫 None

🍴 PIZZERIA CALISTO
$

PIAZZA DI SAN CALISTO 9, 00153
TEL. 06 581 8256
Huge pizza bases come with a range of toppings, including the standards but also some innovations, such as fresh tomatoes with salted *ricotta*. Don't be daunted by the massive diameters, the pizzas are very light and easy to get through.

🔳 60 seats 🚍 8, 23, 44, 75, 280 🕐 Closed Mon. & L daily 🚫 All major cards

FORUM BOARIUM TO AVENTINO

This green, leafy hill just outside the center has been one of the most sought after residential areas of Rome since ancient times and now contains some excellent, tranquil hotels. Many of the nearest restaurants are in the popular Testaccio area or the Ghetto.

HOTELS

🏨 DOMUS AVENTINA
$$$ ●●●

VIA DI SANTA PRISCA 11/B, 00153
TEL. 06 574 6189
FAX 06 5730 0044
Near the old town wall, this elegantly simple hotel is imaginatively decorated throughout with trompe l'oeil in the lobby. The bedrooms are spacious and the bathrooms comfortable.

🛏 26 🚍 Metro: Circo

Massimo; Bus: 175, 715 🔲
🚫 All major cards

🏨 AVENTINO
$$ ●●

VIA DI SAN DOMENICO 10, 00153
TEL. 06 574 5174
FAX 06 578 3604
A simpler, more economical version of its sister Sant' Anselmo and Villa San Pio, here too you'll find a peaceful sanctuary in the green of the Aventine.

🛏 23 🚍 175, 715 🅿 🔳
🚫 All major cards

🏨 SANT'ANSELMO
$$ ●●●

PIAZZA DI SANT'ANSELMO 2, 00153
TEL. 06 574 3547
FAX 06 578 3604
The lush garden with its orange trees makes the perfect setting for unwinding after a day's sightseeing. Public and private rooms are attractively decorated and there are plenty of little corners for a quiet read or chat. Breakfast is extra.

🛏 46 🚍 175, 715 🅿
🚫 All major cards

RESTAURANTS

🍴 CHECCHINO DAL 1887
$$$$

VIA DI MONTE TESTACCIO 30, 00153
TEL. 06 574 6318
True Roman cuisine has always made much use of offal and this long-established restaurant (run by the same family for more than a hundred years) is recognized by aficionados as the place to eat *rigatoni* with calves' intestines, ox-tail, and tripe, as well as dishes for the more squeamish—stewed, roasted, and grilled meats and an excellent range of cheeses.

🔳 95 seats 🚍 95, 170, 780 🅿 🕐 Closed Mon., Aug., Christmas, & D Sun. 🔲
♿ 🚫 All major cards

🍴 GIGGETTO AL PORTICO D'OTTAVIA
$$$$

VIA DEL PORTICO D'OTTAVIA 21A, 00186
TEL. 06 686 1105
The main street of the Jewish ghetto, under the ruins of an ancient portico, is the perfect setting for sampling traditional Jewish Roman cuisine—starting with fried cod, anchovies, zucchini flowers, and artichokes and finishing with cheesecake and blueberry sauce.

🔳 80 seats 🚍 23, 60, 63, 280 🕐 Closed Mon. & July 🚫 All major cards

🍴 SORA LELLA
$$$$

VIA DI PONTE QUATTRO CAPI 16, 00186
TEL. 06 686 1601
Romantically set on the pretty Isola Tiberina between the Ghetto and Trastevere, this is a welcoming little restaurant serving appetite-busting Roman fare such as pasta with potatoes or with chickpeas and clams, cuttlefish and artichokes, and delicious desserts that include a salami of chocolate. No outdoor dining.

🔳 45 seats 🚍 23, 60, 63, 280 🕐 Closed Sun. & Aug.
🔲 🚫 All major cards

🍴 PERINI A TESTACCIO
$$$

VIA MARMORATA 39, 00153
TEL. 06 574 2415
A classic neighborhood trattoria in the classic neighborhood of Testaccio (under the Aventine Hill). People come from miles around and booking is recommended. Efficient, friendly service for authentic, well-prepared standard Roman dishes. No outdoor dining.

🔳 90 seats 🚍 23, 75, 95, 170, 280, 716, 780 🕐 Closed Wed. & Aug. 🔲 🚫 None

🍴 SAN TEODORO
$$$

VIA DEI FIENILI 49, 00186

TEL. 06 678 0633

An all-round winner—lovely setting and atmosphere (both inside and out), charming service, good selection of wines, and, last but not least, delicious innovative cuisine that's based on some of the most appealing ingredients and dishes from all over Italy.

 80 seats 81, 160, 204, 628 Always open All major cards

LA BOTTEGA DEL VINO DE ANACLETO BLEVE
$$
VIA SANTA MARIA DEL PIANTO 9A, 00186
TEL. 06 686 5970

This well-stocked wine shop turns itself into an excellent buffet restaurant at lunchtime and on some evenings. Delicious baked vegetable dishes, cold meats, cheeses, *carpaccio*, and salads. Good service.

50 seats 8, 60, 63 Closed D Mon., Tues., & Sat., & all Sun. All major cards

FUORI LE MURA (OUTSIDE THE WALLS)

Several of these hotels are ideal for those who want the sort of facilities they'd usually find in the country. The few restaurants listed are also worth making a journey for.

HOTELS

CAVALIERI HILTON
$$$$$ ✪✪✪✪✪
VIA A. CADLOLO 101, 00136
TEL. 06 35091
FAX 06 3509 2241

A shuttle service takes guests in and out of central Rome, leaving you free to enjoy facilities and peace that only an out-of-center location could afford. All the well-equipped rooms have balconies and there are tennis courts and a jogging track

among a wide range of features typical of this top-of-the-market chain. Breakfast is extra.

358 and 18 suites All major cards

SHANGRI LA CORSETTI
$$$ ✪✪✪✪
VIALE ALGERIA 141, 00144
TEL. 06 591 6441
FAX 06 541 3813

A peaceful setting surrounded by greenery in the geometrically planned EUR district, which was based on town planning designs commissioned by Mussolini. This attractive modern hotel offers excellent service and facilities.

52 All major cards

TURNER
$$$ ✪✪✪
VIA NOMENTANA 29, 00161
TEL. 06 4425 0077
FAX 06 4425 0165

A superb combination of historic charm (in a late 19th-century *palazzo*) and modern comfort. Decor is elegant and welcoming and the staff are efficient and friendly.

38 including one suite 36, 37, 60, 62, 136, 137, 317 All major cards

VILLA DEL PARCO
$$ ✪✪✪
VIA NOMENTANA 110, 00161
TEL. 06 4423 7773
FAX 06 4423 7572

Comfortable, homely hotel just out of the center which has been run by the same friendly family for decades. The late 19th-century villa is set in its own garden. Bedrooms and bathrooms are tastefully decorated and spacious and snacks are served when and wherever you like.

24 6, 37, 60, 62, 136, 137, 317 All major cards

RESTAURANTS

SOMETHING SPECIAL

LA PERGOLA DE L'HOTEL HILTON

Generally accepted to be the best restaurant in Rome at the moment thanks to its chef, Heinz Beck. Although he's German rather than Italian, the masterpieces he turns out for a menu that changes every day are strongly Italian influenced. Add to this superbly attentive service and one of the best views of Rome, and the night's sure to be a success.

$$$$$
VIA A. CADLOLO 101, 00136
TEL. 06 3509 2211
75 seats Closed Sun., Mon. & L Tues.–Sat. All major cards

CECILIA METELLA
$$$
VIA APPIA ANTICA 125, 00179
TEL. 06 511 0213

Summer lunchtimes are the best times to enjoy the rural charms of this restaurant's huge, pretty, shady garden. In winter, there's an open fire in the dining room. The menu changes seasonally.

180 seats Closed Mon. All major cards

TRAM TRAM
$$
VIA DEI RETI 44, 00185
TEL. 06 490 416

Reservations are essential at this popular, noisy trattoria. The frequently changing menu is oriented toward Pugliese cuisine but makes the most of whatever's available—spaghetti with baby octopus, anchovy and endive tart, bean and chicory purée. Good service but a bit chaotic when it gets busy.

50 seats Closed Mon. & Aug. All major cards

SHOPPING IN ROME

Rome is, generally speaking, a pleasant place to shop. Prices are usually clearly displayed in windows and on or near individual goods. Not all (but by now most) shops accept payment by credit card. Non-EU citizens can claim back the sales tax on personal purchases over L.300,000 made at shops displaying the Europe Tax Free sticker. Make sure you keep the till receipt (*scontrino*) and ask for a tax-back form from the shop.

OPENING HOURS & SERVICE

The opening hours of individual shops have not been listed here. Neither have the days closed. Shop opening hours and days are in a state of flux (see p. 241). A great many of the shops mentioned here are open all day and also on Sunday for at least part of the year. However, before making a special journey on a Sunday, or over the afternoon break (from 1–5 p.m.) check that the shop you want is open by phoning.

Italian shop assistants can seem brusque and offhand (not to say rude) to those used to North American standards of service. Try not to be offended or to get angry, but be ready to assert yourself with a clearly pronounced, smiling "*Mi scusi*" when you're tired of waiting for the assistants to finish their chat. In the shops listed here the service is nearly always attentive, and sometimes positively charming.

DEPARTMENT STORES

Department stores haven't really caught on in Italy where the small, family-run business reigns supreme. Exceptions are Rinascente, with branches at Via del Corso (Bus: 60, 62, 63, 81, 85, 95, 117, 160, 175, 492, 628, 850), Piazza Fiume (Bus: 3, 4, 56, 58, 319, 490, 495) and Coin, housed in an attractive old beer factory at Via Mantova 1 (Bus: 38, 58). They all have wide selections of clothing, accessories, and cosmetics and Coin and the Rinascente at Piazza Fiume also have kitchen and home departments.

ANTIQUE SHOPS & MARKETS

The antique and fine art shopping streets (in the historic center) are Vias del Babuino, dei Coronari, dell' Orso, and Giulia. You'll find gorgeous pieces but dealers know the values and these streets are not for bargain hunters.

Neither, really, is Rome's most famous flea market—Porta Portese held on Sunday mornings in the streets to the east of Viale Trastevere (Bus: 8, 44, 75). Love it or hate it, it's certainly got its own atmosphere with stalls selling everything from old motor parts to organic foodstuffs (hang on to your valuables while you're here—pickpockets are among those who love Porta Portese).

There are markets of various types and sizes all over Rome. Those worth looking at include the brightly colored food, flower, and domestic goods market in Campo dei Fiori (Mon.–Sat morning, bus: 46, 62, 64, 116); the antique book and print market at Piazza Borghese (Mon.–Fri. 9 a.m.–5:30 p.m., Sat. 9 a.m.–7 p.m. Bus: 70, 81, 115, 186, 628); the food market at Piazza Vittorio Emanuele where goodies from all over the world are sold (Mon.–Sat. mornings. Metro: Vittorio Emanuele); and Testaccio Market (Mon.–Sat. mornings. Bus: 23, 75, 280, 716) where cut-price shoes and clothes are sold alongside an impressive array of fresh produce.

CLOTHING

Italy leads the world when it comes to designer fashion. Most of the main houses are based in Milan but one or two (including Fendi and Valentino) have their headquarters in Rome and all of them have major branches here. The chicest shops are in the grid of streets south of Piazza di Spagna—especially in Vias Condotti, Babuino, and Borgognona. Less exclusive clothes' shops are on and around Vias Cola di Rienzo, Nazionale, and del Corso.

Arsenale Via del Governo Vecchio 64, 00186. Tel 06 686 1380. Bus: 46, 62, 64.
Quirky, feminine fashions using swathes of luxurious and unusual fabric.

Datti Via Bocca Leone 89, 00187. Tel 06 678 9942. Bus: 116, 117, 590; Metro: Spagna.
Small but great shop selling tailored clothing and elegant casual wear for men; nearly all made in Italy, in spite of some of the English-sounding labels.

Davide Cenci Via Campo Marzio 1–7, 00186. Tel 06 678 4537. Bus: 81, 115, 117, 204, 590, 628.
Top-quality, elegantly conservative gentlemen's outfitters. There's also a women's department.

Degli Effetti Piazza Capranica 79 and 93, 00186. Tel 06 679 1650 and 06 679 0202. Bus: 60, 62, 63, 81, 85, 95, 117, 160, 175, 492, 628, 850 (Via del Corso).
A selection of the latest offerings from Italian and other fashion houses; one shop for men, one for women.

Dolce e Gabbana Via Borgognona 7, 00187. Tel 06 678 2990. Bus: 116, 117, 590; Metro: Spagna.
Dramatically stylish clothes for women from this designer duo.

Emporio Armani Via del Babuino 140, 00187. Tel 06 322 1581. Bus: 117; Metro: Spagna.
Wearable well-tailored separates for men and women, plus fashion accessories, toiletries and other lines from this highly regarded designer.

Energie Via del Corso 486, 00187. Tel 06 321 4846. Bus: 60, 62, 63, 81, 85, 95, 117, 160, 175, 492, 628, 850 (Via del Corso).
Street fashion aimed at Italian under-25s but appealing to anybody with an eye for the latest, and a sense of fun.

Etro Via del Babuino 102,
00187. Tel 678 8257. Bus: 117;
Metro: Spagna.
For men and women who like
flashes of originality in what are,
basically, conventionally smart
clothes. Gorgeous patterned
silks and other fabrics are also
used for ties and scarves.
Fendi Via Bourgognona 36–40,
00186. Tel 06 679 7641. Bus: 116,
117, 590; Metro: Spagna.
Rome-based designers whose
imposing store sells everything
from fur coats to gifts.
Gianni Versace (Men) Via
Borgognona 24, 00187. Tel 06
679 5037. Bus: 116, 117, 590;
Metro: Spagna. (Women) Via
Bocca di Leone 27, 00187. Tel 06
678 0521. Bus: 116, 117, 590;
Metro: Spagna.
Gianni may have passed away,
but his name lives on in the
flamboyant color schemes and
styles beloved of Hollywood
stars and the international
glitterati.
Giorgio Armani Via dei
Condotti 77, 00187. Tel 06 699
1460. Bus: 116, 117, 590; Metro:
Spagna.
The king of understated
elegance for men and women.
Laura Biagiotti Via
Borgognona 43–44, 00187. Tel 06
679 1205. Bus: 81, 115, 117, 204,
590, 628.
Pretty, wearable high-fashion for
women.
Max Mara Via Condotti 17–19,
00187. Tel 06 6992 2104. Bus:
116, 117, 590; Metro: Spagna.
Very wearable, slightly sporty,
reasonably priced suits and
separates for women.
Prada Via Condotti 92–95,
00187. Tel 06 679 0897. Bus: 116,
117, 590; Metro: Spagna.
Cutting-edge women's clothes
and accessories with a massive
international following among
fashion journalists.
Replay Via della Rotonda 25,
00186. Tel 06 683 2963. Bus: 46,
60, 62, 64, 70, 81, 87, 115, 186,
492, 628, 640, 810 (Largo
Argentina).
Rome's answer to The Gap? The
prices are a little higher but then
so's the styling.

Scala 14 Via della Scala 14,
00153. Tel 06 588 3580. Bus: 8,
23, 44, 75, 280.
Women come from far and wide
for these deliciously original but
wearable clothes for all
occasions, unlike anything you'll
find elsewhere.
Valentino (Men) Via Condotti
13, 00187. Tel 06 678 3656. Bus:
116, 117, 590; Metro: Spagna.
(Women) Via Bocca di Leone
15–18, 00187. Tel 06 679 5862.
Bus: 116, 117, 590; Metro: Spagna.
Chic elegance from Rome's most
famous and best-loved
homegrown fashion house.

SHOES

You can't leave Italy without
buying at least one pair of shoes.
The shops listed here are the
very best but you'll find well-
made, attractively designed shoes
in virtually any shop you look in.
Borini Via dei Pettinari 86,
00186. Tel 06 687 5670. Bus 23,
280.
Massive range of colors and
fashionable youngish styles for
women. Excellent prices.
Bruno Magli Via Gambero 2,
00187. Tel 06 679 3820. Bus: 52,
53, 60, 61, 62, 63, 71, 95, 115, 116
(Piazza San Silvestro). Other
branches around town.
Beautifully made shoes for fairly
conservative but still fashion-
conscious men and women.
Ferragamo Via Condotti 66,
00187. Tel 06 678 1130.
The most famous shoe designers
in the world, based in Florence,
have extended into the designer
clothes and accessories markets
for men and women.
Fragiacomo Via Condotti 35,
00187. Tel 06 678 8780. Bus: 81,
115, 117, 204, 590, 628.
Wide selection of elegant men's
and women's shoes for all
occasions.
Fausto Santini Via Frattina
120, 00187. Tel 06 678 4114. Bus:
116, 117, 590; Metro: Spagna.
Trend-setting luxurious styles
ranging from the everyday
wearable to the downright
eccentric, all exquisitely made.
Last season's lines are available
at massively discounted prices at

Via Santa Maria Maggiore 165,
00185. Tel 06 488 0934. Bus: 4, 9,
70, 71, 75, 204, 590, 714; Metro:
Termini.
Gucci Via Condotti 8, 00187. Tel
06 679 0405. Bus: 116, 117, 590;
Metro: Spagna.
The ultimate in smart, top-
quality shoes and accessories.

LEATHER & OTHER ACCESSORIES

That the Italian leather industry
is the best in the world is a well-
established fact, and the range of
bags, belts, and wallets you'll find
in Rome has something for all
tastes and pockets. Silk ties and
scarves are another specialty.
Alberto Valentini Piazza Santa
Apollinare 36, 00186. Tel 06 686
1238. Bus: 70, 81, 87, 115, 116,
186, 204, 492, 628 (Corso del
Rinascimento).
Rome's best selection of ties.
Arfango Via dei Prefetti 42,
00186. Tel 06 687 3593. Bus: 81,
115, 117, 204, 590, 628.
Stunningly beautiful leather
goods (including shoes, bags, and
clothes). Among the best in Italy.
Bulgari Via Condotti 10, 00187.
Tel 06 679 3876. Bus: 116, 117,
590; Metro: Spagna.
The company for the very latest
and chicest in fashion and
costume jewelry.
Furla Piazza di Spagna 22,
00187. Tel 06 6920 0363. Bus:
116, 117, 590; Metro: Spagna.
Lovely smart bags that look as
though they cost twice as much
as they did. There's also a range
of costume jewelry and other
accessories. Branches all over
Rome.
Mandarina Duck Via
Nazionale 227, 00184. Tel 06 485
914. Bus: 64, 70, 71, 115, 116,
170, 640; Metro: Repubblica.
Well-priced, trendy luggage, bags
and other accessories made in
real and imitation leather.
Branches all over Rome.
Sermoneta Piazza di Spagna
61, 00187. Tel 06 679 1960. Bus:
116, 117, 590; Metro: Spagna.
Massive range of gloves in all
colors and styles, with or
without linings of silk, cashmere,
or wool.

Troncarelli Via della Cuccagna 15, 00186. Tel 06 687 9320. Bus: 46, 62, 64.
Olde worlde hat shop that stocks high-quality versions of all the traditional hats—panamas, berets, hombergs—as well as umbrellas and gloves.

CHILDREN'S CLOTHES & TOYS

Children's clothes don't come cheap in Italy. However, like their adult counterparts, they all have that inimitable touch of style.
La Cicogna Via Frattina 138, 00187. Tel 06 679 1912. Bus: 116, 117, 590; Metro: Spagna. Other branches all over town.
Maternity, babies', and children's wear from this nationwide, quality chain store.
Città del Sole Via della Scrofa 65, 00186. Tel 06 6880 3805. Bus: 70, 81, 87, 115, 116, 186, 204, 492, 628 (Largo Argentina).
Massive selection of toys, books, and games, of a vaguely educational nature.
Mettimi giù Via Due Macelli 59e, 00187. Tel 06 678 9761. Bus: 116, 117, 590; Metro: Barberini, Spagna.
Baby- and child-sized versions of designer clothes and accessories.
Al Sogno Piazza Navona 53, 00186. Tel 06 686 4198. Bus: 70, 81, 87, 115, 116, 186, 204, 492, 628 (Corso Rinascimento).
Gorgeous, cuddly soft toys, some of them life-size, for the truly affectionate child. For collectors there are exquisitely dressed reproduction Victorian dolls, and models, including a miniature version of virtually every Ferrari that's been designed.
Testa e Co. Via Santa Chiara 54, 00186. Tel 06 686 1735. Bus: 46, 60, 62, 64, 70, 81, 87, 115, 186, 492, 628, 640, 810 (Largo Argentina).
Traditional children's clothes of the smocking dresses and sailor suit variety will make even the most thuggish of children look like little angels.

FOR THE HOME

For decades, Italian style has reigned supreme in the interior design industry. Although minimalist furniture may not be on your holiday shopping list, you can still find plenty of smaller items to take home. Look out in particular for ceramics, glassware, household linen and furnishing fabrics, and cooking utensils that are hard to find elsewhere.
Azi Via San Francesco a Ripa, 00153. Tel 06 588 3303. Bus 8, 44, 75.
A little, white shop selling trendy and fun small accessories and equipment for kitchens and bathrooms as well as some very original gift ideas.
Cesari Via del Babuino 195, 00187. Tel 06 361 3451. Bus: 117; Metro: Spagna.
Refined household linen for the dining room and bathroom.
Cucina Via del Babuino 118a, 00187. Tel 06 679 1275. Bus: 117; Metro: Spagna.
Top-quality, expensive kitchen equipment from all over the world. Emphasis on being functional rather than decorative but the overall look is starkly pleasing.
KA International Via del Babuino 45, 00187. Tel 06 321 4190. Bus: 117; Metro: Spagna.
Fashionable, ethnically influenced furnishing fabrics and wall coverings in sunny, natural colors.
Richard Ginori Via del Tritone 177, 00187. Tel 06 679 3836. Bus: 52, 53, 60, 61, 62, 63, 71, 95, 115, 116 (Via del Tritone).
Italy's finest porcelain manufacturers (founded in the 18th century in Tuscany) sell everything for the best-dressed traditional table—cutlery, crystal, and silverware.
Spazio Sette Via dei Barbieri 7, 00186. Tel 06 686 9747. Bus: 8, 60, 63.
Easy to miss from outside, this is a three-story maze of a shop offering the latest word in style and gadgetry for the home.

GIFTS & SOUVENIRS

Carmignani Via della Colonna Antonina 42, 00186. Tel 06 679 5449. Bus: 60, 62, 63, 81, 85, 95, 117, 160, 175, 492, 628, 850 (Via del Corso).
A smoker's paradise specializing in pipes and other gentlemanly accouterments.
Casamaria Via della Scrofa 71–72, 00186. Tel 06 683 3074. Bus: 70, 81, 87, 115, 116, 186, 204, 492, 628 (Corso di Rinascimento).
Vast selection of cosmetics, beauty products, and scents for men and women, most at discounted prices.
Palazzo delle Esposizioni Via Milano 9, 00184. Tel 06 482 8001. Bus: 64, 70, 71, 115, 170, 640.
More sharp Italian design, this time used for stationery, jewelry, and desk accessories among other smart but practical gift ideas.
De Ritis Via dei Cestari 48, 00186. Tel 06 686 5843. Bus: 46, 60, 62, 64, 70, 81, 87, 115, 186, 492, 628, 640, 810 (Largo Argentina).
You may not need the clerical outfits and regalia that this and other shops nearby specialize in. However, the nativity scenes in high-quality, hand-painted epoxy resin make a nice (reasonably priced) souvenir of your stay in the home of Catholicism. Pieces are sold singly or in basic sets. Luxury versions come in wood or porcelain.

BOOKS & MUSIC

There are some excellent English-language bookstores in Rome, most of them with large sections on Rome and Italy. Several larger Italian stores also have selections of books in English.
Anglo-American Bookshop Via della Vite 102, 00187. Tel 06 679 5222. Bus: 116, 117, 590; Metro: Spagna.
Especially good for non-fiction titles catering for a wide range of special interests.
Archivio Fonografico Viale Aventino 59, 00153. Tel 06 574 1293. Metro: Circo Massimo.
Serious classical music store with a small selection of jazz. The owner's knowledge is encyclopedic—you just have to hum a few bars of the CD or cassette you're looking for and he'll find you at least one, and usually several, recordings to chose from.

Bibli Via dei Fienaroli 27, 00153. Tel 06 588 4097. Bus: 8, 44, 75. Italian books with a big section on Italian history (also books on, among others, computing, cinema, philosophy, psychology, health, fiction). Some titles in English, mainly classic literature. There's a very pleasant bar for coffees and light meals, and downstairs an Internet center.

Corner Bookshop Via del Moro 48, 00153. Tel 06 583 6942. Bus: 8, 23, 44, 75, 280. A treasure trove. Stacks of books from floor to ceiling entice you to browse through fiction, poetry, biography, film, history, and a wide range of other categories. If you're looking for anything in particular, ask—miraculously the owner and her staff seem to know the exact whereabouts of every book in the store.

Economy Book and Video Center Via Torino 136, 00184. Tel 06 474 6877. Bus: 64, 70, 71, 115, 116, 170, 640; Metro: Repubblica.
Its cluttered noticeboard of adverts for jobs, accommodations, and household sales is a contact point for the English-speaking community in Rome. Good selection of books covering a variety of subjects and genres, including secondhand paperbacks. English-language videos to rent or buy.

Feltrinelli Largo Torre Argentina 5a, 00186. Tel 06 6880 3248. Bus: 46, 60, 62, 64, 70, 81, 87, 115, 186, 492, 628, 640, 810 (Largo Argentina). Other branches throughout Rome. Three floors of Italian books covering everything—art, economics, history, sociology, travel, computing. English-language fiction plus a good selection of general and specialized guidebooks to Rome and Italy.

Feltrinelli International Via V.E. Orlando 84, 00185. Tel 06 482 7878. Metro: Repubblica. Books in a wide variety of languages, including English.

Ricordi Via Cesare Battisti 120c, 00187. Tel 06 679 8022. Bus: 64, 70, 170, 640.

Good selection of CDs and cassettes of all kinds of music. There's also a sheet-music section and a section selling musical instruments.

STATIONERY
For more than 500 years, Italian paper has been sought after for its high quality. Look out for products from Florence, Venice, and the Amalfi coast—paper-making and decorating centers.

Campo Marzio Penne Via Campo Marzio 41, 00186. Tel 06 6880 7877. Bus: 81, 115, 117, 204, 590, 628, 913, 926. Unbelievably vast selection of pens, including some exquisite glass creations, and elegant writing materials.

Cartoleria Pantheon Via della Rotonda 15, 00187. Tel 06 687 5313. Bus: 46, 60, 62, 64, 70, 81, 87, 115, 186, 492, 628, 640, 810 (Largo Argentina). Sumptuously decorated printed paper is used for personal stationery and to cover photo-albums, note and address books, and desk accessories.

Vertecchi Via della Croce 38 and 70, 00187. Tel 06 322 6942. Bus 117.
From the most traditional to the latest word in stationery and office equipment, it's all here, including a good pen selection and a massive range of writing papers to suit all personal styles.

TASTE TREATS
As well as the places listed here, try some of the wine bars listed in Eating and Entertainment for off-license sales of excellent wines and other drinks.

Bar Sant'Eustachio Piazza Sant'Eustachio 82, 00186. Tel 06 6861309. Bus: 46, 60, 62, 64, 70, 81, 87, 115, 186, 492, 628, 640, 810 (Largo Argentina). Probably the best coffee in central Rome is sold as beans or ready-ground in a variety of gift packs—and by the cup for a taste at the bar. There is also an interesting range of chocolates and other traditional Italian candies.

Castroni Via Cola di Rienzo 196, 00192. Tel 06 687 4383. Bus:

32, 81, 590; Metro: Lepanto. Unusual jams, honeys, pastas, and other Italian specialties as well as a wide range of hard-to-find foreign goods. If you really can't survive without a taste of home, this may be the place to find it.

Il Fornaio Via dei Baullari 5–7, 00186. Tel 06 6880 3947. Bus: 46, 62, 64, 116.
Leave your diet at the door and feast on these imaginatively named traditional Italian cakes and pastries—dolce del marinaio (sailor's dessert), baci di dame (ladies' kisses), and pangialli (yellow bread) to name but a few. Rest assured, too, that they're all so natural and wholesome that you're almost bound to be boosting your supplies of some essential nutrient, whichever you choose to eat. Incidentally, most of them keep very well for several days at least, as long as you keep them wrapped up between feeding frenzies.

Franchi Via Cola di Rienzo 200, 00192. Tel 06 686 4576. Bus: 32, 81, 590; Metro: Lepanto. Mouth-watering selection of ready prepared dishes and delicacies to take away or eat at the bar on the premises.

Ai Monasteri Piazza delle Cinque Lune 76, 00186. Tel 06 6880 2783. Bus: 70, 81, 87, 115, 116, 186, 204, 492, 628 (Corso Rinascimento).
When they're not contemplating the infinite, Italy's monks and nuns are busy preparing a surprisingly hedonistic range of gourmet goodies—luxury jams, liqueurs, and chocolates—as well as herb-based cosmetics and health products. This attractive shop sells the output of several convents and monasteries.

Volpetti Via della Scrofa 31–32, 00186. Tel 06 686 1940. Bus: 70, 81, 87, 115, 116, 186, 204, 492, 628. Closed Sunday.
Packed with some of the best of Italy's cheeses, salamis, oils, and other delicacies. An attached tavola calda offers a wide range of lunch dishes to eat at tables in the basement and afternoon snacks to grab at the bar (try the spinach croquettes).

ENTERTAINMENT

Compared to other major cities, Rome doesn't have a particularly active or varied night life, but there is certainly enough to stop all but the most difficult to please visitors from becoming bored.

Details of what's on where for the following week are published on Thursday in the magazine *Roma C'è* (which includes a section in English) and in the *TrovaRoma* and *Metro* free inserts that come with Thursday's editions of *La Repubblica* and *Il Messaggero*, respectively. The monthly *Time Out Roma* gives some idea but isn't really frequent enough to be reliable. For a selection of concerts, exhibitions, and some other events, see the English-language fortnightly *Wanted in Rome*.

Much of cultural and social Rome packs up for the summer but, to make up for this, there are lots of outdoor arts festivals all over the city; the Estate Romana, for instance, puts on important theater, dance, and music from some of the world's best companies while Massenzio is a film and music jamboree in the park opposite the Palatine. Some of the more establishment nightclubs move to outdoor locations on the coast at Fregene.

Ticket agencies are still something of a novelty in Italy and frequent distribution problems sometimes hamper the brave pioneers such as Orbis (Piazza Esquilino 37, 00184. Tel 06 482 7403. Bus: 4, 9, 16, 70, 71, 75, 204, 590, 714). Other than cinemas the vast majority of the places listed here are shut on Mondays.

THEATER

Nearly all theater is in Italian. *Wanted in Rome* has details of any English-language drama that's taking place.
Argentina Largo Argentina 52, 00186. Tel 06 6880 4601/2. Bus: 8, 46, 60, 62, 63, 64, 70, 87, 186, 204, 640, 810.
A beautiful, restored 18th-century theater is home to lo Stabile Roma, one of the city's leading companies directed by

Luca Ronconi. The repertoire is mainly Italian classics in grand (not to say grandiose) style.
Colosseo Via Capo d'Africa 7, 00184. Tel 06 700 4932. Bus: 13, 30b, 81, 85, 87, 117, 175, 186, 673, 810, 850 (Via Labicana, Piazza del Colosseo).
Many of today's big names in Italian theater and cinema cut their teeth at this long-established home of experimental productions (some more experimental than others). It also stages concerts, short films, and dance.
Della Cometa Via Teatro Marcello 4, 00186. Tel 06 678 4380. Bus: 8, 44, 46, 57, 81, 95, 160, 170, 628, 640, 715, 716, 810 (Via Teatro Marcello).
Pretty, smallish but perfectly formed theater where accessible, but by no means banal, new and nearly new works dominate the program.
Eliseo and **Piccolo Eliseo** Via Nazionale 183, 00184. Eliseo: Tel 06 488 2114; Piccolo: Tel 06 488 5095. Bus: 57, 64, 70, 71, 81, 170, 640.
Well-loved classics from Italy and elsewhere (in translation) are the mainstay of both these theaters which also host visiting companies. Casts often include Italian stage and screen stars.
Nazionale Via del Viminale 51, 00184. Tel 06 485 498. Bus: 64, 70, 71, 115, 116, 117, 170, 492, 640 (Piazza del Cinquecento).
This is the place to see the most successful productions of the most acclaimed directors and actors. Very varied range of events includes concerts given by international names of classical, jazz and other music.
Quirino Via M. Minghetti 1, 00187. Tel 06 679 4585. Bus: 60, 62, 63, 81, 85, 95, 117, 160, 175, 492, 628, 850 (Via del Corso).
One of two theaters operated by the Italian National Theater Company (see Valle). Top-quality productions of classics and the

best of contemporary theater are accompanied by art exhibitions, meetings and conferences on theater, and the productions currently being staged.
Rossini Piazza Santa Chiara 14, 00186. Tel 06 6832 281. Bus: 81, 115, 117, 204, 590, 628, 913, 926 (Largo Argentina).
Folkloric, old-style Roman music hall, much of it in dialect, aimed at Italian-speaking tourists.
Sistina Via Sistina 129, 00187. Tel 06 420 0711. Metro: Barberini.
Vast barn of a place specializing in unsophisticated versions of Italian and other musicals (in translation) often starring Italian television actors and personalities.
Valle Via del Teatro Valle 23, 00186. Tel 06 6880 3794. Bus: 46, 62, 64, 70, 81, 87, 115, 116, 186, 492, 628 (Corso del Rinascimento).
The second of the national theaters (see Quirino) has its headquarters in one of the oldest theater buildings in Rome (inaugurated in 1727). The program here concentrates on Italian and international contemporary drama and includes the occasional non-Italian play in original language.

OPERA, DANCE, & CLASSICAL MUSIC

As well as the places listed here, look out for posters announcing details of free classical concerts held in historic churches. These are often of extremely high standards and the settings are superb.
Accademia di Santa Cecilia (concerts at) Auditorio, Via della Conciliazione 4, 00193. Tel 06 6880 1044. Bus: 23, 34, 62, 64.
Italy's best symphony and chamber orchestra, at present directed by Myung-Whun Chung, offers a rich program of classical music including guest appearances by some of the world's greatest conductors, soloists, and orchestras. The purpose-built Auditorio also hosts non-classical music

ENTERTAINMENT

concerts by such established stars as James Taylor, Madredeus, Keith Jarrett, and Bruce Springsteen. In summer, concerts are held under the stars in the romantic setting of Villa Giulia, Piazzale di Villa Giulia 9, 00196. Bus: 19, 30, 225.

Il Gonfalone Via del Gonfalone 32 a, 00186. Tel 687 5952. Bus: 28, 116, 280, 870.

A glorious, appropriately 16th-century setting for camera and choral music with the emphasis on the baroque. Some concerts held in the Sala Grande of Palazzo della Cancelleria, Piazza della Cancelleria, 00186. Bus: 46, 62, 64, 116.

Olimpico Piazza Gentile da Fabriano 17, 00196. Tel 06 323 4890. Bus: 1, 2, 48, 201, 204, 220, 225, 232, 280, 301, 446, 910, 911 (Via Flaminia, Lungotevere delle Nave).

As well as being the concert hall of the Rome Philharmonic Orchestra (who perform here on Thursday nights during the season), this is the place to come for major dance events (visiting companies from all over the world), jazz, and other music as well as large-scale theater productions.

Teatro dell'Opera Piazza B. Gigli, 00184. Tel 06 4816 0255. Bus: 64, 70, 71, 115, 116, 170, 640 (Via Nazionale).

Rome's Opera and Ballet Company are re-establishing a good reputation after years of mismanagement and financial turbulence led to a loss of prestige. Recent productions have been original and success-ful, both musically and visually. In summer, opera and ballet are performed outdoors in suitably atmospheric surroundings—the exact location varies from year to year but is sometimes the Baths of Caracalla, the Orangery on the Aventine Hill or the arena of Piazza di Siena in Villa Borghese.

Teatro Brancaccio Via Merulana 244, 00184. Tel 06 487 4563. Bus: 16, 714, 204.

The ballet company of the Teatro dell'Opera sometimes performs in this large theater which also stages concerts and other events.

Il Tempietto Concerts in winter at: Sala Baldini, Piazza Campitelli 9, 00186 and Basilica di San Nicola in Carcere, Via del Teatro Marcello 46, 00186. In summer: Teatro Marcello, Via del Teatro Marcello 44, 00186. Tel (for all) 06 481 4800. Bus: (for all) 44, 60, 63, 81, 95, 160, 170, 204, 628, 715, 716, 780 (Via del Teatro Marcello).

Lively classical musical association that puts on concerts every Saturday and Sunday throughout the winter and every night (in the atmospheric outdoor surroundings of the ancient theater of Marcellus) in summer. Hosts choirs, soloists, and music groups from all over the world.

Vascello Via G. Carini 72, 00132. Tel 06 588 1021. Bus 8, 44, 75, 710.

Pleasant arena theater for visit-ing dance groups of all kinds—Japanese, Indian, contemporary European.... The theater program is also worth checking out; there's a bit of everything from the classics, through contemporary and the experimental to original multimedia events.

LIVE MUSIC

Surprisingly, not all major musicians include Rome in their tours of Italy—it's something to do with a dearth of suitable venues. However, many Italian and international music stars do come here and perform at the football stadium, the disused air terminal at Ostiense station, or some other, often unusual, setting. Many of the following spots also attract some extremely interesting (and famous) acts.

Alexanderplatz Via Ostia 9, 00192. Tel 06 3974 2171. Bus: 23, 51, 907, 991; Metro: Ottaviano.

One of Italy's most important and well-known jazz clubs is plastered with photos of visiting performers. Dinner (Italian cuisine) is served to those who want it. In summer the club moves to the outdoor setting of Villa Celimontana. Bus: 30b, 75, 81, 117, 175, 204, 673.

Alpheus Via del Commercio 36, 00154. Tel 06 574 7826. Bus: 23, 716.

Three different music spaces all under one roof (more or less): Momotombo is for Latin American and Caribbean; Red River, for blues, soul and cabaret; and Mississippi for rock and other bigger concerts. Food served.

Big Mama Vicolo San Francesco a Ripa 18, 00153. Tel 06 581 2551. Bus: 8.

The self-styled "Home of the Blues in Rome" offers an interesting selection of more than 200 concerts a year featuring up-and-coming musicians and great names of the past and present—both Italian and international.

Caffè Latino Via Monte Testaccio 96, 00153. Tel 06 5728 8384. Bus: 23, 75, 170, 175, 280, 716, 780; Metro: Piramide.

Concerts, most of them by local bands, nearly every night, followed by a disco playing mainly funk, acid jazz, and black music. On the same street are two similar places: Caruso (at No. 36. Tel 06 574 5019) concentrates on Latin American music; while Radio Londra (at No. 65b. Tel 06 575 0044) is more interested in rock, blues, and dance.

Locale Vicolo del Fico 3, 00186. Tel 06 687 9075. Bus: 46, 62, 64, 70, 81, 87, 115, 116, 186, 204, 492, 628 (Corso del Rinascimento). Chaotically lively and friendly place to hear new, mainly Italian, bands late in the evening—earlier there are occasional theatrical performances. Frequent exhibitions of photos or paintings are hung on the walls.

New Mississippi Jazz Club Borgo Angelico 18, 00193. Tel 06 6880 6348. Bus: 19, 23, 49, 51, 81, 492, 982, 990; Metro: Ottaviano.

In fact, at slightly over 30 years old, this is one of Rome's oldest jazz clubs. Open only on Fri.

and Sat., it's the place to come to hear the greats of the Italian jazz scene.

Palladium Piazza B. Romano 8, 00154. Tel 06 511 0203. Metro: Garbatella.

One of Rome's larger live music venues hosts dance events as well as rock, ethnic, acid, and a wide range of other concerts by some interesting musicians. Standing/dancing room only downstairs; there are seats upstairs on the balcony.

Villagio Globale Lungotevere Testaccio, 00153. Tel 06 5730 0329. Bus: 95, 170, 780.

A spectacular 19th-century slaughterhouse makes an exotic venue for open-air world music concerts in the summer and a variety of cultural events all year round.

BARS AND NIGHT CLUBS

Rome's club scene is relatively unchanging from year to year. There are exceptions but nightclubs tend to be either slightly stiff and full of important people getting themselves seen, or rather bland versions of the American and London scenes. Bars are often a safer bet for an enjoyable evening with or without music. Many of the bars listed here are open all day.

Alibi Via Monte Testaccio 40, 00153. Tel 06 574 3448. Bus: 23, 75, 170, 175, 280, 716, 780; Metro: Piramide.

One of Rome's earliest gay discos is also one of its most popular with both hetero- and homosexuals.

Alien Via Velletri 13, 00198. Tel 06 841 2212. Bus: 3, 4, 58, 63, 319, 490, 495.

Famous, conventionally trendy disco particularly popular with young Romans and a few fairly minor starlets who come here to be seen.

Bar della Pace Via della Pace 4, 00186. Tel 06 686 1216. Bus: 46, 62, 64, 70, 81, 87, 115, 116, 186, 204, 492, 628 (Corso del Rinascimento).

Beautifully furnished old bar in an attractive corner behind

Piazza Navona. It's long been one of the places to see and be seen late in the evening. Customers include visiting Hollywood stars and other international show-biz VIPs. Open all day.

Bar della Scala Via della Scala 60, 00153. Tel 06 580 3763. Bus: 8, 23, 280.

Throbbing nightspot (especially on Fri. and Sat. nights) whose vast clientele includes ex-pats and young Romans. There's a restaurant, a pub, and a cocktail bar among its many different rooms, and live music or other entertainment is sometimes arranged.

Bella Blu Via L. Luciani 21, 00197.

Chic nightspot in the elegant Parioli residential area. There's a small dance floor and a lot of comfortable corners for sitting in. Also a restaurant.

Bevitoria Navona Piazza Navona 72, 00186. Tel 06 6880 1022. Bus: 46, 62, 64, 70, 81, 87, 115, 116, 186, 204, 492, 628 (Corso del Rinascimento).

Definitely one of the more genuine establishments on Piazza Navona, this wine bar gives you plenty of choice for an aperitif or after-dinner stop. Outdoor tables on the piazza. Open all day.

Caffe di Marzio Piazza Santa Maria in Trastevere 15, 00153. Bus: 8, 23, 280.

Wonderful place for an after-dinner drink or ice cream in the piazza facing the mosaics and frescoes of the facade of Santa Maria in Trastevere. Open all day.

Il Fico Piazza del Fico 26, 00186. Tel 06 686 5205. Bus: 46, 62, 64, 70, 81, 87, 115, 116, 186, 204, 492, 628 (Corso del Rinascimento).

Trendy and fashionable without being intimidating, this cocktail bar is at its liveliest on summer evenings when customers sip drinks under the fig tree. Also pleasant for an early evening aperitif. Open all day.

Fiddler's Elbow Via dell'Olmata 43, 00184. Tel 06 487 2110. Bus: 4, 9, 16, 70, 71, 75,

204, 590, 714 (Piazza Santa Maria Maggiore).

One of the longest-established of hundreds of nominally Irish pubs all over the city. It may not be the real thing but it's an excellent example of a pub *alla Italiana*.

Follia Via Ovidio 17, 00193. Tel 06 6830 8435. Bus: 34, 49, 280, 492, 990.

A fashionable disco and piano bar frequented by smart young Romans. Its parties (some of them to celebrate new films, theater, or television programs) and themed evenings are particularly spectacular and popular.

Giardino dei Ciliegi Via dei Fienaroli 4, 00153. Tel 06 580 3423. Bus: 8, 44, 75.

This mellow cocktail bar and well-supplied tea room that serves snacks and light meals is particularly pleasant in summer when it fills the shady outside courtyard. Popular with the Roman theater world, it also has special events such as tarot card and horoscope readings. Open all day.

Gilda Via Mario dei Fiori 97, 00187. Tel 678 4838. Bus: 116, 590.

Long-established as the place to see the great and the good of Italian politics, culture, and society at dignified play, in a slightly restrained and conservative atmosphere. Comfortable seating surrounds the dance area and there is also an elegant piano bar.

Jazz Cafe Via Zanardelli 12, 00186. Tel 06 686 1990. Bus: 70, 81, 87, 115, 116, 186, 204, 492, 628 (Corso del Rinascimento).

In spite of its name, this is not a great place for listening to jazz— instead it's a lively, sophisticated, well-stocked cocktail bar with a loyal regular clientele and live music several times a week on the lower floor.

Jonathan's Angels Via della Fossa 16, 00186. Tel 06 689 3426. Bus: 46, 62, 64, 70, 81, 87, 115, 116, 186, 204, 492, 628 (Corso del Rinascimento).

Not for shrinking violets as you may be roped into one of the semi-impromptu evening floor shows that sometimes take place at this chaotic, packed cocktail bar. The decorations—wall paintings, statuettes—must be seen, especially the gorgeous bathroom. Open all day.

Nuvolari Via degli Ombrellari 10, 00193. Tel 06 6880 3018. Bus: 34, 49, 280, 492, 990.
As well as extensive wine and cocktail menus, this pleasantly relaxed bar also serves light meals and offers live jazz, and cabaret several times a week.

Ombre Rosso Piazza San Egidio 12, 00153. Tel 06 588 4155. Bus: 8, 23, 280.
Open from the crack of dawn until late at night, this bar caters to virtually all refreshment needs (including light meals, tea, and delicious cakes). Mellow atmosphere and an attractive, flower-lined terrace on the piazza.

Piper Via Tagliamento 9, 00198. Tel 06 841 4459. Bus: 3, 4, 63, 319.
This historic Dolce Vita discotheque has moved with the times and now attracts mainly young Romans. It has gay nights on Saturday (check first as this may change).

Vineria Reggio Piazza Campo dei Fiori 15, 00186. Tel 06 6880 3268. Bus: 46, 62, 64, 116.
The Campo dei Fiori wine bar has long been an obligatory port of call for ex-pats, tourists, and Romans who flock here to quaff reasonably priced wines and other drinks at the bar or outside on the pavement.

CINEMA
Sadly, Italy is proud of its dubbing tradition and even serious film fans would often rather see a film dubbed than have to bother with subtitles. English-speakers are better off than other language groups, however, because several cinemas now screen films in "original language" on one night a week or even every day.

Alcazar Via Merry del Val 14, 00153. Tel 06 588 0099. Bus: 8, 44, 75.

Womb-like, red upholstered cinema showing the latest releases; in original language (usually English) on Mondays.

Intrastevere Vicolo Moroni 3a, 00153. Tel 06 588 4230. Bus: 23, 280.
Tiny labyrinth where three screens are packed into the available spaces in a former theater. "Arty" international films dominate the program—usually in or dubbed into Italian but English-language films are sometimes shown in their original language for a week or two.

Nuovo Olimpia Via in Lucina 16, 00186. Tel 06 686 1068. Bus: 81, 115, 117, 492, 590, 628.
Cult cinema of the 1960s has been imaginatively restructured and now has two screens where restored old Italian and other films are often shown (along with recent releases, nearly always in Italian).

Nuovo Sacher Largo Ascianghi 1, 00153. Tel 06 581 8116. Bus: 8, 23, 44, 75, 280.
A mecca for cinema fans. Director Nanni Moretti owns this cinema which is named after his favorite cake. He screens interesting mainstream European and American releases as well as works by (as yet) little-known directors from various parts of the world. Films shown in original language (by no means always English) on Mondays. Outside arena for summer screenings.

Pasquino Piazza San Egidio 12, 00153. Tel 06 580 3622. Bus: 8, 23, 280.
The Pasquino has been a point of reference for anglophones in Rome for decades. It's been completely (and attractively) revamped and now has no fewer than three screens showing recently released films in English every day.

Quirinetta Via M Minghetti 4, 00187. Tel 06 679 0012. Bus: 60, 62, 63, 81, 85, 95, 117, 204, 492, 628, 850 (Via del Corso).
Recent English-language releases in original language, every day; occasionally Italian films are shown with English subtitles.

ICE CREAM
Forget any preconceived ideas you may have about ice cream being kids' stuff—in Italy it's for everybody (taste it and you'll soon understand why), especially to accompany an after-dinner stroll through the historic center.

Alberto Pica Via della Seggiola 12, 00186. Tel 06 6880 6153. Bus: 8, 56, 60.
About 50 different flavors include some imaginative inventions (green apple, rice with cinnamon, rosewater) as well as classic favorites. There are also some interesting combinations of several flavors.

Cremeria Monteforte Via della Rotonda 22, 00186. Tel 06 686 7720. Bus: 46, 60, 62, 64, 70, 81, 87, 115, 186, 492, 628, 640, 810 (Largo Argentina).
Delicious real ice cream from this tiny, packed little shop. The *semi-freddi* and chocolate and orange ice cream are among the proclaimed favorites here.

Giolitti Via Ufficio del Vicario 40, 00186. Tel 06 699 1243. Bus: 60, 62, 63, 81, 85, 95, 117, 204, 492, 628, 850 (Largo Argentina).
Right next to Parliament, this is where the establishment buys its ice cream, which comes in about 50, mainly traditional, delicious flavors. Tea, pastries, and, of course, exotic ice cream mixes are served in the charmingly faded splendor of the tea room.

San Crispino Via della Panetteria 42, 00187. Tel 06 679 3924. Bus: 52, 53, 58, 60, 61, 62, 63, 95, 116, 175, 204, 492, 590 (Via del Tritone).
Constantly changing and expanding range of flavors include some true innovations such as meringue and hazelnut or pink grapefruit with whisky.

Tre Scalini Piazza Navona 28, 00186. Tel 06 6880 1996. Bus: 70, 81, 87, 115, 116, 186, 204, 492, 628 (Corso Rinascimento).
The highlight here are the *tartuffi*, rich, chocolatier-than-chocolate blobs of ice cream with glacé cherries and chunks of chocolate embedded in them, served with cream.

LANGUAGE GUIDE

USEFUL WORDS & PHRASES

Yes *Si*
No *No*
Excuse me (in a crowd or asking for permission) *Permesso*
Excuse me (asking for attention) *Mi scusi*
Hello (before lunch) *Buon giorno*, (after lunch) *Buona sera*
Hi or Bye *Ciao*
Please *Per favore*
Thank you *Grazie*
You're welcome *Prego*
Have a good day! *Buona giornata!*
OK *Va bene*
Goodbye *Arrivederci*
Good night *Buona notte*
Sorry *Mi scusi* or *Mi dispiace*
here *qui*
there *lì*
today *oggi*
yesterday *ieri*
tomorrow *domani*
now *adesso/ora*
later *più tardi/dopo*
right away *subito*
this morning *stamattina*
this afternoon *questo pomeriggio*
this evening *stasera*
open *aperto*
closed *chiuso*
Do you have? *Avrebbe?*
Do you speak English? *Parla inglese?*
I'm American (man) *Sono americano*, (woman) *Sono americana*
I don't understand *Non capisco*
Please speak more slowly *Potrebbe parlare più lentamente?*
Where is...? *Dov'è...?*
I don't know *Non so*
No problem *Niente*
That's it *Ecco*
Here/there it is (masculine) *Eccolo*, (feminine) *Eccola*
What is your name? *Come si chiama?*
My name is... *Mi chiamo...*
Let's go *Andiamo*
At what time? *A che ora?*
When? *Quando?*
What time is it? *Che ora è?*
Can you help me? *Mi può aiutare?*
I'd like... *Vorrei...*
How much is it? *Quanto costa?*

MENU READER

breakfast *la (prima) colazione*
lunch *il pranzo*
dinner *la cena*
appetizer *l'antipasto*
first course *il primo*
main course *il secondo*
vegetable, side dish *il contorno*
dessert *il dessert*
wine list *la lista dei vini*
the bill *il conto*
I'd like to order *Vorrei ordinare*
Is service included? *Il servizio è incluso?*

PASTA SAUCES

all'amatriciana tomato sauce with chili and bacon
all'arrabbiata ("angry") tomato and chili sauce
alla carbonara with bacon, eggs, and pecorino cheese
alla gricia carbonara without the eggs
alla scoglia ("seashore") with prawns, mussels, and clams

MEAT

l'abbacchio lamb
l'anatra duck
la bistecca beefsteak
ben cotta well-done
non troppo cotta medium
appena cotta rare
al sangue very rare
il filetto fillet steak
il carpaccio finely sliced raw cured beef
il cinghiale wild boar
il coniglio rabbit
il fegato liver
le lumache snails
il maiale pork
il manzo beef
misto di carne mixed grill
il pollo chicken
le polpette meatballs
la porchetta cold roast pork with herbs
il prosciutto ham, *crudo* raw, *cotto* cooked
i rognoni kidneys
la salsiccia fresh, spicy (usually pork) sausage
saltimbocca allo Romano veal and ham in a creamy mushroom sauce
straccetti pan-fried strips of beef or veal

lo stufato stew or casserole
il tacchino turkey
la trippa tripe
il vitello veal

FISH

l'alici/acciughe anchovies
l'aragosta/astice lobster
il calamaro squid
le cozze mussels
i gamberi prawns
i gamberetti shrimp
il granchio crab
le ostriche oysters
il polipo octopus
il salmone salmon
le sarde sardines
la sogliola sole
la spigola bass
il tonno tuna
la trota trout

VEGETABLES

l'aglio garlic
gli asparagi asparagus
il carciofo artichoke
la carota carrot
il cavolfiore cauliflower
la cipolla onion
i fagioli dried beans, usually haricot or borlotti
i fagiolini fresh green beans
i funghi (porcini) mushrooms
l'insalata mista/verde mixed/green salad
la melanzane eggplant
le patate potatoes
le patate fritte or *le patatine* potato chips
il peperone pepper (vegetable not condiment)
i piselli peas
i pomodori tomatoes
il radicchio bitter reddish lettuce
il riso rice
gli spinaci spinach
il tartufo truffle
le zucchine zucchini

FRUIT

l'albicocca apricot
l'ananas pineapple
l'arancia orange
le cilegie cherries
le fragole strawberries
la mela apple
la pera pear
la pesca peach
la pescanoce nectarine
il pompelmo grapefruit
l'uva grapes

ILLUSTRATIONS CREDITS

Abbreviations for terms appearing below: (t) top; (b) bottom; (l) left; (r) right; (c) center.

Cover (tl), Corbis UK Ltd/John Heseltine. (tr), AA Photo Library/Dario Mitidieri. (bl), Images Colour Library. (br), (spine), SuperStock. 1, Gettyone/Stone. 2/3, Steve McCurry/National Geographic Society. 4, Steve McCurry/National Geographic Society. 9, Robert Harding Picture Library. 11, AA Photo Library/Jim Holmes. 12/13, Steve McCurry/National Geographic Society. 14/15, James Stanfield/National Geographic Society. 16/17, Marka. 19, James Stanfield/National Geographic Society. 20/21, O. Louis Mazzatenta/National Geographic Society. 23, The Entry of St. Ignatius into Paradise, ca.1707 (fresco) by Andrea Pozzo (1642–1709), Church of St. Ignatius, Rome, Italy/Bridgeman Art Library. 24, Corbis UK Ltd/Bettmann. 25, Rex Features. 26/27, Victor Boswell/National Geographic Society. 28/29, James Stanfield/National Geographic Society. 30, AA Photo Library/Jim Holmes. 32, British Film Institute. 34, Gettyone/Stone. 35, Robert Harding Picture Library. 38/39, Riccardo Musacchio/Farabolafoto. 40/41, Corbis UK Ltd/Carmen Redondo. 44/45, Steve McCurry/National Geographic Society. 46, Corbis UK Ltd/Carmen Redondo. 47, De Camillis/John Sims. 48, Corbis UK Ltd/Carmen Redondo. 51(t), Augustus and the Tiburtine Sibyl (oil on canvas) by Antoine Caron (1520–99), Louvre, Paris, France/Peter Willi/Bridgeman Art Library. 51(bl), Gold coin of the Roman Emperor Nero (A.D. 54–68), Private Collection/Bridgeman Art Library. 51(br), Robert Harding Picture Library. 52, Corbis UK Ltd/Sandro Vannini. 54, Corbis UK Ltd/Vittoriano Rastelli. 55, Corbis UK Ltd/Archivo Iconografico, S.A. 58/59, Corbis UK Ltd/Carol Havens. 61(t), Robert Harding Picture Library. 61(b), Corbis UK Ltd/Archivo Iconografico, S.A. 62, Gettyone/Stone. 63, Corbis UK Ltd/Michael S. Yamashita. 64, Corbis UK Ltd/Vanni Archive. 65, Corbis UK Ltd/AFP. 67, Marka. 68/69, AA Photo Library/Jim Holmes. 70(t), Corbis UK Ltd/Ruggero Vanni. 70(b), Corbis UK Ltd/Archivo Iconografico, S.A. 73, AA Photo Library. 76, Mecky Fögeling. 77, Mecky Fögeling. 78/79, Corbis UK Ltd/Vanni Archive. 80, John Sims. 81, De Camillis/John Sims. 82,

Marka. 84, Marka. 85, John Heseltine. 86, Museo Nazionale Romano. 86/87, Museo Nazionale Romano. 88, Museo Nazionale Romano. 89, Corbis UK Ltd/Vanni Archive. 90, Musacchio/Farabolafoto. 91, Vannini/Speranza. 95, Robert Harding Picture Library. 96, Robert Harding Picture Library. 97(tl), Corbis UK Ltd/John Heseltine. 97(tr), Franca Speranza Srl. 97(c), AA Photo Library/Jim Holmes. 97(b), Marka. 98, Corbis UK Ltd/Hubert Stadler. 99, Musacchio/Farabolafoto. 100, Scala. 101, Corbis UK Ltd/Araldo de Luca. 102/103, Travel Library. 105, Corbis UK Ltd/Nicolas Sapieha; Kea Publishing Services Ltd. 107, Marka. 108/109, Steve McCurry/National Geographic Society. 111(t), Corbis UK Ltd/ Vittoriano Rastelli. 111(bl), Corbis UK Ltd /Vittoriano Rastelli. 111(br), Travel Library. 112, Corbis UK Ltd /Hubert Stadler. 113, Franca Speranza Srl. 114, The Conversion of St. Paul, 1602 (oil on canvas) by Michelangelo Merisi da Caravaggio (1571–1610), Santa Maria del Popolo, Rome, Italy/Bridgeman Art Library. 115, Scala. 116, Corbis UK Ltd/Vanni Archive. 117, Corbis UK Ltd/Massimo Listri. 119(t), Robert Harding Picture Library. 119(bl), Corbis UK Ltd/John Heseltine. 119(br), John Sims. 120/121, Corbis UK Ltd/Michael S. Yamashita. 122, Corbis UK Ltd/ Massimo Listri. 123, Corbis UK Ltd/ Dennis Marsico. 124, Robert Harding Picture Library. 127, Corbis UK Ltd/Vanni Archive. 131(t), PowerStock/Zefa. 131(bl),Mecky Fögeling. 131(br), Robert Harding Picture Library. 132, Axiom. 133, PowerStock/Zefa. 134, Anthony Blake Photo Library. 136, Corbis UK Ltd/ Francesco Venturi; Kea Publishing Services Ltd. 137, AA Photo Library/ Jim Holmes. 138, Sandro Vannini/ Franca Speranza Srl. 139, Sasso/ Farabolafoto. 141, Corbis UK Ltd/ Michael S. Yamashita. 142, Corbis UK Ltd/Franz-Marc Frei. 144/145, Gettyone/Stone. 145, Corbis UK Ltd/ John Heseltine. 146/147, Lanni/ Farabolafoto. 148, The Martyrdom of St. Matthew, 1599–1600 by Michelangelo Merisi da Caravaggio (1571–1610), San Luigi dei Francesi, Rome, Italy/Bridgeman Art Library. 149, AA Photo Library/Dario Mitidieri. 150, Axiom. 152/153, John Sims/Anthony Blake Photo Library. 153, Mecky Fögeling. 154, Marka. 154/155, The 'Galleria di Carracci' (Carracci Hall) detail of Jupiter and Juno, 1597–1604 (fresco) by Annibale Carracci (1560–1609), Palazzo Farnese, Rome, Italy/Bridgeman Art Library. 155, Corbis UK Ltd/John

Heseltine. 156, Mecky Fögeling. 159, Robert Harding Picture Library. 161, James Stanfield/National Geographic Society, 163, Steve McCurry/National Geographic Society. 164, Jim Holmes/ Axiom. 166/167, Corbis UK Ltd/ Archivo Iconografico, S.A. 168, Robert Harding Picture Library. 168/169, Corbis UK Ltd/Franz-Marc Frei. 170, James Stanfield/National Geographic Society. 172, Corbis UK Ltd/Vittoriano Rastelli. 173, Sistine Chapel Ceiling, 1508–12 (fresco) (post restoration) by Michelangelo Buonarroti (1475–1564), Vatican Museums and Galleries, Vatican City, Italy/Bridgeman Art Library. 174/175, James Stanfield/National Geographic Society. 175, Victor Boswell/National Geographic Society. 177, Corbis UK Ltd/Sandro Vannini. 179, AA Photo Library/Jim Holmes. 182, Scala, 182/183, John Heseltine. 184, Franca Speranza Srl. 186, AA Photo Library/ Dario Mitidieri. 187, Corbis UK Ltd/ Massimo Listri. 188, John Heseltine. 189, John Heseltine. 190/191,John Sims, 192, John Heseltine. 192/193, John Heseltine. 194/195, Corbis UK Ltd/Franz-Marc Frei. 195, Corbis UK Ltd/Ali Meyer. 197, Corbis UK Ltd/ Christel Gerstenberg. 199, Jim Holmes/Axiom. 200, Marka. 201, Axiom. 202, Marka. 204, Corbis UK Ltd/Hubert Stadler. 205, Robert Harding Picture Library. 206, PowerStock/Zefa. 207, John Heseltine. 208/9, Jim Holmes/Axiom. 211, Robert Harding Picture Library. 212, Corbis UK Ltd/Carmen Redondo. 213, The Grape Harvest (mosaic), Santa Costanza, Rome, Italy/Bridgeman Art Library. 214, AA Photo Library/Peter Wilson. 217, Hubert Stadler/Corbis UK Ltd. 218, Sandro Vannini/Franca Speranza Srl. 219, Corbis UK Ltd/Araldo de Luca. 220, AA Photo Library/Jim Holmes. 221, Corbis UK Ltd/Ruggero Vanni. 222, Ceiling decoration with flowers and birds (mosaic) Santa Costanza, Rome, Italy/Bridgeman Art Library. 223, Robert Harding Picture Library. 225, Robert Harding Picture Library. 226, AA Photo Library/Clive Sawyer. 228/229, AA Photo Library/Clive Sawyer. 231, Robert Harding Picture Library. 232, Corbis UK Ltd/ acduff Everton. 232/233, PowerStock/Zefa. 235, AA Photo Library/Clive Sawyer.

Published by the National Geographic Society
John M. Fahey, Jr., *President and Chief Executive Officer*
Gilbert M. Grosvenor, *Chairman of the Board*
Nina D. Hoffman, *Senior Vice President*
William R. Gray, *Vice President and Director, Book Division*
David Griffin, *Design Director*
Elizabeth L. Newhouse, *Director of Travel Publishing*
Barbara A. Noe, *Associate Editor*
Caroline Hickey, *Senior Researcher*
Carl Mehler, *Director of Maps*
Joseph F. Ochlak, *Map Coordinator*
Lise Sajewski, *Editorial Consultant*
Gary Colbert, *Production Director*
Richard S. Wain, *Production Project Manager*
DeShelle Downey, *Staff Assistant*

Edited and designed by AA Publishing (a trading name of Automobile
Association Developments Limited, whose registered office is Norfolk
House, Priestley Road, Basingstoke, Hampshire, England RG24 9NY.
Registered number: 1878835).
Betty Sheldrick, *Project Manager*
David Austin, *Senior Art Editor*
Allen Stidwill, *Senior Editor*
Bob Johnson, *Designer*
Inna Nogeste, *Senior Cartographic Editor*
Amber Banks, Peter Smith, *Cartographers*
Richard Firth, *Production Director*
Steve Gilchrist, *Prepress Production Controller*
Picture Research by Zooid Pictures Ltd.
Area maps drawn by Chris Orr Associates, Southampton, England
Cutaway illustrations drawn by Maltings Partnership, Derby, England

Library of Congress Cataloging-in-Publication Data
Gilbert, Sari.
   The National Geographic Traveler : Rome / Sari Gilbert and Michael Brouse.
     p. cm.
    Includes index.
    ISBN 0-7922-7566-7
     1. Rome (Italy)--Guidebooks. I. Brouse, Michael. II. Title.

   DG804 .G55 2000
   914.5'63204929--dc21

                          00-021915
                          CIP

Printed and bound by R.R. Donnelley & Sons, Willard, Ohio.
Color separations by Leo Reprographic Ltd., Hong Kong.
Cover separations by L.C. Repro, Aldermaston, U.K.
Cover printed by Miken Inc., Cheektowage, New York.

Visit the Society's Web site at http:/www.nationalgeographic.com

THE NATIONAL
GEOGRAPHIC TRAVELER

A Century of Travel Expertise
in Every Guide

- **Australia** ISBN: 0-7922-7431-8
- **California** ISBN: 0-7922-7564-0
- **Canada** ISBN: 0-7922-7427-X
- **The Caribbean** ISBN: 0-7922-7434-2
- **Florida** ISBN: 0-7922-7432-6
- **France** ISBN: 0-7922-7426-1
- **Great Britain** ISBN: 0-7922-7425-3
- **Italy** ISBN: 0-7922-7562-4
- **London** ISBN: 0-7922-7428-8
- **Miami and the Keys** ISBN: 0-7922-7433-4
- **New York** ISBN: 0-7922-7430-X
- **Paris** ISBN: 0-7922-7429-6
- **Rome** ISBN: 0-7922-7566-7
- **San Francisco** ISBN: 0-7922-7565-9
- **Sydney** ISBN: 0-7922-7435-0

AVAILABLE WHEREVER BOOKS ARE SOLD